XI'AN
FAMOUS
FOODS

西安
名吃

XI'AN FAMOUS FOODS

The Cuisine of Western China, from New York's Favorite Noodle Shop

JASON WANG with Jessica K. Chou

photography by Jenny Huang

ABRAMS, NEW YORK

Contents

Recipe List

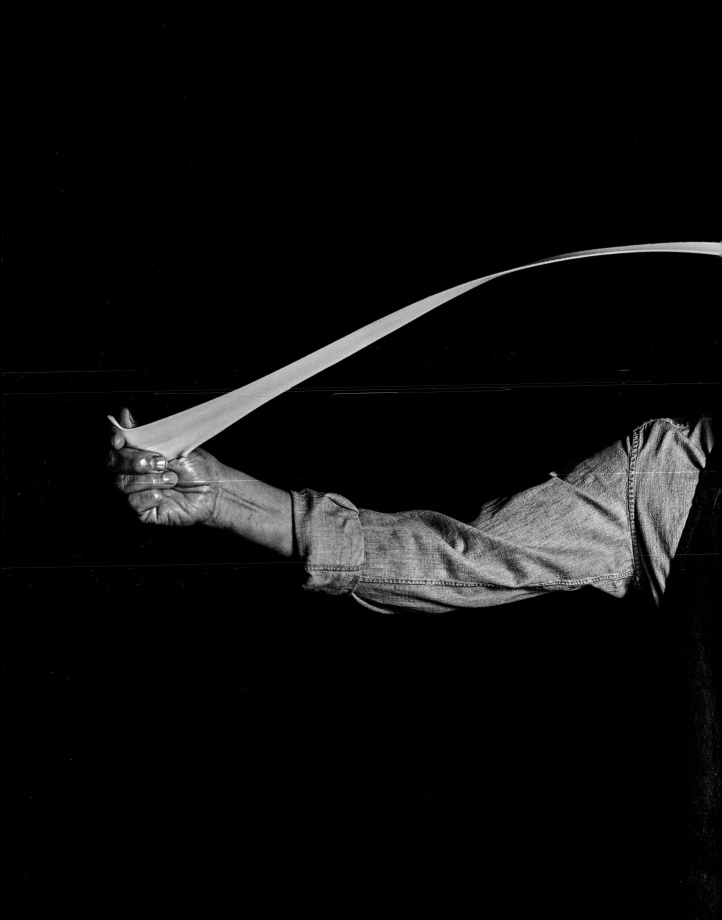

Introduction

A YOUNG JASON IN CHINA, PREPARING FOR HIS ADVENTURE ABROAD.

IF YOU'RE A FOOD FAN IN NEW YORK CITY, YOU MIGHT ALREADY KNOW A BIT ABOUT THE XI'AN[1] FAMOUS FOODS STORY. IT GOES A LITTLE LIKE THIS: In the winter of 2005, a hardworking immigrant named David Shi (aka my dad) opened a shop in Flushing, New York, to sell *boba*, or bubble tea—you know, those chewy tapioca pearls plopped into a mixture of sugar, powdered tea, and water, sometimes with flavored syrup for that fake mango taste. But in New York City, even back then, bubble tea shops were a dime a dozen, and competition was fierce. So my dad, ever the hustler, pivoted. He rented a tiny little space and started selling the food of our hometown: Xi'an, China.

The rest, as they say, is history. Word on the street started to spread about the man in a tiny basement stall banging out noodles and other cheap street eats rarely seen this side of the Pacific. We're talking chewy, cold ribbons of *liang pi* doused in a spicy, bright vinegar sauce, fresh-pulled *biang-biang* noodles with a heat so intense it makes you sweat, and caramelized pork stuffed between flatbread, easy enough to eat with one hand while swiping your MTA card, running to catch the next train. Customers took notice, and the food soon outsold the boba. People were lining up to scarf down the noodles, slurping up the leftover sauce just to make sure they didn't waste a single drop. Then, the camera crews showed up. Anthony Bourdain dropped by, as did Andrew Zimmern, along with the food bloggers of Chowhound and Serious Eats, *New York* magazine and the *New York Times*. And then, more camera crews, more food bloggers,

1 Also, if you're not in the know, it's pronounced *shee-ahn*.

more celebrities. The cycle continued; business boomed. Lines stretched around the basement food court, up the stairs, and around the street corner. Expansion seemed like a no-brainer, so after college, I signed on to helm the XFF

eating lamb soup dotted with broken-up bits of bread for lunch. On weekends, I'm sitting on my dad's bicycle handlebars, riding to the street markets where shop owners peddle stick-skinny skewers and *rou jia mou* (burgers).

So my dad, ever the hustler, pivoted. He rented a tiny little space and started selling the food of our hometown: Xi'an, China.

empire, putting the dishes of my childhood on America's culinary map like never before.

It's a good story. But like most American dreams, the beginnings of Xi'an Famous Foods started long before that.

Our first stop, of course, is in Xi'an, a dry, dusty city in northwestern China. In the past, it held a coveted status as the capital of multiple ancient Chinese dynasties, and as the start of the Silk Road, Xi'an became an epicenter of trade that connected China with the Middle East, bringing an influx of people into the city—and their food. While coastal cities like Guangzhou and Fuzhou developed regional dishes with crab, shrimp, and fish, Xi'an took on the flavors and ingredients of western China and the Middle East. This meant gamey lamb, not often seen in some regions of China, and earthy spices like cardamom and star anise. This is my city of fiery desert food, and this is where I'm born. On weekdays, I'm playing hide-and-seek in (seemingly) cavernous apartment complexes,

I see charcoal smoke and smell spicy cumin lamb and eat rough, ragged street noodles swimming in bright red chili, my senses on overload, tingling from peppercorn.

But then we do a full 180. When I'm eight years old, my parents announce a move to America for a better education, a better future. I'm excited, expecting annual trips to Disneyland and a magical elixir known as hot chocolate (Starbucks hadn't made it to Xi'an just yet). We're dropped into the snowy woods of Michigan, and I see my childhood of concrete and smoke replaced with cookie-cutter houses, painted red and blue and yellow, with porches and lawns and the tallest oak and evergreen trees I'd ever seen. My life turns into a "coming to America" reel. In one scene, my mom and I stare open-mouthed at a tiny "Asian food" section at our local grocery store. In another, we're trying to defrost imitation crab and mixing white vinegar with soy sauce, hoping to re-create the complex black vinegar of home. In a third, we're bribing a family friend, Uncle Feng, to

My life turns into a "coming to America" reel. In one scene, my mom and I stare open-mouthed at a tiny "Asian food" section at our local grocery store. In another, we're trying to defrost imitation crab and mixing white vinegar with soy sauce, hoping to re-create the complex black vinegar of home.

drive three hours to the closest major city for cumin and some actually decent soy sauce. I have my first taste of hot chocolate, and it's overwhelmingly, sickeningly sweet.

Our family lasts three years in Michigan before we take off for the suburbs of Connecticut—another promise of a better education, a better future. I enroll in a Catholic middle school and become a latchkey kid while my parents work multiple jobs to make ends meet. I roll out of bed, walk to school, let the racist jokes roll off my back. Come back to an empty home, heat up some dinner from the freezer, chat aimlessly on AIM, watch *The Simpsons* until bed. My dad's working weeks at a time at random Chinese restaurants all across the East Coast, jumping ship from Pennsylvania to New Jersey to Maryland. He's cooking sweet-and-sour pork, beef and broccoli, fried rice with too much soy sauce—the type of Americanized Chinese food we'd never eat at home. Every few months, he shows up at our doorstep, having been fired because his boss can't stand him, or quit his latest gig because he can't stand his boss. My mom's

taking on odd jobs here and there, whatever she can get, and leaving me notes to find the *hong shao rou* in the freezer, the dumplings ready to be boiled for dinner.

Once a month, we head to Flushing, New York, filled with people who look kind of like me and walk and talk kind of like me. Sometimes you'll hear Mandarin and Cantonese on the streets, and sometimes you'll hear Fujianese and Shanghainese, with different cadences and tones and accents that are gibberish in my brain. Still, there are grocery stores with vegetables I recognize, barbers who actually know how to cut my east Asian hair well, and shops where you can buy snacks like chicken feet marinated in chili oil, doled out in vacuum-sealed plastic bags. But there's nothing that tastes like the charcoal and fire and cumin of Xi'an cuisine—yet.

Even when we move to Queens for my high school (same deal: better education, better future), I feel like an outsider. Sure, there are more Asian Americans, but I don't live in a house like everyone else and don't have family meals. My dad's barely home; he's chasing every extra hundred dollars, even if it means washing dishes for ten hours straight at some buffet restaurant two hours away. He's scrambling to scrimp and save, making just enough to pay rent for our tiny basement apartment on time, saving just enough to get his only son a straight shot to a stable white-collar job at some corporate firm.

In fact, only when I'm halfway through college does he dare pursue his unspoken dream—his own spot, specializing in our hometown eats. So first he splurges on a bubble tea franchise. Then he goes all in and drops around two thousand dollars on a literal hole-in-the-wall space next to the Q58 bus stop and starts with two dishes: spicy and sour liang pi "cold skin noodles" and rou jia mou, our soon-to-be-signature "burgers." He knows instinctively that the local market is itching for authentic street food, intensely flavorful yet quick and cheap. So he starts making the food at home, pushing it over in a cart, and then praying it doesn't rain so he can stay open all day and break even.

Eventually, the community catches on. My dad makes enough to snag that soon-to-be iconic space in Flushing's Golden Shopping Mall and expands the menu. That's when the lines start forming. He's working twenty-hour days, pulling noodles and making burgers in Flushing, while old high school friends are calling me up, asking if I can get them the hookup. I believe the hype; my dad's liang pi is my first authentic taste of Xi'an in more than a decade. I head back to school dreaming about it, knowing we hit on something big, something bigger than

Flushing, and potentially bigger than New York. And then, one day in my junior year, I'm chilling in my dorm room in St. Louis playing Counter-Strike, and I get a call from my dad. "There's a tall, old white dude here with a film crew. Do you know who he is?"[2]

This is a cookbook about the recipes behind the Xi'an Famous Foods empire, but it's also the story of the XFF family, a guide to where we came from, the food we grew up with. It's the reason why this all exists; you can't have one without the other. The following dishes trace our path from the building blocks of Xi'an cuisine to the novel and exciting flavor combinations found in America. They're home-style meals, new takes on street food, and expanded versions of my favorite recipes, all with the flavors, textures, and spices of

ANTHONY BOURDAIN WITH MY FATHER AT OUR ORIGINAL FLUSHING STORE CIRCA 2011.

2 It's Bourdain.

Xi'an Famous Foods as a backbone. And while many of these dishes aren't on our menu, they were staples during my childhood, dishes I return to over and over again. You'll find the makings of family feasts that can be easily slapped together, sizzling woks best enjoyed buzzed with friends, and last-minute dinners to slurp down when you only have fifteen minutes between gigs.

So, yes, you're going to get the secret to several incredible bowls of noodles, but you're also going to get a story about immigrants leaving a place called home and creating a new one, both in China and in the United States. You're going to get recipes that showcase the malleable language of food, the transformations that take place through time and through space, and the magical powers familiar flavors have in unfamiliar environments. And you're going to get a story about my family—my mother, who managed to find nostalgic flavors in foreign ingredients; my stubborn father, who tested and retested recipes until perfection; and me, a scrawny, ambitious kid who had to grow the fuck up to actually make it in the grimy, dirty, rapid-fire kitchens of New York City. It's a story about

leaving behind the world of suits and ties and adapting my white-collar training to the frenetic kitchens of Chinatown, the unruly restaurant scene in Flushing, and envisioning not just one tiny two-hundred-square-foot stall but storefronts in Manhattan, Brooklyn, *and* Queens. But let me tell you, as much as my Aston Martin might make this life look like an endless party, I had to squash countless cockroaches while cleaning out shitty kitchen basements to get here.

Sometimes I wonder how we managed to do it. How did we make the food of Xi'an—so spicy and sour and not sweet at all—not just palatable but popular enough to spawn lines down the block? How did we do it in America, the world of beef and broccoli and General Tso's chicken? And, more important, how did I do it with my father, the most impulsive hothead I know?

So here it is, the never-been-told version of how the XFF empire came to be—the random, weird pit stops along the way; the family drama behind the scenes; the labor hidden in the secret recipes; and, yes, some *really* fucking good spicy cumin lamb.

. . . you're going to get the secret to several incredible bowls of noodles, but you're also going to get a story about immigrants leaving a place called home and creating a new one . . .

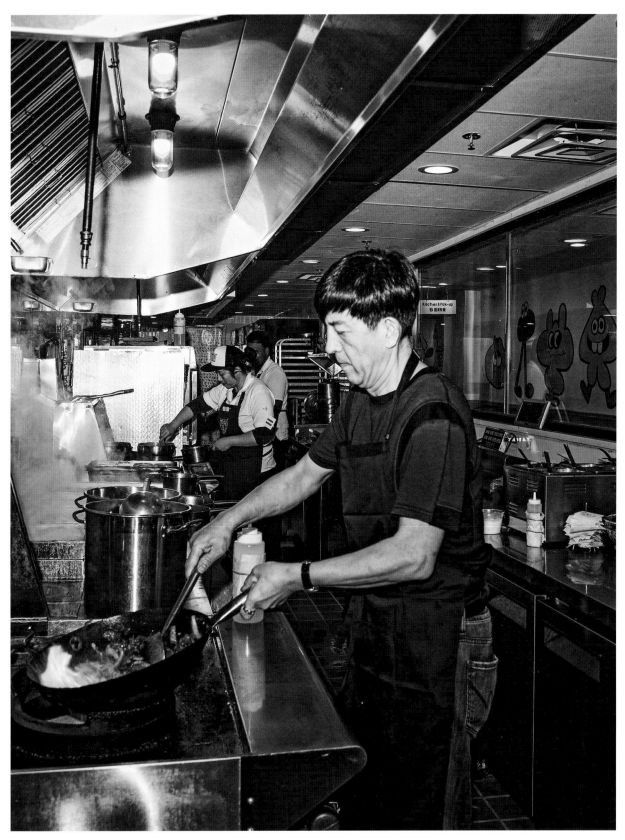

MY FATHER, DAVID SHI, HOPPING IN AS A LINE COOK AT ONE OF OUR MANHATTAN STORES, ON 43RD STREET.

1 | THE ORIGINAL TRACK

Laying the Foundations in Xi'an

LEFT: THE KITCHEN AT MY GRANDMOTHER'S HOUSE IN XI'AN. **ABOVE:** A GIRL ENJOYING A BOWL OF NOODLES AT A NEARBY VILLAGE.

ABOVE AND RIGHT: ON MY LAST TRIP TO XI'AN, I MADE SURE TO STOP BY THE MUSLIM QUARTER FOR MY FAVORITE LAMB SKEWERS.

MY OBSESSION WITH LAMB STARTED WITH ONE DISH: RAZOR-THIN LAMB SKEWERS CRISPED UP, SPRINKLED WITH CUMIN, BROWNING OVER THE RED GLOW OF CHARCOAL. It's almost Pavlovian— one whiff of the smell of burning coals and I'm transported to the front of my dad's bicycle, my five-year-old self anticipating those skewers as we weave through the city blocks. Gradually, the smell of smoke overwhelms my senses, followed by a slightly metallic wildness of lamb, a sharp bite of cumin, before, finally, a hit of roasted chile peppers that travels all the way to the back of my throat, a sign that we've arrived at the jam-packed, dusty streets of the Muslim Quarter. We jostle for a spot on a stool next to aunties and uncles slurping up noodles, or some drunk guys in their twenties eating *pao-mo* soup and drinking *erguotou baijiu*,[1] their faces barely lit with the yellow streetlamps. My focus zeroes in on the skewers, glistening in fat and oil, lit in red.

Truthfully, those lamb skewers were almost the only thing I would eat as a kid. They were irresistible to me—smoky, savory, spicy, with a touch of char, snapping with crushed cumin seeds. Every other dish I tried paled in comparison.

And yet, the food would be there, a daily constant, just like the red scarf I wore to school every day and the morning salute to the Chinese flag. On weekdays, I'd walk to school, hum the Chinese national anthem, learn some grammar and math, and walk home for lunch with my grandfather, who always had a bowl of lamb pao-mo ready for me. After a nap, I'd head back to school again, and then arrive home just as my mother put on a pot of hong shao ribs and started washing rice for dinner, all

---

1 *Baijiu,* a strong white liquor, is the go-to alcohol in China. It's what *soju* is in Korea, or vodka in Russia. *Erguotou baijiu* is one of the cheaper, low-grade types, which can sometimes be found for the same price as a beer.

the while yelling at me to practice piano. On weekends, I'd go to my grandmother's house, where I watched my aunt tend to the garden, harvest eggs from the chicken coop, and pick loquats and walnuts from the trees framing the front door.

I didn't know how good I had it. That invigorating bowl of lamb soup? It was left to congeal in its bowl while I snuck off to attend to my Transformers or dinosaur toys (I loved dinosaurs). More often than not, I'd eschew dinner, preferring to catch crickets in the courtyard of our building or play hide-and-seek with my neighbors in the cavernous stairwells. Family meals meant eating as quickly as possible so I could get back to the sunroom filled with my grandfather's birds, where I'd play with our pet baby chicks that we bought from street vendors.

Despite my childhood ambivalence toward food, however, the dishes I ate as a kid created the flavor palate that is my foundation. It's my comfort food—what I crave when I'm sick, or when the weather's shitty, or when work is too much. Instead of Grandma's chicken noodle soup, I ate grandpa's pao-mo (page 161). In lieu of spaghetti and meatballs, I had heavily spiced hand-ripped noodles (page 58). And an afternoon snack was never a plate of sliced apples or "ants on a log," but rou jia mou, an English muffin-like bun stuffed full of fatty soy-braised pork (page 169).

So to understand the Xi'an Famous Foods story, you have to understand my childhood first. And to do that, you have to understand where we came from and what forces made the food of my hometown so special, how migration and geography and various dynasties' power plays collided. And then, you have to master the basic building blocks and flavors that make the foundation of our cuisine. It's not always going to be pretty. I grew up eating dishes full of mouth-puckering vinegars and aggressive chili oils, chickens with jagged broken bones, freshly slaughtered in our backyard and drained of their blood, all served over rough, hearty buns and dense, chewy noodles that demand to be made—and eaten—quickly. It's food that makes you sweat for it, but—as you'll soon learn—it's always worth it.

A Brief Guide to the Flavors of Xi'an

XI'AN HAS ALWAYS BEEN KIND OF A BIG DEAL. Formerly known as Chang'an, my hometown was the longest-serving ancient capital of China. Dynasties rose and fell, but the area's importance remained constant.

It's the reason why our food is unique. A long time ago,[2] some hotshot emperor[3] decided to make a deal with a native tribe farther west in order to fight their enemy at the time, the Xiongnu. The messenger Zhang Qian ended up being captured, but when he finally escaped ten years later, he brought back stories of the food, culture, and legendary "winged" horses[4] found in the west.

Naturally, more people were sent out, more returned. The paths became the Silk Road, a caravan trade route between China and the West, and when the Tang dynasty came to power, Xi'an became the cultural epicenter of the country. Our silks and spices and teas were passed merchant to merchant, winding through the less-traveled region of Xinjiang, marching past the Taklamakan Desert, branching out into networks and crossing Afghanistan, through Iraq, and eventually making the journey across the Mediterranean Sea to the Roman Empire and beyond. And in return, Xi'an, like modern-day metropolitan areas, found itself flush with newcomers who brought their foods, flavors, and traditions with them. Eventually, a sizeable Muslim population set up shop in what is now the Muslim Quarter; their descendants became known as Hui, one of China's many ethnic groups.

After the Tang dynasty fell, the rest of the world zoomed away, focusing on newer capitals, cities like Nanjing and Beijing, while the coastal city of Shanghai gained prominence as an important trade stop. But the city of Xi'an continued to hum along, serving as an important manufacturing and agricultural hub in central China in the modern day, and continuing its role as a connector between the eastern and western parts of the country. And in the meantime, the food, the mishmash, the swirling of cultures in Xi'an thrived. The flavors I grew up with, explained briefly here, are the result of this vibrant culture.

2 141–87 BCE.
3 Emperor Wudi of the Han dynasty.
4 A fancy way of saying really freakin' fast horses.

SOUR

Almost any chef will say great food requires a balance of acid—and our acid of choice is vinegar. Specifically, **black vinegar**, a tangy, rich kick so ingrained in our cooking, so deified, artisans were trained to make it specifically for the imperial court during the Zhou dynasty.

Now black vinegar is everywhere. In Xi'an, we'd have our pick of local vinegars, but stateside, the easiest bottle to buy is the rice-based Zhenjiang vinegar, or Chinkiang vinegar, which you can snag at any Asian supermarket.

SPICY—THE HOT KIND

Contrary to popular belief, our food isn't supposed to burn your face off. Instead, Xi'an food tends to use spice for fragrance, flavor, and depth. Nevertheless, we do incorporate two types of sinus-clearing heat. The first comes from **Tianjin peppers**, also referred to as **Chinese red chile peppers**. These capsaicin-loaded fruits are typically spicier than cayenne, but not quite as explosive as habanero chile peppers. The Tianjin pepper lacks some of the more complex, earthy notes of other varietals, but makes up for it with heat, smokiness, and eye-catching color. You could chop up these red peppers and toss them straight into any dish for extra fire, but I prefer to turn them into a chili oil, roasting both the membrane and the seeds to really amp up the flavors. For a spicy crunch but slightly milder hit, we'll also thinly slice red or green **longhorn peppers**, tossing the slivers into a stir-fry or raw into salads.

The second wave of heat comes from **Sichuan peppercorns**, named for the nearby province known for its humidity, heat, and intensely hot food. If you want truly mind-numbing, taste-bud-obliterating spicy food, Sichuan is your North Star, with dishes that will simultaneously burn your mouth and numb it. The latter sensation comes from the peppercorns, which are neither black pepper nor chile peppers, but rather dried berries from a citrus tree. So, while Sichuan peppercorns don't have capsaicin like spicy peppers, they do include another compound that triggers a vibrating, intense tingle—the "*ma*," or tingly sensation, to pair with the spicy "*la*" in "*ma la*."[5]

SPICY—THE SAVORY KIND

Now *this* is where the food gets interesting. While many parts of China use Sichuan peppercorns, Tianjin chile peppers, and black vinegar (call it the holy trinity), the food of Xi'an is unique in that it embodies the Silk Road's history. So, in addition to those three core flavors, we're also drawing in spices from the Mediterranean, India, and the Middle East, plus the core spices that are native to China. **Star anise**, a key ingredient in Chinese five-spice powder, often gets paired with **cinnamon** for its spicy sweetness and **cloves** for their earthy intensity, all simmered with soy sauce to tenderize and flavor heavy meat stews. **Dried tangerine or orange peel**, a staple from the Guangdong region with a pithy bitterness softened with aging, is frequently used to cut through those heady spices, while powdery **white pepper** adds a bright, clean kick as a final flourish.

Meanwhile, flavors from abroad gradually made their way into the foundation of our cuisine, brought in by traders along the Silk Road. Both black cardamom and white cardamom, traveling from their native home of India, are used to add warmth to our sauces and stocks. **Black cardamom**, with its smoky, dried flavor, pairs especially well in meaty, savory components with a punch of umami. **White cardamom**, or Siam cardamom, adds a delicate floral spice to lighter dishes and soup stocks.

The most important spice, however, might be **cumin**. I'm biased, given my love for cumin lamb, but historians have identified cumin as one of the most ancient ingredients in the world, so commonly traded that the origins of the ingredient are a little muddy, its path to Xi'an a geographical adventure. First, cumin had to be transported from the Mediterranean down the Persian Gulf, through India along the Silk Road, becoming a staple in Uighur cuisine in Xinjiang, until its merchants finally reached the farthest eastern point of Xi'an. With its strong, earthy punch, flavorful enough to mask the metallic flavors sometimes found in lamb, cumin became a staple ingredient in this region's cuisine, making its home alongside the chili oil, black vinegar, Sichuan peppercorns, and myriad sweet-savory spices that have created the landscape of Xi'an's cuisine.

---

5 I like to think I coined the phrase "spicy and tingly"—no other place described *ma la* this way before we did, as far as I know.

Your First Cooking Lessons

HOW TO COOK RICE

Even though Xi'an cuisine traditionally revolves around noodles and breads, my family's meals also used rice as a base. The grain is historically preferred in southern Chinese cuisine instead of northern, but by the time I was born, it was easily accessible—and easier to cook for feeding a crowd.

In restaurants, you'll see a lot of jasmine rice, but at home my family prefers short-grain or sushi rice, which is slightly sweeter on its own. And how it tastes is essential; we don't add seasonings to the rice as it cooks, since it's meant to balance the saltier toppings and side dishes of a meal.

Personally, I plan out my bowl to make sure there's enough grain to soak up the flavors and the salt, but not too much to make the overall meal bland. It's a tricky balance, like getting the right ratio of chips and dip.

In a Rice Cooker

I learned to use a rice cooker before I learned to boil water, and let me just say, they're pretty genius—foolproof enough to be used by a seven-year-old (aka me).

Still, there's an art to the whole practice. You can use almost any rice except for glutinous rice, which is too sticky. Measure out the number of cups you need using the plastic cup provided by the rice cooker of your choice. Cover your rice in cold water, swirl it around with your hand to get all those dusty bits worked up, and then pour out the milky liquid, catching any grains of rice in between your fingers. Repeat two more times until the water runs clear—but do this more than three times and you risk washing out the fragrance of the rice.

Finally, add enough water to cover for cooking, using a 1½ to 1 ratio of water to rice. It's possible to approximate this by sight and feel. The adults used to tell me to put my palm flat against the surface of the washed grains in the rice cooker to measure how much water I needed to add. For more of a bite, you add enough water to just barely cover your knuckles. If you want the rice to be softer, add a bit more. Pros will let the rice soak for an hour, but hey, if you're starving, just push that button and go about your business.

In a Pot

Not going to lie, prior to writing this book I had never cooked rice in a pot. But I learned for you—and it's pretty damn easy. Just wash the rice in a pot, cover it with water in that same 1½ to 1 ratio as you would with a rice cooker, and then bring the pot of rice and water to a boil with a lid on. Immediately drop the temperature to a simmer and simmer for 20 to 30 minutes, until the liquid is absorbed and the rice is soft.

FIVE RULES TO BOILING NOODLES

Whether you're working with dried noodles or fresh, store-bought or homemade, the steps are the same. Bring a large pot of water to a boil and drop in the noodles, and never, ever break these rules:

1. Make sure the water is at a rapid boil and there's enough room to allow the noodles to separate and "swim freely."

2. Don't salt the water. We're not Italian.

3. Use chopsticks or tongs to make sure the strands don't stick to the bottom. This is especially important when you first drop the noodles in.

4. Test (aka eat a strand), and make sure it's "QQ," a common Chinese phrase that means chewy or toothy. Basically, our version of al dente. Don't overcook.

5. Change the water if you are cooking more than two batches. Once the water gets too starchy and bubbly, the noodles will cook differently, so after a few servings, start a fresh pot.

What's in Your Pantry

NO CHINESE KITCHEN IS COMPLETE WITHOUT AN ARRAY OF MYSTERIOUS JARS FULL OF FUNKY SAUCES AND BRIGHT RED PASTES, OR BOTTLES OF DARK LIQUIDS THAT ALL LOOK LIKE SOY SAUCE AT FIRST GLANCE. Though this collection might seem extravagant, each of these condiments adds an extra dash of flavor to our dishes, creating a base layer of umami or a top note of acid to finish off a bite. Here's what you'll need to get your Xi'an pantry started.

BLACK VINEGAR
Zhenjiang vinegar, also known as Chinkiang vinegar, is the most common Chinese black vinegar you'll find. It's neither sweet nor thick like balsamic, but does have a slightly fruity, sour kick.

CHILI SAUCE OR CHILI GARLIC SAUCE
While our XFF Chili Oil goes for roasty, toasty, spicy goodness, sometimes you need a little kick of acid and vinegar. Enter this bright red chili sauce, which adds the taste of fresh peppers to dipping sauces. You could go for any chili sauce, but Huy Fong is my reliable go-to. And if you want an extra punch, opt for the chili garlic version.

DARK SOY SAUCE
While light soy sauce might be used for cooking and stewing, aged, or dark, soy sauce is often used as a finishing touch. The aging process darkens the sauce, deepening the flavor for a less salty, slightly sweeter finish, making this an essential last step in getting the right color for many of our dishes.

FERMENTED BLACK BEANS
Not what you'd find in the canned bean section, *douchi*, or dry, fermented black soybeans, are typically used as a flavoring agent, bringing an extra layer of salty, almost funky umami to a stewed dish. These beans also get pounded into a black bean paste, sometimes with garlic and soy sauce.

LIGHT SOY SAUCE
Your go-to soy sauce. If we don't specify what type of soy sauce to use in the recipe, this is what we're referring to.

OSMANTHUS SYRUP
Not a must-have, but definitely a favorite for desserts, this sweet, floral syrup brings to mind flavors of chamomile and chrysanthemum (minus whatever medicinal notes you might associate with those blooms).

OYSTER SAUCE

When I was younger, my mom told me that oyster sauce was made from oysters (it kind of is), and since oysters were rare in Xi'an, I always thought that oyster sauce was something to be coveted. It also helped that this sauce was sweet, savory, and rich. Every time we brought out a bottle, tapping it at a specific angle as you would ketchup, my mom would let me lick the remnants off the rim before putting it back in the fridge, an illicit (and, yes, bacteria-friendly) taste that I still remember.

PIXIAN BEAN SAUCE

Warning: This sauce can get spicy. Named after the Sichuan district of Pidu (formerly Pixian) in Chengdu, this paste is typically made from fermented beans, chile peppers, wheat flour, and salt. The coarse, deep red paste adds a complex, savory undertone to dishes when cooked, with a slow build of heat.

SHAOXING COOKING WINE

Our primary cooking wine, made from fermented rice, is most often used to combat strong meat aromas while adding some depth of flavor.

SESAME PASTE

Our version of tahini, used to add a thick, nutty base to sauces. Over time, this condiment has become more popular in Xi'an with the rise of sesame-dressed liang pi (page 247). It's also excellent in hot pot dipping sauces (page 141).

SWEET FLOUR SAUCE

If you've ever had Peking duck, you've likely smeared this on the pancakes before tossing on the crispy duck skin and green onions. The thick, black, paste-like condiment is also the base for meat sauces like *zha jiang mian* (page 91) and a flavoring agent on our Chinese *juan bing* (page 83). While it's salty enough to be treated like soy sauce, there's a roasted maltiness to the paste, reminding tasters that the main ingredient is, in fact, flour.

TOASTED SESAME OIL

I rarely use sesame oil to fry or sauté. Instead, toasted sesame oil is added as an aromatic to meats, dipping sauces, and dressings for its nuttiness and fragrance. A little will go a long way.

Roasted Sesame Seeds
烤芝麻籽

My family's pantry was rarely without sesame seeds, which act as flavor, texture, aroma, *and* aesthetic. My mom would keep a jar of roasted seeds, refilling as needed, and sprinkle these crunchy, toasty bites over almost every dish—sweet or savory. We'd have them on dumplings, noodles, and bread just as soon as we'd have them with sweet, sticky rice cakes. Coarsely crush them after roasting to open up the flavor components and then use them as quickly as possible.

Makes
2 cups
(300 g)

2 cups (300 g) white sesame seeds

In a large skillet set over low heat, add the sesame seeds and roast for 8 to 10 minutes.

When the seeds are golden and fragrant and start making popping sounds, remove from the heat and carefully transfer them to a cutting board to cool.

Once cooled, coarsely crush the sesame seeds against the cutting board using a rolling pin. Store in a sealed container for up to 6 months, longer if refrigerated, although the seeds are best used fresh.

Red Chili Powder
辣椒粉

If you buy chili powder from the supermarket, chances are you're getting other spices in there—ground-up garlic, cumin, dried onions. That stuff's aight, but it's nothing compared to home-ground chili powder. Trust me.

The trick here is to get the best quality dried Tianjin red chile peppers you can find—look for peppers that are vibrant and red.[6] Then we go through the extra step of roasting the peppers, gently releasing all of the flavors, before cooling and grinding them into a powder. Yes, it'll take more time—but it'll save you money, be ten times more delicious, and give a little extra burn to all of your dishes.

Note: Wear gloves, and never touch your face after handling the powder until you've thoroughly washed your hands. I say this from experience. You'll want to wash the spice grinder very carefully afterward, too. If you can take it apart, do so and thoroughly clean out the machine per the manufacturer's instructions. I've also used coffee grinders in a pinch, cleaning out the system afterward by grinding up raw grains of rice in the machine two or three times, emptying it out in between. Even then, you might end up with a lingering chili powder flavor. If you truly want to be safe, reserve a spice grinder specifically for making chili powder.

Makes
1 cup
(450 g)

1 pound (450 g) dried Tianjin red chile peppers (typically labeled as Chinese dry red chiles in markets)

½ cup (120 ml) canola or vegetable oil

Preheat the oven to 200°F (90°C).

Wash the peppers in cold water and blot with paper towels to dry.

In a large bowl, toss the peppers in the oil and place them in a single layer on a baking sheet. Roast in the oven for 15 minutes, shaking the pan occasionally to avoid sticking.

Cover a plate with paper towels. Remove the peppers from the oven and carefully set on the paper towel–lined plate to cool.

Once cooled, use a spice grinder to grind the peppers into powder form, and store at room temperature in an airtight container for up to 1 month.

6 Most of the time, you'll find these peppers wrapped in plastic, but if you can, I'd recommend testing their quality by crumbling one so the flavor is released, smelling it, and then tasting it. The pepper should immediately be fragrant and spicy; stale peppers lose both their flavor and their heat.

What's in Your Fridge

Your Aromatics

CHINESE CELERY

Chinese celery is smaller, crunchier, and more flavorful, with a strong peppery bite packed into thin, fibrous stalks, as if a stalk of conventional celery were drained of 50 percent of its water and compressed. In all the recipes in this book, Chinese celery is preferred, but only absolutely necessary when noted.

CHINESE CHIVES

Unlike hollow onion chives, which are typically used in Western cooking, Chinese chives, or garlic chives, are flat-leaved. And just like how onion chives are slightly delicate versions of onions, garlic chives have a light garlic flavor. When used in bulk, however, that punch is strong. You can use both the leaves and the flowers, the latter if you want a bigger kick.

GREEN ONIONS

A dish is rarely finished without a sprinkling of chopped green onions on top. Typically, the white parts of the stalk are added earlier in the cooking process to slowly soften the oniony flavor; the green parts are added in the final stages of cooking as a flourish.

Garlic Puree
蒜泥

Okay, so I admit, this is hardly a recipe. But it requires some work. The traditional method would be pounding this out with a mortar and pestle, but a garlic press also does the trick. Make a batch and store it away, like I do, and soon you'll be adding a dab into your dumpling sauce, a scoop into your noodles, a tablespoon into vegetable stir-fry, and an obscene amount into a sharp dressing over cucumbers. Who knows? You might find yourself liking the taste of garlic so much, you'll be nibbling a clove in between dumpling bites. Heck, you might even find yourself mixing whole cloves of garlic into your bowl of noodles, like a true Xi'an local. It's too good to pass up, even when it causes heartburn.

Note: If you find yourself in the middle of a recipe without garlic puree on hand, 1 teaspoon of this powerful stuff equates to roughly 1 garlic clove, peeled and finely chopped.

Makes about ½ cup (170 g)

2 heads of garlic

Separate all the cloves from the heads of garlic and easily peel them by smashing them with the flat side of a knife. The skins should just fall away. Trim the root ends from each clove.

Place a few cloves at a time in a mortar or garlic press and pound or press them until you have a smooth paste.

Transfer the paste to a glass or plastic storage container as you work your way through the rest of the cloves. One batch should last 3 days refrigerated in an airtight container.

Chili Oil Is Your Friend

NOT AS SPICY = NOT AS GOOD

I GET IT. NOT EVERYONE HAS THE SAME SPICE TOLERANCE I HAVE. BUT I WOULD NEVER COOK OR ORDER XI'AN FOOD WITHOUT A SINGLE HIT OF CHILI OIL. Our foods are known for being spicy and flavorful, and our chili oil is an important player in that. This isn't just about burning your face off, by the way; this is as much about heat as it is about taste and aroma, the toasted cloves and bay leaves, the fragrance of the spices. Without chili oil, many of the dishes will end up being too bland. It's just not XFF.

- X
- F
- F
-

Think of it this way: I used to take drawing lessons, and I learned there are two ways of drawing. One is to draw lines—strong marks that depict an image. Another way is to shade in the contours, the shadows, and create an image through the implied shapes. XFF is the former—every flavor, every spice, is meant to be accentuated, to pack a punch. There's nothing subtle about our food.

So, when you're making the dishes in this book, pay attention to when chili oil is listed as an ingredient. Some recipes will call for just the oil; some just for the seeds (for a little extra kick without the fat). Others will let you make that adventurous decision for yourself. But even if you're a wuss and you think you can't stand the heat, don't skip it.

CHILI OIL IS YOUR FRIEND—without it, you won't be getting the full flavor expected of a true XFF experience.

STILL SCARED? Here's a guide to getting your dosage right. It's a rough estimate, since some of the dishes in this book already have peppers or chili powder added, but it's a good start to building up your tolerance.

The Least You Could Do: Drizzle at least 1½ teaspoons of chili oil on your dish, and maybe a touch more if you think you can handle it.

Mild: For a little more, add 1 tablespoon of chili oil (no seeds) for a kick. You'll still sweat, but you won't be crying.

Regular: If you're a spice fiend, top your noodles with 2 tablespoons of chili oil and 1 tablespoon of seeds—because the seeds are where the real oomph is.

Extra Spicy: If you think you can handle it, pour on 2 tablespoons of chili oil plus 2 tablespoons of seeds per serving. Then hit me up; we should hang.

XFF Chili Oil
秘制辣椒油

While most sauces like sriracha aim to get the bright, acidic bite of fresh peppers, we go for that deep, fiery, earthy heat of roasted chile peppers. So while our chili oil might look red and intimidating, it actually caps off quite early in terms of spice level, and instead focuses on the flavor and fragrances of spices like star anise, cloves, and bay leaves. I add it to eggs, congee, and any and all noodles. A drop or two will add a small but powerful kick; a splash will make your mouth water; a spoonful will make you sweat. And let's not even get started on the chile pepper seeds that soak in this powerful stuff.

This type of heat doesn't come easy. In the stores, we go all out with thirty different ingredients sourced from all over the world, but at home, I make this pared-down version that's just as good and not as annoying to make—although it's still pretty annoying, to be honest. The recipe calls for oil to be heated up to 450°F (232°C), ready to give you some severe burns or start a fire if you don't watch yourself. My recommendation: Deck yourself out with all the protective gear possible (*definitely* do *not* cook naked with just an apron on), and have a fire extinguisher on standby. And if you live in a tiny NYC apartment, your smoke detector *will* go off.

Note: Make sure none of your pots are near any open flames and are all set securely on stable surfaces. You want to make sure the pot won't tip over when you're pouring out the hot oil. Serious burn injuries may be sustained if the oil touches your skin—it's happened to me, and it's not fun.

Makes slightly less than 1 quart (960 ml)

2 cups (455 g) Red Chili Powder (page 35)

4 cups (960 ml) canola or soybean oil

1 tablespoon Sichuan peppercorns

4 star anise pods

4 cloves

5 bay leaves

1 green onion, trimmed and coarsely chopped

¼ medium red onion, peeled and roughly chopped

2-inch (5 cm) piece fresh ginger, peeled and roughly sliced

Splash of black vinegar

TOOLS:

High-temperature infrared or probe thermometer that goes up to at least 450°F (232°C)

Small fine-mesh strainer

Place the red chili powder into a large, heat-safe pot or bowl big enough to pour the hot oil into later. Set aside on a stable surface.

Add the oil to a second pot and set over medium heat. Heat until the thermometer registers 300°F (150°C).

Add the Sichuan peppercorns, star anise, cloves, and bay leaves. Immediately after, carefully place the green onion, onion, and ginger into the hot oil as well. This will bring the temperature of the oil down; bring the temperature of the oil up to 350°F (177°C) and maintain it there by carefully moving the pot off the heat if too hot and putting back on the heat if too cool. Fry the spices at 350°F (177°C) in the oil for about 3 minutes, until the spices are fragrant but not blackened. Use a strainer to remove everything solid from the oil (reserve these aromatics to enhance a broth or stew later).

Heat the oil up to 450°F (232°C), then turn off the burner and carefully remove the pot from the heat.

You might want to wear long sleeves for this next step. Very carefully, while wearing oven mitts, gradually pour the hot oil into the bigger pot with the red chili powder, stirring carefully to make sure every bit of the chili powder is cooked by the hot oil. This will create a lot of smoke, so if you can, do this step outdoors or be ready to deal with smoke alarms. Don't inhale the smoke.

The temperature of the oil will drop quickly. Add a splash of black vinegar to add more flavor but also to bring down the temperature so the chili powder doesn't get burnt.

Leave the oil to cool to room temperature, and let it rest, covered, for 10 to 12 hours or overnight. Store in an airtight container at room temperature for up to 1 month.

Bone Broth
骨头汤

A childhood in the States has taught me that chicken soup can cure the soul, but my family relied on beef and lamb for that comfort. Unlike meat broths, where hunks of meat can be quickly boiled for a clean and flavorful soup, the cooking mantra for this is low and slow.

Which is all to say, this shit takes time. This isn't some ten-minute Instant Pot recipe. This is the stuff grandmas are known for. For the most flavorful version, you have to soak the bones for an hour, boil them to clean them, and then start all over with the aromatics.

I like to keep quart containers of this broth in my freezer to use as the base for hot pot (pages 139–40), pao-mo (page 161), and even instant ramen (page 70). On sick days, I'll just drink it up with some chopped green onions, salt, and a sneeze-inducing dash of white pepper. But save the actual broth making for a boring day at home; your future self will thank you.

**Makes
2 quarts
(2 L)**

4 ounces (115 g) beef or lamb femur or marrow bones

4 ounces (115 g) beef or lamb rib bones

4 ounces (115 g) any cut of beef or lamb with both fatty and lean meat (optional)

1-inch (2.5 cm) piece fresh ginger, peeled and thickly sliced

2 green onions, trimmed and cut into 2-inch (5 cm) segments

2 bay leaves

2 star anise pods, broken

1 teaspoon Sichuan peppercorns

4 white cardamom pods

3½ quarts (3.3 L) cold water

TO TASTE AT END:
Salt

White pepper powder

In a large pot, add the bones and, if you're using it, the meat. Cover with cold water to submerge and soak for 1 hour.

Remove the bones and meat from the pot and set aside. Discard the water and clean the pot thoroughly to remove any residue and impurities. Add the bones and meat back to the pot and cover with fresh water until submerged.

Cover, set the pot over high heat, and bring to a boil. Once boiling, turn off the heat. Carefully remove the bones and meat once more and set them aside. Dump the water and clean the pot again.

Add the bones, meat, and the remaining ingredients to the clean pot. If you have a larger capacity pot, you *can* add more water, but leave extra room to prevent the broth from boiling over.

Set the pot over high heat and bring everything to a boil. Once boiling, turn down the heat to low, keeping the broth at a simmer, and cover the pot. Simmer for 6 hours. Strain all of the solids from the broth before using. If you're drinking it straight, add salt and white pepper, to taste. The broth can be stored in an airtight container for up to 3 days in the refrigerator, or 1 month in the freezer.

The Key Sauces

YOU MIGHT LOOK AT THESE SAUCES AND SEE NO DIFFERENCES—BUT THE BEAUTY IS IN THE DETAILS. Each blend of soy sauce and vinegar has the perfect amount of salt, savoriness, and bite, with the right texture and mouthfeel to grip onto the surface you're dressing.

XFF Noodle Sauce
秘制调面汁

For dense hand-pulled noodles, you're going to want the sauce to be saltier and spicier, balancing out the thick wheat noodles with extra aromatics for depth of flavor.

Makes
1½ cups
(360 ml)

- X
F
F
-

1 cup (240 ml) soy sauce

⅓ cup (75 ml) black vinegar

1 tablespoon oyster sauce

½ teaspoon sugar

1 star anise pod

½ teaspoon Sichuan peppercorns

1 bay leaf

½ teaspoon salt

1 teaspoon fennel seeds

1½-inch (4 cm) piece fresh ginger, peeled and sliced

Dash of white pepper powder

In a saucepan, combine all of the ingredients with ¼ cup (60 ml) water and mix to combine. Bring to a boil over high heat.

Once boiling, turn the heat down to a low boil and cook for 2 minutes. Then turn off the heat, cover the pot, and let sit for 10 minutes.

Strain the sauce and use immediately, or let cool and store in an airtight container, refrigerated, for up to 3 days.

XFF Liang Pi Sauce
秘制凉皮汁

Traditionally, liang pi purveyors only dress liang pi with salt and vinegar, letting the chewy ribbons shine on their own. At XFF, however, we found that the salt grains would interrupt the slick mouthfeel of cold skin noodles. Our compromise? Soy sauce, and a generous dose of vinegar.

Makes
1½ cups
(360 ml)

½ cup (120 ml) soy sauce

1 cup (240 ml) black vinegar

1 teaspoon sugar

2 star anise pods

1 teaspoon Sichuan peppercorns

2 bay leaves

1 black cardamom pod

1-inch (2.5 cm) piece cinnamon stick

1½ teaspoons salt

In a small saucepan, combine all ingredients with ⅓ cup (75 ml) water and mix to combine. Bring to a boil over high heat.

Once boiling, turn the heat down to a low boil and cook for 2 minutes.

Turn off the heat, cover the pot, and let sit for 10 minutes.

Strain the sauce and use immediately, or let cool and store in an airtight container, refrigerated, until ready to use, for up to 3 days.

XFF Dumpling Sauce
秘制饺子汁

The balance for this sauce is important: A stronger vinegar to soy sauce ratio helps cut the fattiness of the dumplings, while the oyster sauce adds a slight velvety finish and a touch of sugar.

Note: Mix in a little Spicy and Tingly Sauce (page 194) for an extra kick.

Makes
1½ cups
(360 ml)

¼ cup (60 ml) soy sauce

1 cup (240 ml) black vinegar

1 tablespoon oyster sauce

1 tablespoon sugar

1 star anise pod

½ teaspoon Sichuan peppercorns

1 bay leaf

4 black peppercorns

1½-inch (4 cm) piece fresh ginger, peeled and sliced

In a small saucepan, combine all of the ingredients along with ¼ cup (60 ml) water. Bring to a boil over high heat.

Once boiling, turn the heat down to a low boil and cook for 2 minutes. Then turn off the heat, cover the pot, and let sit for 10 minutes.

Strain the sauce and use immediately, or let cool and store in an airtight container, refrigerated, until ready to use, for up to 3 days.

Your Carb Bases

Daily Bread
馍

Walk into any Xi'an market and you'll see this bread in all shapes and sizes—and smell it, too. But it hardly feels fair to call this bread, since you don't use an oven to bake it. Instead, we use a skillet, frying it like a pancake. The result is almost a flatbread, with a slightly fluffy center and a little extra crisp on the outside. You could have this by itself for a quick snack, but I also toss this into Hoolah Soup (page 236) or onto the grill (page 201) to revive the next day. Most important, this bread is the main component of our XFF burgers (page 60), bookending our classic Stewed Pork (page 169) or Spicy Cumin Lamb (page 173).

Makes
4
breads

2 cups (250 g) all-purpose flour or high-gluten flour

¼ teaspoon active dry yeast

⅛ teaspoon baking powder

⅛ teaspoon granulated sugar

½ cup (120 ml) room-temperature water

TOOL:
A thin, evenly cylindrical rolling pin, roughly 1½ inches (4 cm) in diameter

In a large bowl, add the flour, yeast, baking powder, and sugar and mix to combine.

Add the water slowly while mixing with one hand, until the texture is fluffy and sandy, almost like feathery snow. Using both hands, knead the dough until it comes together in a smooth ball, 3 to 5 minutes.

Cover the dough with plastic wrap and let rest at room temperature for 20 minutes.

After resting, remove the plastic wrap and knead the dough a few more times, either inside the bowl or on a countertop. Cover with plastic wrap and let rest for another 10 minutes.

After resting, divide the dough into 4 evenly sized pieces.

To shape the dough, take one piece and place it on an unfloured work surface. Lightly grip the dough and firmly roll against the work surface into a smooth, round mound.

When round, flatten the ball of dough with the palm of your hand against the work counter. Use a rolling pin to flatten it into a round cake, about 4 inches (10 cm) in diameter. Repeat with the remaining dough.

Set a small dry skillet over medium heat. Preheat for 3 minutes.

Once hot, turn the heat down to low and put a cake (or if you are confident with your skills, a few cakes) into the pan. Cover the skillet and cook the bread for about 1 minute on each side, until some brown spots appear. Flip and cook once more on each side to ensure the dough is fully cooked. If you see any parts that look gray or raw, it's not quite ready. It should be slightly crisp on the outside and steaming inside. The bread is best served fresh and warm, but can be cooled to room temperature, wrapped in a zip-top bag or plastic wrap, and stored in the refrigerator for up to 3 days.

Longevity Noodles
长寿面

Most of our fans know us for biang-biang noodles that are hand-pulled, ripped, and purposefully disheveled, but the goal of longevity noodles is to create a long, slick, uniform strand, gently pulled over and over again until you get the right thickness. Pros will feed the noodle straight into the pot while pulling in quick, seamless motions, but unless you do this a hundred times a day, you'll end up with an unevenly cooked strand—al dente on one end, mushy on the other. To avoid that, this recipe calls for folding the noodle over itself, pulling the strand like a cat's cradle, and finally tossing it in all in one go.

Note: You can serve these noodles with any of our main toppings as described on page 61, but I particularly enjoy these with Concubine's Chicken (page 165). And if you don't like slurping, you might want a different dish (or book), because cutting these noodles into more manageable strands is considered bad luck.

Makes 2 very long noodles, enough to serve 2 *Lady and the Tramp* style

2 cups (250 g) all-purpose flour or high-gluten flour

½ teaspoon salt

¾ cup (180 ml) room-temperature water

Canola or vegetable oil as needed

2 cups (480 ml) cold water, divided

In a large bowl, add the flour and salt and mix well to combine.

Add the room-temperature water slowly while mixing the dough with your hands. Using both hands, knead the dough until it comes together in a smooth ball, 3 to 5 minutes.

When the dough is formed, cover the dough with plastic wrap and let it rest at room temperature for 20 minutes.

After resting, remove the plastic wrap and knead the dough in the bowl a few more times. Cover again with plastic wrap and let it rest for another 15 minutes.

After the second rest, brush a bit of the oil on the dough and place it on a cutting board or work surface. Cut the dough in half, and using your hands, roll each piece of dough into a long, snake-like cylindrical shape, a little over ½ inch (12 mm) in diameter.

Lightly coat a large container with oil. Store the dough inside by forming each piece into a spiral (like a resting snake). Brush the dough with a bit of extra oil to prevent sticking. Cover it with plastic wrap and rest in the refrigerator for at least 30 minutes (if using immediately) or up to 1 day.

When ready to use, remove the dough from the refrigerator and let it rest at room temperature for 10 minutes.

Fill a large pot with water, enough for the noodles to swim freely in. Set the pot over high heat and bring to a boil.

Work with one coil of dough at a time (see illustration step 1). Pick up one end of the dough coil with one hand, then grab it about 4 inches (10 cm) down the strand with your other hand (step 2).

Using your first hand, pull the end of the dough out and away from your second hand, to stretch it without breaking it (step 3). Continue pulling the dough with your first hand, stretching it out with the other (step 4). This should lengthen and slim the dough without breaking it. After you have finished stretching the length of the noodle, the dough should be less than ½ inch (12 mm) in diameter, roughly 8 feet (2.5 m) long.

Loop the dough into a large ring roughly 18 inches (46 cm) in diameter. You might have to loop the dough several times (step 5). With your hands shoulder-width apart, pick up the dough ring with both of your hands, cradling it with your fingers. Make sure not to tangle the strand.

With both hands holding the dough, pull the noodle ring outward while slapping it up and down on the work counter (step 6). Pull until the individual strand is less than ¼ inch (6 mm) in diameter. (You could go thinner, but it requires skill.) Be careful not to break it; if the noodle snaps, simply pick up where the strand breaks and resume pulling. Each noodle should end up being roughly 27 feet (8 m) long.

Repeat the stretching, pulling, and slapping process with the second half of the snake coil.

Once done pulling both pieces of dough, throw the noodles into the boiling water right away, stirring so the noodles don't stick to themselves or the side of the pot.

When the water comes back to a rapid boil, pour 1 cup of cold water into the pot. Bring back to a boil and cook for 1 minute before adding another cup of cold water. Once the pot boils again, carefully fish out the noodles using a hand strainer or spider. The noodles should have boiled for 2 to 3 minutes in total.

Liang Pi "Cold Skin Noodles" 凉皮 and Seitan 面筋: What It Is and How to Make It

Makes
2 to 3
servings

The name *liang pi*, which translates into "cold skin," refers not to the noodle's ingredients, but its texture. Typically served at room temperature, liang pi is bouncy, chewy, and slippery, akin to the delightfully slick texture of the skin on a Chinese poached chicken.

So despite its name, these noodles are not made from the skin of an animal. Instead, it's a cold noodle that is steamed and then sliced, rather than pulled and boiled. While you're making a dough, the goal is to isolate the starch in that dough by washing it. The washed dough becomes seitan, a spongy, almost tofu-like mass of protein perfect for soaking up dressings (like in our seitan salad, page 111), and that starchy water is what makes your noodles. Trippy, right?

It took us many years and many experiments to get to the right ratio of starch and water for that perfect, chewy bite. Too much water and you end up with slush; too little, and your noodles turn brittle and break. But don't worry; if I can make batches of this in a shitty college apartment (which I did one summer), you can make it anywhere. It just might take a few tries.

Note: This recipe will give you batches of liang pi and seitan, as they're two halves of the same recipe. You can use the liang pi noodles for our most famous dish, the classic liang pi (page 162), as well as our stir-fried liang pi (page 164), and if you wanted to be an overachiever, sub out the noodles in the sesame version (page 247). The seitan can be used in our seitan salad (page 111), a perfectly tasty consolation prize if you end up with inedible noodles.

FOR THE DOUGH:

5 cups (625 g) all-purpose flour

¼ teaspoon salt

1¾ cups (420 ml) cold water

FOR THE SEITAN:

Washed dough

½ teaspoon active dry yeast

FOR THE LIANG PI:

Reserved starchy liquid (from washing the dough)

¼ cup (60 ml) vegetable oil

TOOLS:

Double-stack steamer pot, which can fit pans with at least a 12-inch (30.5 cm) diameter

2 to 4 deep dish-pans, 9 inches (23 cm) in diameter

Pair of tongs, at least 8 inches (20 cm) long

Chopsticks

Brush (for oil)

1. To make the dough: In a large bowl, add the flour and salt and stir to combine. Slowly add the cold water in a stream while mixing with one hand to form a dough. When the dough is formed, continue to knead, making sure that all of the flour is incorporated. The dough should be springy and elastic. Cover with a wet towel and let rest for 30 minutes.

After 30 minutes, uncover and knead for 1 more minute. Cover again and let rest for another 30 minutes.

Uncover the dough and place it in a large bowl. Pour 3 cups (720 ml) water over the rested dough and "wash" the dough, massaging, poking, and squeezing the mass with your fingers to release the starch into the water. After about 2 minutes, carefully pour the water into a large container and set aside.

Repeat the washing process through five washes total. This will leave you with a smaller mass of washed dough and a vat of starchy water. Place the starchy water in the fridge and allow it to settle for at least 1 hour, up to 8 hours. Cover and store the washed dough in the fridge until you're ready for the next steps. Now you're ready for both seitan and liang pi.

2. To make the seitan: Place your washed dough into a large bowl and pour 3 cups (720 ml) water over the dough. Wash again, but this time discard the starchy water. Repeat five times. After the last wash, the water should run clear and you should be left with a mass that looks a little like a brain—a beige clump, with visible rubbery strands of gluten. This is your uncooked seitan.

Transfer the seitan to a bowl and sprinkle the yeast over it. Rub the yeast into the seitan and knead with your hands into a cohesive mass, evenly dispersing the yeast throughout. Cover with a wet towel and let it rest for 30 minutes.

Use one level in your steamer. Fill your steamer with water and bring to a boil. Place the seitan on the first stack and steam for 30 minutes. Let it cool until ready to cut and serve. The cooked seitan will last 1 to 2 days, refrigerated, in an airtight container.

3. To make the liang pi: Carefully take your reserved starchy water out of the fridge. It should have settled and separated, with a layer of water on top.

Remove about 11 cups (2.6 L) of the water layer from the top and discard. Stir the starchy mass at the bottom to form a smooth mixture.

In the double-stack steamer, fill the bottom of the steamer with water, about 6 cups (1.4 L), and bring to a boil. In the meantime, brush one of your steamer's deep-dish pans with vegetable oil.

Scoop ½ cup (120 ml) of the starchy mixture into the prepared pan and smooth it out into an even layer. Place the pan on the lower stack of the steamer pot and cover immediately. Steam for 3 minutes. When bubbles begin forming on the now-translucent sheet of liang pi, it is done.

Prepare an ice bath for your deep-dish pan. Carefully remove the pan from the steamer with tongs and place on the ice bath to cool completely.

Prepare a flat pan for liang pi storage by brushing it with vegetable oil.

Use chopsticks to loosen the sides of the liang pi, then carefully peel the sheet off with your hands. If the sheet comes off as a whole piece without breaking, and can be folded without cracking, you've succeeded! Put the cooked liang pi on the prepared pan to prevent sticking.

If the sheet breaks, however, your liang pi is too dry. Add water (¼ cup/60 ml at a time) into the reserved starch mixture and try again. If the noodle doesn't form, the mixture has too much water. Let the starch settle once more, remove the top layer of water, and try again. In general, it's better to err on the side of removing too much water than too little at first.

Repeat the steaming process with the remaining liang pi batter, using ½ cup (120 ml) of mixture per metal pan. If you're feeling confident, you can use multiple pans and steamer stacks at once. Store the cooked liang pi sheets stacked on top of each other, brushing plenty of oil between each sheet to prevent sticking. These noodles are best eaten fresh (like on page 162), so wait to cut the sheets into thin ribbons until you're ready to serve them. If you must refrigerate the sheets, you can opt for stir-fried liang pi instead (page 164).

See pages 111, 162, and 164 for dishes that use the seitan.

Biang-Biang (or Hand-Ripped) Noodles

Makes 2 to 3 servings (2 if you're feeling particularly hungry)

The name *biang-biang* refers to the sound of the noodle hitting the counter as it's being pulled, but you might also notice that there isn't a Chinese title to this recipe. This is because the onomatopoeia isn't technically in the Chinese dictionary. The character, biang, with fifty-six strokes, is more of a picture made up of several other words, all jammed into one. There are a lot of stories around this character, and one story is actually an old poem, written specifically so people could remember how to draw it. It's sort of like when you're a kid and your parents teach you to tie your shoes with a bunny metaphor; the poem is the same way, a mnemonic device that teaches you to draw "biang." So when you see the employees in our stores pulling these, slapping them against the counter, think of those fifty-six strokes as a symbol of how much history these noodles have.

Having these pulled to order isn't a gimmick, though; you simply cannot pre-pull these fuckers. They're finicky. Hold pulled dough for too long and the noodles will lose their shape and stretch. Once cooked, the noodles should be eaten immediately, or they'll stick to each other and get mushy. In a perfect world, the dough would go straight from being pulled into a pot of boiling water, before being dressed and devoured. So while these wide, thick noodles are great—perfectly chewy, raggedy vehicles for sauces and spice—they can be a pain in the ass to make, especially if you're planning on serving at a dinner party. You'll be standing around banging these noodles out one by one, while the rest of your friends chow down. I've been there. It sucks.

Luckily, it's not that hard to master the dough, and once you get the technique down, you can dish bowls of these out in no time. It just takes some practice, but soon you'll find yourself keeping stacks of noodle dough in your fridge and whipping these out for a toothy, perfectly "QQ" last-minute meal.

Note: **New York** ***magazine says these would be just as good slathered in ketchup, but I prefer you serve them with any of our main XFF main dishes, like Spicy Cumin Lamb (page 173). At the very least, add on our XFF Noodle Sauce (page 43) and XFF Chili Oil (page 40).***

3⅓ cups (405 g) all-purpose flour or high-gluten flour

½ teaspoon salt

¾ cup (180 ml) room-temperature water

Vegetable oil, to keep the dough pieces from sticking

TOOLS:

Stand mixer with dough hook attachment (optional; you can mix this by hand, too)

Rolling pin

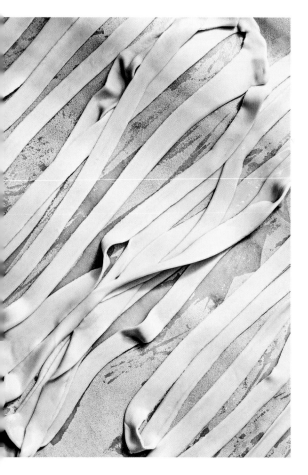

To make the dough: Place the flour in a stand mixer with the dough hook attachment.

In a Pyrex measuring cup or a container that has a mouth to pour, stir the salt into the room-temperature water until dissolved.

Start the mixer at a low speed. Slowly add the salt water at the side of the mixer until all of the water is evenly incorporated. Keep running the mixer until the sides of the mixing bowl are flour-free and the dough is smooth. If the dough doesn't seem to be coming together, you can add up to ¼ cup (60 ml) more water, a little at a time.

Alternatively, if mixing by hand in a bowl, add the water ¼ cup (60 ml) at a time, using your hands to knead the mixture into a ball of dough. Knead until a dough is formed, 8 to 10 minutes.

Remove the dough from the mixing bowl and knead on a floured board. You'll need to use a bit of muscle, as the dough will be quite tough at first, but it will get smoother and springier the longer you work it. Knead until relatively smooth and springy.

Cover with a moist towel and let rest for 5 minutes. Then uncover and knead the dough for a minute or so with clean hands on a floured board. Repeat this rest-then-knead process twice more. In total, you should have rested the dough for 15 minutes and kneaded it three times.

After the final rest, flatten the dough into a rectangle to the best of your ability and cut the dough into 3½-ounce (100 g) pieces (about 6 pieces for one batch of dough). Use a rolling pin to roll each piece into a flat rectangle, a little over ¼ inch thick, 4 to 5 inches long, and about 1½ inches wide (or 6 mm thick, 10 cm to 12 cm long, and 4 cm wide).

Brush the dough with vegetable oil and store without stacking them on top of each other. In the stores, we pack the un-pulled pieces on their edge, like books, sideways in a container. Rest, covered with plastic wrap and refrigerated, for at least 1 hour, up to 3 days.

To pull and cook the noodles: These noodles cannot sit after being pulled, and are best eaten fresh. Be prepared to immediately boil, sauce, and slurp them down.

Take the pieces of dough out of the refrigerator and let them warm up to room temperature.

Bring a large pot of water to a boil. On a clean counter, warm up the pieces of dough by flattening them on the counter with your hands, until the dough feels stretchy and elastic.

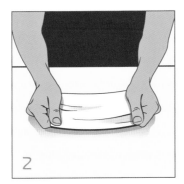

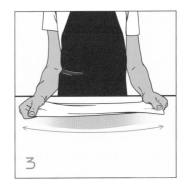

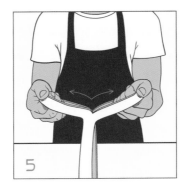

Evenly press the dough into a flat rectangular shape until it is about 6 inches long and 3 inches wide (15 cm long and 7.5 cm wide); see step 1 illustration above.

Grab the ends of the rectangle with your thumbs and forefingers, as if you are checking if a bill is counterfeit in the light (step 2).

Pull the dough gently, stretching it until it is about shoulder-width long (step 3).

Start to slightly pull and bounce the noodle flat against the counter in an up-and-down motion (step 4). Pull and slap the dough against the counter until the dough is almost 4 feet (1.25 m) long. Be careful not to pull too quickly or grip too tight, as you'll break the noodle. If the noodle does break, just grab onto the broken part and try to pull from there.

When the noodle is the right length (4 feet/1.25 m), pick it up at the middle and rip it into two pieces like string cheese (step 5). Pull until you almost reach the end, but don't pull all the way through. You'll end up with a giant noodle ring. Carefully press the ends of the strands to stretch and even them out if they are too thick.

Pull and rip the remaining noodles and throw all strands into the pot of boiling water at the same time (step 6). Stir with tongs to make sure they do not stick. They should be "swimming" in the water (see Five Rules to Boiling Noodles, page 29).

Boil for 2 minutes. If the water is about to spill out, turn the heat down slightly but keep it at a boil. Add cold water to the pot if necessary. Your total boiling time should be capped at 2 minutes.

Strain out the noodles and serve as directed on the next page or as described on page 61.

Ready? Now you can make one very important dish . . .

Hot Oil–Seared Biang-Biang Noodles
油泼辣子面

In Xi'an, a traditional street vendor will always have a pot of boiling water for noodles *and* a pot of oil kept right below smoking point, just so they can make this dish. In fact, this is the most old-school way to prepare biang-biang noodles. You know how a burger is just a burger? Biang-biang noodles are just *this*—fresh hand-ripped strands topped with fragrant aromatics and spices, doused in the aforementioned hot oil, and quickly tossed to coat. Slurp it up fast, bowl in one hand, chopsticks in another. Try not to burn your tongue. Feel that? That's what street food should be like.

Serves
1

3 pieces of Biang-Biang Noodle Dough (page 55)

2 leaves green or napa cabbage, coarsely chopped

⅓ cup (75 ml) vegetable oil

¼ cup (60 ml) XFF Noodle Sauce (page 43)

1 tablespoon Red Chili Powder (page 35)

1 teaspoon Garlic Puree (page 37)

½ green onion, trimmed and chopped

½ stalk celery, diced

1 Chinese chive, diced

Bring a large pot of water to a full boil over high heat.

Pull the biang-biang dough into three noodles, following the process on page 57. Add to the boiling water and cook for 2 minutes. Remove the noodles from the water and set aside to drain.

Cook the cabbage briefly in the noodle water. Strain out and place with the noodles.

In a small metal skillet (preferably cast-iron), heat the vegetable oil over high heat until it just starts to shimmer but before it starts to smoke, 1 to 2 minutes.

Meanwhile, add the noodles, noodle sauce, and cabbage to a serving bowl and stir to combine. Then place the chili powder, garlic puree, green onion, celery, and chive in a little pile on top of the noodles.

Carefully and slowly drizzle the still-hot oil a little at a time over the pile of aromatics on the noodles, making sure every bit gets sizzled. Stir quickly and serve immediately.

How to Use This Book

VERY RARELY IS A MAIN DISH IN THIS BOOK MEANT TO BE SERVED SOLO, LIKE A STEAK. Instead, the recipes are versatile, to be paired with rice, noodles, *or* bread. So if you see these symbols accompanying our main dishes, like Spicy Cumin Lamb (page 173) or the Spicy and Tingly Beef (page 168), it means you can serve them in the following ways:

OVER RICE

Rice is one of the easiest and most common bases of any Chinese meal. Simply cook one raw cup (or more) of white or brown rice per person, as instructed on page 29. Divide the rice into individual bowls and serve your main dish (and potentially a side salad like our Spicy and Sour Carrot Salad, page 104) in the center of the table for diners to portion as they please.

AS A BURGER

These aren't the fat, crazy burgers you might find all over social media, with five patties and extravagant toppings on soft potato rolls. XFF burgers, or 肉夹馍 rou jia mou, are heartier and more rugged, sandwiching our stewed meats with our crispy soft Daily Bread (page 46) before pressing it down to meld all the flavors together. One bite and you'll see why Sloppy Joes felt really familiar to me as a kid.

---

1 Daily Bread bun (page 46)

3½ ounces (100 g) main dish

Slice your Daily Bread bun in half, as you would a bagel, but don't cut all the way through. Leave a ½-inch (12 mm) connection at the end.

If you're serving the Stewed Pork (page 169), chop it up so you end up with tiny pieces of pork, roughly ½ inch (12 mm) large. If you're using other proteins, leave as is.

Stuff as much of your filling as you can into the bread.

In a small skillet, toast the burger slightly on both sides over medium heat. Serve immediately so the bread doesn't get soggy; it should be crispy on the outside and fatty, meaty, and juicy inside.

WITH NOODLES

I like to think there aren't a lot of rules with our food. So while some main sauces in this book might have traditional pairings (Mt. Qi Pork on page 175, for example, is historically served with thinner noodles), at XFF, we do what we like. If you see this icon, it means you can pair the dish with either Biang-Biang Hand-Ripped Noodles (page 55) or Longevity Noodles (page 49). The former offers a slightly more unwieldy (and fun) eating experience, with wide ribbons of dough to cling on to and scoop up the sauce. Longevity noodles, on the other hand, are a little more uniform, dense, and slick, and they're especially great if you're making more than one serving. Neither is better than the other; it's just a matter of personal preference. In either case, you'll need an extra dash of noodle sauce and chili oil to finish off the dish.

---

1 serving noodles (2 pieces Biang-Biang Noodles, page 55, or 1 piece Longevity Noodles, page 49)

¼ cup (50 g) cabbage or bok choy, roughly chopped into 2-inch (5 cm) pieces

1 teaspoon chopped Chinese chives

1 green onion, trimmed and chopped

1 tablespoon chopped celery

2 tablespoons liquid stew from main dish in cases where applicable (like with Stewed Pork, page 169)

4¼ ounces (120 g) main dish

2 tablespoons XFF Noodle Sauce (page 43)

XFF Chili Oil (page 40)

Pull and cook your noodles according to the recipe. Strain out from the water.

Cook the cabbage or bok choy briefly in the noodle water. Strain out and place on top of the noodles.

Mix in the remaining ingredients. Serve immediately.

WITH NOODLES IN SOUP

Turn our stews into a noodle soup with bone broth and some sesame oil for a nutty, sweet fragrance. You could even use hot water, if you're in a pinch. And, same as before, either Biang-Biang or Longevity Noodles work.

---

1 serving noodles (2 pieces Biang-Biang Noodles, page 55, or 1 piece Longevity Noodles, page 49)

¼ cup (50 g) cabbage or bok choy, roughly chopped into 2-inch (5 cm) pieces

2 tablespoons liquid stew from main dish, in cases where applicable (like with Stewed Pork, page 169)

2 tablespoons XFF Noodle Sauce (page 43)

½ teaspoon salt

1 teaspoon chopped Chinese chives

1 green onion, trimmed and chopped

1 tablespoon chopped celery

2½ cups (600 ml) hot Bone Broth (page 42) or noodle water

4¼ ounces (120 g) main dish

XFF Chili Oil (page 40)

Drizzle of toasted sesame oil

1 sprig cilantro, chopped (optional)

Pull and cook your noodles according to the recipe. Strain into your serving bowl. Cook the cabbage or bok choy in the hot water and strain into your serving bowl.

Add the liquid stew, noodle sauce, and salt to your bowl. Toss in the Chinese chives, green onion, and celery.

Add your broth (beef broth if your main protein is beef; lamb broth if it's lamb) or the water you cooked the noodles in if your dish is neither beef- nor lamb-based.

Top with your main dish, chili oil, and sesame oil. Garnish with cilantro, if desired.

2 | THE REMIX

Making It Work in Middle-of-Nowhere America

Hold up, THAT'S our plane?!
How is THAT going to

THIS WAS THE FIRST "WAIT, WHAT?" MOMENT OF MY AMERICAN LIFE, AND IT WAS A SIGN THAT THINGS WEREN'T GOING TO BE WHAT I EXPECTED.

When I was seven, my parents sat me down and explained that we were going to move to America. At first, I wasn't thrilled. I had just started developing my first crush (on a cute girl named Natasha—or the Chinese version of that name) and making a friend circle (thanks to my extensive collection of more than a hundred dinosaur toys). I was even kind of popular. I didn't want to leave that all behind.

But then my English tutor told me about a magical playground,[1] where my favorite Disney movies came to life and chocolate became liquid and drinkable. And my classmate's mom, overhearing my news, told me about a job in America where boys my age could deliver newspapers and get five-dollar tips. I did the dollar-to-yuan conversion in my head. *Holy crap, I could buy ALL the Transformers toys*. And Natasha? You could tell she was impressed by all my America talk. I got on board with the plan. I put up a world map, marked where Disneyland was with Mickey Mouse ears, and started to prep for my international adventure.

Which brings us back to the plane. Once our international flight landed, I started getting the tiniest inkling that I was being tricked. My first clue was our connecting flight. As we began to board, I couldn't help but think that our plane looked like a toy, with twelve tiny seats and a small propeller that looked fragile enough to be blown off by a particularly forceful gust of wind. It was a dinky little baby compared to the Boeing 747 we just disembarked from. I started asking an even bigger question: If *this* is the plane, how small is the city at the end of the ride?

Very small, as it happened. Our town in Michigan was mostly known for being in the middle of nowhere—albeit a beautiful middle of nowhere, great

---

1 I had always followed Disney. I watched *The Lion King* every freaking day, no exaggeration. It was to the point where I was worried that the cassette was going to get worn out and break. I spent too many hours of my childhood trying to figure out how to make copies.

get us to Disneyland?

for winter sports and summer lakeside activities. We moved at the end of summer, and as I took in the looming green trees framing the highway, the Victorian-style homes with immaculate, lush lawns, the blue skies with cotton candy clouds, I thought, *Well, this might not be Disneyland, but it certainly feels like it.*

A distant family friend helped us get settled in a quaint one-bedroom apartment on the first floor of a house, and I woke up each morning disoriented, taking in the faded paint, brown shaggy carpet, and wood-paneled walls. Instead of hopping on a bike and zooming around a dusty, concrete city, we hitched rides with family friends (back then in Xi'an, cars were only for the rich) or walked everywhere, marveling at the sheer amount of open space the suburbs provided.

At first, it was exciting. Phone calls home were filled with adventures: There were so many wild berries to eat, so many new bugs to capture, so many places to see.

Once the novelty wore off, though, the newness became a daily frustration. The parent-child dynamic in my life had shifted. Back in Xi'an, my mom was the head of the household. She ran everything—the meals, the activities, my piano practice sessions. But

when we moved, she went from being completely in control to not being in charge at all. She no longer had piano to hold over my head (thankfully, I might add). She couldn't understand a word of English, save for "Hi" and "How are you?" She couldn't drive, couldn't read, couldn't speak. And back then, she couldn't even Google.

On the other hand, I had the luxury of a few English classes, and even if they weren't always helpful, I was younger and malleable and picked up the language and the customs quickly. So there I was, eight years old, learning the rules of the new supermarkets, the new street signs, and the new schools for the both of us. I was walking my mother through doctors' forms to get my immunization shots, helping her study for DMV tests, practicing the English phrases she kept trying to memorize from her tapes and books.

School wasn't easy for me, though. My first day of school was a "movie day," and I walked in thinking, *I could get used to this.* But I was soon told I would have to spend several hours a day reading Dr. Seuss books with an ESL teacher, and man, I found those illustrations creepy. One day I had to go to the bathroom but I couldn't remember the words, so I creatively gestured with my hands until another kid caught on and asked the teacher for me.

I tried to say "breath," but it came out like "breast," and it became a running joke for months (that joke got old real fast, too). I quickly realized it was going to be a long journey to fit in here.

Pretty soon, I started to miss home. I tried pizza for the first time and almost threw up; I tried Twinkies and was overwhelmed by the sugar. I saw a jar of pickles, took a bite, and thought, what the hell, this is definitely not *paocai*.[2] I missed the comfort of knowing what things were when I saw them, missed the independence I had back in Xi'an, missed my relatives, my grandmother's house, the street vendors with their baby chicks. And I started to miss lamb skewers, dumplings in vinegar, noodles, sour hawberry candies—heck, I even started to miss the lamb pao-mo soup I always ignored as a kid. But I knew not to ask for it. I knew what our grocery stores looked like. I knew how dismal the "Asian section" was, how finding lamb was like finding gold.

So we learned to make do for a little hit of the familiar. We learned to eat chicken breast, packaged in plastic and Styrofoam. We learned to swap out beef for lamb in our favorite recipes. And we learned the importance of community. One friend brought us into the fold of a group of international students studying at the nearby university, students from all over China who banded together to make a place that felt a little like home. Once a month, one person would make a massive grocery run, braving the three-hour drive to the closest "large" city. We'd put in orders for black vinegar, soy sauce, and actually decent rice, and we learned to ration our supplies to last us until the next haul. And then we learned to experiment with new and unusual flavors (e.g., our makeshift vinegar on page 69), creating dishes that formed a new flavor profile for my childhood. Slowly, the phone calls home became more mundane. *Are you doing well in school? Yes. Are you listening to your mom? Yes. What did you have for dinner? Something bad that mom tried to make.*[3]

But then, one sunny day, we had a big lakeside barbecue planned and those university students wanted to do something special. They went out of their way to procure some lamb. They hoarded some cumin and some chile flakes. After months of talk, they were tired of hearing about those mythical lamb skewers and asked me to make the skewers, to show them the flavors of Xi'an. I didn't know exactly what I was doing, but I had a basic idea; I had, after all, spent many nights of my childhood watching the streetside vendors work as I patiently waited for my food to be cooked. So when I found myself with a golden opportunity, some lamb, some cumin, and a charcoal grill by the lake, I was not going to waste it.

The adults painstakingly sliced the meat by hand into thin pieces, threading them carefully onto skewers. They fired up the grill and waited for the coals to get hot enough. And then, as the adults looked on, I placed the skewers onto the hot grill, sprinkling on the precious cumin and salt. I watched them closely, making sure not to let them burn. And the minute one was done, crispy, dripping,

2 Chinese pickled cabbage.
3 It was Brussels sprouts (page 76). I was eight. I didn't understand the struggle.

fragrant, I took a bite. It tasted—magically, surprisingly—of home. I was once again five years old, riding the front of my dad's bike, on my way home from the Muslim Quarter.

On that sunny summer day, as I happily grilled away, the heat drying water off my swim shorts, I realized that re-creating it all was possible. Sure, the setting was a little different, the ingredients in different forms, the cooking tools in different sizes and shapes. But the flavors, the elements, those were all still attainable. We didn't have to be cramped up next to some drunk bros in the Muslim Quarter of Xi'an. We could re-create the taste of Xi'an in this middle-of-nowhere town. It would be difficult, but possible.

This section embodies what it really means to be a kid addicted to black vinegar stuck in a place where soy sauce was "exotic," in an era when Amazon and Yamibuy didn't exist. The dishes you'll read about here were combinations born out of desperation, out of creativity, out of coming from one place and entering another. My family and I dreamt these up when toying around with the wrong tools to create the right flavors, and there were plenty of questionable choices and pretty disgusting disasters. But there were a lot of pleasant surprises as well, some truly delicious combinations we wouldn't have thought of otherwise, family meals that

demanded less work but delivered just as much flavor. These are the dishes that quickly became our go-tos, our new favorites. They take on the sweet-and-sour combinations of Chinese American cooking, mix it with my dad's affinity for spicy and sour, and showcase what it means to create something that is simultaneously new and familiar. I wouldn't really call these dishes authentically Xi'an, but they hit the right notes and flavor profiles. And you know what? They're pretty spot on, too.

YOUNG JASON GRILLING CUMIN LAMB SKEWERS IN MICHIGAN, PREPARING TO BLOW THE MINDS OF ALL THESE BIG KIDS.

It tasted—magically, surprisingly—of home.

Some Foods I Actually Liked (It Wasn't All Bad!)

IT MIGHT SOUND LIKE I HATED ALL AMERICAN FOOD WHEN I FIRST MOVED HERE, AND SURE, SOME DISHES WERE NOT MY FAVORITE. But there were several that I loved right off the bat (and I did learn to love pizza eventually, in part because of Lunchables).

CHOCOLATE CHIP COOKIES

I'd buy these for twenty-five cents a pop at school, and they were nothing like the crunchy chocolate chip cookies sold in stores or the chewy, dense desserts of Xi'an. These were fresh, soft, melty, and almost without a bite entirely. I was obsessed. During recess, I'd play and win marble matches, and then sell my winning marbles to the other kids so I could buy these cookies with the money.

PANNU KAKKU

In my little town, there was a modest population of Finnish descent, which explains how I started eating this custardy, crepe-like Finnish pancake. This breakfast was oftentimes served at school with a blueberry sauce, and was one of the few dessert-like options that did not feel too sweet for me.

THIMBLEBERRIES

I hated raspberries, associating the fruit with the fake sugary flavor found in raspberry candy. But then I tried thimbleberries, which I picked off the side of a small road while riding my bike, and the tartness became my go-to mid–bike-ride snack. (Huckleberries were also a favorite, and also grew on the side of the road.)

SLOPPY JOES

The first time I saw a sloppy joe, I thought it was a quintessential American dish. But then I took a closer look, and something about the orange sauciness, the ground-up meat wrapped in bread, looked very appealing to me, almost familiar. In my kid brain, I associated it a bit with Mt. Qi pork, and decided to try it out. I was not let down.

HOT DOGS

In many Chinese bakeries you'll find links wrapped in a soft, buttery dough, and that was the only hot dog version I ever saw in China back then. In the States, though, we could only find plain hot dogs in the grocery store, so it ended up being a typical afternoon snack. I'd simply get home from school, pop one in a microwave, and cut it up.

Makeshift Vinegar
自制醋

When I was a kid, I associated black vinegar with health. Have a fish bone stuck in your throat? Drink a shot of vinegar to wash it down. Feeling a little queasy? Sip just a little bit and take a nap. It was a lifesaver—an elixir of sorts. I would drink it out of the bottle when my mom wasn't looking, or surreptitiously slurp up leftover dipping vinegar after a meal. Then, we moved to America, where the closest thing we could find was white vinegar. Let me tell you, that shit burns if you try to drink it straight up. My mom knew she had to do *something*.

This concoction was her cure for homesickness. She started off with regular white vinegar and doctored it with soy sauce and spices, hoping to create something that looked and tasted like the elixir of home. The results weren't perfect, but it was close enough, and in dire times you do what you gotta do.

If you find yourself in a distant land with a paltry Asian grocery section and no delivery, or you simply don't want to run to the grocery store, you can use this recipe to create a little taste of Xi'an in a pinch.

Makes
2 cups
(480 ml)

2 cups (480 ml) white vinegar

2 tablespoons soy sauce

2 star anise pods

In a small saucepan, add all ingredients and set over medium heat. Bring to a boil. Let boil, uncovered, for 1 minute. Turn off the heat and cover the pot. Let cool to room temperature.

Once cooled, remove the star anise and discard. Pour the vinegar into a nonreactive (glass, ceramic, or plastic) container and store in the refrigerator for up to 1 week.

XFF Ramen
家常方便面

Before highbrow ramen became relatively mainstream in the States, there was instant ramen, and it was the shit. As a kid, I would eat the noodles dry, broken into bits, with the powdered seasoning sprinkled on for little bursts of umami and salt. When we moved to America, it became a nostalgic treat. Even in the "whitest" grocery stores, where there were more tomato sauce options than soy sauce, you could still scrounge up some bright orange packets of dehydrated noodles. My mom never really taught me how to cook, but she did teach me how to doctor up some instant ramen like no other.

Some people might just drop in an egg, but if you're going to do it the XFF way, you have to go all out. We're talking black vinegar for a mouth-puckering bite, tomatoes for a little fruity sweetness, and yes, our XFF Chili Oil to taste (I douse it, obviously). Toss in some bok choy, and you could trick yourself into thinking you have a balanced meal.

Serves
1

1 package dried instant ramen and seasoning packet (any brand)

½ tablespoon black vinegar, plus more to finish

XFF Chili Oil (page 40)

¼ large tomato, roughly cut into wedges

¼ green onion, trimmed and chopped

¼ stalk celery, chopped

1 egg

1 baby bok choy or ½ cup (115 g) napa cabbage ripped into bite-sized pieces

Toasted sesame oil

Salt

Bring a medium pot of water to a boil.

Meanwhile, add half of the dry seasoning packet (or as much as you desire based on your sodium preference; I usually use half, otherwise I find it too salty) to a large soup bowl, along with the black vinegar and chili oil to taste. Stir to combine.

When the water starts boiling, add the dried instant noodles and wait until the water comes up to a boil again.

Add the tomato, green onion, and celery to the pot and stir to submerge. Immediately move aside the noodles and vegetables to create a pocket of space, crack the egg into the boiling water, and poach it for 1 minute. You could also separately fry the egg sunny-side up instead.

Toss in the bok choy or napa cabbage. Cook for up to 1 minute, then remove from the heat.

Carefully ladle some of the cooking water into your serving bowl with the dry seasoning, black vinegar, and chili oil. This will control how much broth your ramen will have.

Transfer the noodles into the serving bowl, mixing with chopsticks or a fork until evenly combined.

Strain out the egg and vegetables from the pot and place on top of the noodles.

Finish with a few drops of sesame oil for fragrance and more chili oil, vinegar, and salt to taste.

Fried Chicken Wings with XFF Spices
香脆炸鸡翅

I spent many afternoons doing homework in the dining rooms of various Chinese restaurants, and during those slow hours my dad would show off his various experiments. One of those experiments turned out to be a precursor of our Spicy and Tingly Cumin Chicken Wing Skewers (page 203), but this version is less about the savoriness of cumin and all about the oily, fatty decadence of chicken skin.[4] Thanks to the double-frying process, the skin pops and crackles with each bite, amplifying the juiciness of the dark meat below. You could make your own fried chicken (as instructed), or you could save yourself time and buy some takeout instead. The key here is the dry spice dip, which is "optional" in the recipe but actually mandatory, adding a dusting of chili and pepper for an extra zing. It's so good, you'll be adding it onto fries, too.

Serves
2 as an
appetizer

FOR THE CHICKEN WINGS:

6 whole chicken wings

1 teaspoon salt

½ teaspoon white pepper powder

2 teaspoons oyster sauce

½ teaspoon garlic powder

2 tablespoons cornstarch

2 tablespoons all-purpose flour

5 cups (600 ml) vegetable oil

FOR THE DIPPING SPICE
(optional, but why would you skip it?):

½ teaspoon Sichuan peppercorn powder

¼ teaspoon white pepper powder

½ teaspoon dried chili powder

⅛ teaspoon salt

TOOL:

Digital instant-read thermometer

To make the chicken wings: Briefly wash the chicken wings to remove debris and blood, then pat dry with paper towels.

Place the wings in a large bowl with the salt, white pepper powder, oyster sauce, and garlic powder. Use your hands to rub the spices and sauce evenly into the wings.

Cover the bowl with plastic wrap and put in the refrigerator to marinate for 2 hours.

Combine the cornstarch and flour in another large bowl. Remove the marinated chicken from the fridge and add the chicken wings to your cornstarch and flour mixture. Toss evenly to combine.

In a large pot, heat the vegetable oil over medium heat until the oil is hot but not smoking (a thermometer should read 375°F/190°C). Carefully put the chicken wings into the oil, working in batches if needed, and fry for 2 minutes. Turn the heat down to 350°F (177°C) and continue frying for 10 minutes more. Be sure to carefully move the wings around with tongs to prevent burning and to fry the chicken evenly on all sides.

Remove the wings from the oil and drain on paper towels. Repeat with the remaining batches, if necessary.

Heat the pot of oil back up to 375°F (190°C). Return the wings back to the pot, working in batches if necessary, and fry for 1 minute, or until crispy and golden.

To make the dipping spice: If desired (it should be), in a small bowl, combine the ingredients for the dry spice dip. Serve alongside the wings.

Note: You could scale up this recipe if you want to make more than 6 wings, but watch the oil. If the frying oil gets too cloudy, you'll have to change it out.

4   Let's be clear: The skin is the best part of fried chicken. When I was in college, I dated a girl who refused to eat fried chicken skin; I'd watch as she meticulously peeled off the crispy, flavorful bits and left them there to waste. That's when I knew we would never work out.

Fiddlehead Fern Salad
凉拌山野菜

Let the record show that we were hip foragers before it became cool. One of my earliest memories is of my mother teaching me to forage for dandelion greens in China; when we moved to Michigan, we'd gather fiddlehead ferns, looking for shoots that were just starting to sprout. These things grew like weeds in the woods, and in the springtime you'd see me running around outside, picking up fistfuls of ferns for a snack.

We didn't eat fiddlehead ferns in Xi'an, but the plant is a staple in other areas of China. So we took the greens we gathered on the other side of the world and prepared it as you would in northern China—blanched, cooled, and then dressed in the classic combination of black vinegar, soy sauce, and sesame oil, with slivers of peppers for a little kick.

Serves
1 or 2 as an appetizer

8 ounces fiddlehead ferns (typically available packaged in Korean grocery stores, in long segments, or in farmers' markets in spring and early summer)

½ red longhorn pepper (or another long, thin, fresh chile pepper), sliced

½ teaspoon salt

½ teaspoon sugar

½ teaspoon soy sauce

½ teaspoon toasted sesame oil

1 teaspoon black vinegar

1 teaspoon Garlic Puree (page 37)

1 teaspoon XFF Chili Oil (page 40; optional)

Note: You could substitute haricot verts if fiddlehead ferns are unavailable.

Fill a pot with enough water to cover the fiddlehead ferns. Bring to a boil over high heat.

Trim the tough ends off of the fiddlehead ferns. Add the trimmed ferns to the boiling water and cook, uncovered, for 2 minutes. Strain from the water and set aside to cool.

Toss the fiddlehead ferns and all the remaining ingredients in a bowl (along with the chili oil, if you like it spicy). Serve immediately.

Hot-and-Sour Soup
酸辣汤

Hot-and-sour soup is one of those dishes in every freakin' Chinese restaurant, and it always tastes exactly the same—sour, a little spicy, silky from cornstarch, and just a touch too salty because it's been evaporating in a hot holding unit all day.

Still, this was one of the few American Chinese dishes my family actually enjoyed on our own, even as my dad spent all day making it at the restaurants where he worked. The home version was slightly dressed up, though. We'd use homemade bone broth, tofu, and fresh vegetables for a healthier, less sodium-intense version, a good dose of sesame oil for fragrance, and a couple extra spoonfuls of vinegar for our family's signature sour kick.

Serves 3 or 4 as an appetizer

2 tablespoons plus 2 teaspoons (65 g) cornstarch, divided

4 ounces (115 g) pork loin, cut into ¼-inch (6 mm) thick matchsticks, roughly 1½ inches (4 cm) long

3 teaspoons soy sauce, divided

½ tablespoon peeled and finely chopped fresh ginger

1 quart (945 ml) unsalted chicken stock or Bone Broth (page 42)

2 ounces (55 g) silken tofu, carefully cut into ½-inch (12 mm) cubes

1 dried shiitake mushroom, hydrated in warm water for 30 minutes, cleaned, and sliced

3 wood ear mushrooms, hydrated in warm water for 30 minutes and sliced

¼ teaspoon salt

1 teaspoon white pepper powder

3 tablespoons (45 ml) black vinegar

2 eggs, beaten

1 tablespoon toasted sesame oil

1 green onion, trimmed and finely diced

1 teaspoon XFF Chili Oil (page 40; optional)

In a small bowl, whisk together 2 tablespoons of the cornstarch with 2 tablespoons water. Mix in one direction to make a smooth slurry and set aside.

In another bowl, mix the pork with 2 teaspoons of the soy sauce and the remaining 2 teaspoons cornstarch.

In a soup pot, add the ginger and stock or bone broth. Cover the pot and bring to a boil over high heat.

Add the pork and stir. Bring back to a boil, uncovered. Boil for 2 minutes.

Add the tofu, both mushrooms, salt, and white pepper powder, along with the black vinegar and the remaining 1 teaspoon soy sauce. Bring back up to a boil.

Stir to unsettle the starch slurry and pour into the soup slowly, stirring constantly as the starch mixture thickens the soup.

Stir in the beaten eggs while stirring constantly. Remove from the heat.

Serve the soup in bowls, topped with sesame oil and green onion along with the chili oil, if desired.

Brussels Sprouts with Shrimp Sauce
虾米炒孢子甘蓝

One of my earliest memories of America is waking up from a winter afternoon nap to a horrible smell—a stench, if you will. Groggy and slightly hungry, I stumbled to the kitchen to find my mother putting together dinner. "I'm using this new vegetable I found," she said, revealing a slimy green and brown concoction. The classic dried shrimp sauce looked familiar, but the vegetables in question were unlike anything I'd seen before. They were small, bitter-smelling, soggy half circles with layers and layers of tiny leaves.[5]

They were, I would come to learn, Brussels sprouts. And they smelled like shit.

The traditional version of this dish is made with bok choy, which works with the light, umami-filled seafood sauce. But Brussels sprouts added an unexpected element, a bitterness and a mushiness and a smell that stunk up the apartment for days. I threw a fit. I remember being forced to eat the sprouts, spitting them out when my mom wasn't looking, crying and complaining the entire time.

Only now do I look back and realize what a brat I was being, and how hard my mom was working to make do with whatever ingredients she could find. And to her credit, she became a better cook over the years. So in her honor, I went back and tried this dish—and to my surprise, it worked. The extra hit of garlic masks the typical Brussels sprouts smell, while the chicken bouillon adds a savoriness to counterbalance the fishiness of the shrimp. I promise, it won't stink up your apartment, but if you're really nervous you could just use bok choy.

Serves
4 as an
appetizer

¼ cup (60 ml) vegetable oil

6 garlic cloves, peeled and chopped

24 Brussels sprouts, halved

2 teaspoons salt

20 dried shrimp, hydrated in ½ cup (120 ml) warm chicken broth or water for 40 minutes (reserve the liquid)

2 teaspoons chicken bouillon powder

In a large skillet, heat the vegetable oil over medium-low heat. Add the garlic and cook until fragrant, about 3 minutes.

Turn up the heat to medium-high and add the Brussels sprouts. Stir-fry for 3 minutes. Add the salt and keep stirring until the sprouts turn bright green.

Add the shrimp and the reserved broth or water, plus the chicken bouillon powder. Stir to combine and cook for 1 to 2 more minutes. Serve.

---

5   She probably thought they were some new type of baby bok choy.

Blistered Tiger Shishito Peppers
虎皮小辣椒

A trick for those with low tolerance for spice: start with whole, blistered peppers. In Xi'an, we would make tiger skin peppers, named for the striped, grilled skin of long green hot peppers. I was intimidated by the dish when I was a kid, scared of getting my mouth burned off, so I started first by eating the vegetal part of the peppers and avoiding the seeds. Gradually, as I became more accustomed to the flashes of spice every now and then, I would up my tolerance. First, I'd allow myself a nibble of the seedy part, then a whole bite, and then I found myself downing these whole, not caring for the occasional fiery pepper[6] that made me run for a drink of water.

Still, I get that not everyone is into the whole "mouth on fire" sensation, so this version swaps out hot peppers for the more mild shishitos while keeping the soy-sugar dressing. You might find yourself running into a hot one every now and then, but just think of it as training.

Serves
4 as an
appetizer

¼ cup (30 ml) vegetable oil

20 shishito peppers

2 tablespoons soy sauce

½ teaspoon sugar

In a large skillet, heat the vegetable oil over medium heat. Once the oil is shimmering, add the peppers and blister on both sides, 1 to 2 minutes.

Remove the skillet from the heat. In a small bowl, add the soy sauce and sugar and mix together. Pour over the peppers in the skillet, stir to combine, and serve.

6   Not all peppers are the same, even within the same variety. Some are spicier, some are milder; it all depends on the circumstances they were grown in. It's a game of roulette, and every pepper is an adventure.

Five-Flavor Beef Shank
五香牛腱

Serves
4 as an
appetizer

My grandfather is an odd eater. I never saw him eat a full meal when I was a kid; he just snacked. I'd get home from school and he'd be watching his Beijing soap operas, fixing himself a glass of baijiu, a plate of salted peanuts, and thin slices of this marinated beef. This is our version of charcuterie, a cold cut with less fat and salt. My grandfather would dip a delicate slice of beef into a garlicky, spicy dip, savor the flavor bomb with a little vinegar bite, and then wash it all down with a burning sip of booze. There was nothing subtle about this ritual; every bite, every sip was a punch to the palate.

The beauty of this dish is that it's easily adaptable to any lean, tough meat. In China, we'd use beef shank, but in Michigan we'd run across cuts of venison that worked as well. One winter afternoon, I came home to my father braising a giant chunk of meat. When I asked him where he got it, he told me: *The side of the road.*

Turns out, he was driving home and saw a freshly killed deer on the side of the road—so fresh the animal was still warm, almost steaming. Feeling it was a waste to leave an animal like that, he rummaged around his car, found a steak knife, and carved out a giant piece of the leg. Once he got home, he got to work, and ended up making five-flavor venison shank. It was so large that we froze most of it. Throughout that winter, we'd carve out an odd piece here and there to defrost, a tiny taste of Chinese food during a time when it was an incredible hassle to find those flavors.

I like this story because it shows just how adaptable our food is, how the essence of it can be reimagined in surprising ways if you're resourceful and a little desperate. But you don't have to go out and find fresh roadkill for this, obviously (in fact, you probably shouldn't). A nice piece of beef shank will do just fine, serving up meaty, spicy goodness. If you have a glass of *baijiu* sitting nearby, well, all the better.

X
F
F

FOR THE BEEF:

1 pound (455 g) beef heel shank or heel of round

1 tablespoon Shaoxing cooking wine

¾ cup (180 ml) soy sauce

½-inch (12 mm) piece fresh ginger, peeled and sliced

2 green onions, trimmed and cut into 1-inch (2.5 cm) segments

2 star anise pods

1 teaspoon Sichuan peppercorn powder

1 bay leaf

3 cloves

1 black cardamom pod

2 white cardamom pods

1 dried red chile pepper (such as Tianjin)

1¾ ounces (50 g) rock sugar

FOR SERVING:

1 tablespoon XFF Dumpling Sauce (page 44)

XFF Chili Oil (page 40)

1 teaspoon Garlic Puree (page 37)

To make the beef: Place the beef inside a large stockpot and submerge in cold water.

Add the rest of the ingredients to the pot, cover, and bring to a boil over high heat. Boil for 10 minutes, then turn the heat down to low to simmer for 50 minutes.

Let the contents of the pot cool to room temperature. If you're in a hurry, prepare an ice bath and place the pot in the bath to speed up the cooling process.

Once cooled to room temperature, reserve the broth and remove the beef.

To serve: To make a dipping sauce, mix together the dumpling sauce, chili oil, and garlic puree, plus 2 teaspoons of the reserved broth.

Thinly slice the beef and serve at room temperature with the dipping sauce.

Pork Juan Bing
酱爆肉丝菜卷饼

This basic snack has many variations—some people fill it with mostly meat, some people focus on veggies—but the premise is always the same: a thin, Chinese crepe/tortilla/*bing*, filled with anything your heart desires and eaten with gusto with your hands.

The ingredients in this dish are fairly basic, meaning that even in the middle of nowhere, we could still scrounge it up every once in a while. The recipe's complexity comes in the prep work, however, and the timing. An experienced cook will make the filling before toasting the bing, since you want to keep the wrappers warm; once they go cold they lose their suppleness. Watching my dad cook the wrappers is like watching a complex dance. He'll put a fresh round of dough in the pan and after the first flip, heap any finished bing on top to keep the steam in while maintaining their warmth. He knows they're done not by color but by the air bubbles that form.

This isn't necessarily a meal to serve everyone at once, though. The best time to eat this is right as the bing comes off the pan. Grab a hot one, fill it to your liking, and take it on the go. And while this recipe calls for pork, if you just use the other ingredients, this makes a satisfying vegetarian wrap.

Note: Please don't call this fusion. We've been doing this for a long time.

Serves 2 or 3 as an appetizer

FOR THE BING:
2 cups (250 g) all-purpose flour

⅓ cup plus 4 teaspoons (100 ml) hot water

⅓ cup plus 4 teaspoons (100 ml) cold water

FOR THE PORK FILLING:
1½ tablespoons sweet flour sauce

3 teaspoons Shaoxing cooking wine, divided

½ teaspoon sugar

10 ounces (280 g) pork tenderloin, cut into thin slivers

½ teaspoon soy sauce

1-inch (2.5 cm) piece fresh ginger, peeled and finely chopped

½ teaspoon cornstarch

2 tablespoons vegetable oil, divided

1 garlic clove, peeled and sliced

1 green onion, trimmed and cut into 1-inch (2.5 cm) segments

FOR THE FIXINGS:
2 tablespoons vegetable oil, divided

½ teaspoon Sichuan peppercorns

1 dried red chile pepper, cut into ¼-inch (6 mm) segments

1 garlic clove, peeled and sliced

1 green onion, trimmed and cut into 1-inch (2.5 cm) segments

½ yellow potato, roughly 3 ounces (85 g), peeled and cut into thin matchsticks

1¼ teaspoons white vinegar, divided

⅜ teaspoon salt, divided

¼ teaspoon sugar, divided

1¾ ounces (50 g) dried kelp slivers, hydrated in warm water

½ teaspoon toasted sesame oil

FOR SERVING:
Sweet flour sauce

2 green onions, trimmed and sliced on the diagonal

TOOL:
Rolling pin

To make the bing: In two separate bowls, add 1 cup (125 g) of the flour to each.

Gradually add the hot water to one of the bowls, mixing by hand until it forms a dough.

In the second bowl, gradually add the cold water until a dough forms—this dough will be drier.

In a bowl or on a flat surface, knead the two doughs together until they form one smooth, evenly incorporated dough, about 4 minutes. The dough should be softer than Play-Doh but not sticky. Cover with a damp towel and let it rest for at least 10 minutes, or store, covered in a damp towel, in the refrigerator until ready to use. Meanwhile, make the fillings (see below).

When you're ready to cook the bing, remove the dough from the fridge. On a cutting board or flat work surface, use your hands to roll the ball of dough into a long, fat cylinder. Cut the cylinder into 6 equal pieces, about 3 ounces (85 g) each. Using a rolling pin, flatten each piece into a thin round about 8 inches (20 cm) in diameter.

Set a flat, wide pan over medium heat. Once hot but not smoking (you should be able to hover your hand just above the surface for about 3 seconds without feeling it burn), add one bing at a time. Cook for 1 minute on each side, or until it develops golden brown spots and begins to develop air bubbles. Repeat with the remaining pieces of dough and stack finished bing on top of a fresh one after the first flip to keep them warm. Alternatively, wrap the finished rounds in cheesecloth and cover in a large bamboo steamer to keep warm.

To make the pork filling: In a small bowl, whisk together the sweet flour sauce with 2 teaspoons of the cooking wine and the sugar. Set aside.

In a large bowl, add the slivered pork, the remaining 1 teaspoon cooking wine, the soy sauce, ginger, and cornstarch and mix together until evenly combined. Store in the refrigerator until ready to cook.

In a medium skillet, heat 1 tablespoon of the vegetable oil over high heat. When the oil is hot but not smoking, add the pork and stir nonstop for 2 minutes. Remove the pork from the pan and set aside.

Wipe out the pan and heat up once more over high heat. Add the remaining 1 tablespoon vegetable oil and heat until hot but not smoking.

Add the garlic and green onion and cook for 30 seconds. Add the prepared sauce. Add the pork back to the pan, stir to combine, and remove from the heat.

To make the fixings: In a large skillet, heat 1 tablespoon of the vegetable oil over high heat until hot but not smoking. Turn the heat down to medium and add the Sichuan peppercorns and dried red chile pepper. Stir-fry for 30 seconds.

Add the garlic and green onion. Cook for 30 seconds more, then carefully remove and discard the spices and aromatics from the pan. Leave the aromatic oil in the pan.

Turn the heat up to high and add the potatoes. Stir-fry until they begin to turn translucent, about 1½ minutes. Turn the heat down to medium and add 1 teaspoon of the white vinegar, ¼ teaspoon of the salt, and ⅛ teaspoon of the sugar. Stir-fry until the potatoes are just tender, about 1 more minute. Remove them from the pan and set aside.

Fill a medium pot two-thirds full of water, cover, and bring to a boil. Add the hydrated kelp and blanch, uncovered, for 30 seconds.

Strain out the seaweed. In a small bowl, mix the seaweed with the remaining ⅛ teaspoon salt, ⅛ teaspoon sugar, ¼ teaspoon white vinegar, and the sesame oil. Set aside.

To serve: Lay a bing on a plate and spread some sweet flour sauce on it. Place your desired amounts of pork, potatoes, and seaweed down the center. Be careful not to overstuff!

Top it all off with sliced green onions. Roll your juan bing up tightly and enjoy.

Pineapple Chicken
菠萝鸡

Our small community of Chinese expats in Michigan was a jumble of families from all over China, so our potlucks were a melting pot of American food, Chinese American food, and traditional Chinese cooking. This dish is a result of those potlucks, a perfect example of how immigration and location can transform cultural flavors. Xi'an might not have a lot of sweet-and-salty combinations, but those flavors developed in other regions in southern China. Add in the influence of Chinese American takeout, and you get this: crispy bits of chicken in your classic sweet-and-sour sauce, with pineapple and ketchup (yes, ketchup). It's exactly what you would think of when you think Chinese American food, but potentially better, fresher, from the takeout joint you wish were near your apartment.

One mother brought pineapple chicken to a Chinese New Year potluck, and my mom snagged the recipe to see if she could make her own version. Nothing about this dish was familiar to me back then, but when I have it now, it reminds me of a time when my family and I were trying so hard to blend into a new place, cooking with new ingredients. We ended up with flavors and combinations that on the surface looked strange but at their core struck something that felt like home (and tasted pretty damn good, too).

Serves
2

page 60

---

5 ounces (140 g) boneless, skinless chicken breast, cut into 1½-inch (4 cm) pieces

½ teaspoon salt, divided

¾ teaspoon Shaoxing cooking wine, divided

⅓ cup plus ¼ teaspoon (48 g) cornstarch, divided

¼ teaspoon plus 2 cups (480 ml) plus 1 tablespoon vegetable oil, divided

1 tablespoon sugar

2 teaspoons white vinegar

⅓ cup (75 ml) ketchup

2-inch (5 cm) piece fresh ginger, peeled and thinly sliced into matchsticks

1 garlic clove, peeled and sliced

½ green bell pepper, cut into ¾-inch (2 cm) squares

½ red bell pepper, cut into ¾-inch (2 cm) squares

3½ ounces (100 g) canned pineapple cubes (if using a fresh pineapple, carefully remove and cut the flesh into ¾-inch/2 cm cubes; reserve the shell)

1 green onion, white part only, cut into slivers

Tenderize the chicken by lightly beating it with the blunt edge of a knife. This improves the texture and lets the seasoning sink into the meat.

In a medium bowl, add the chicken along with ¼ teaspoon of the salt and ¼ teaspoon of the cooking wine. Mix well to combine.

In a small bowl, make a slurry by combining ⅓ cup (45 g) of the cornstarch with 3 tablespoons water to form a paste. Mix in one direction to combine. Add ¼ teaspoon of the vegetable oil and stir to combine.

In another small bowl, add the remaining ¼ teaspoon salt and the remaining ½ teaspoon cooking wine, along with the sugar, white vinegar, and ketchup. Mix evenly in one direction. This is your sweet-and-sour sauce.

In a large skillet, pour in the 2 cups (480 ml) vegetable oil and set over medium heat. Make sure the slurry is not settled by stirring it in one direction. Right before the oil reaches the smoking point (about 400°F/200°C, or when you see it start to shimmer), dip each piece of chicken in the cornstarch slurry and then carefully place into the oil. Make sure not to overcrowd the pan, working in batches if necessary.

Cook the chicken on one side for 1½ minutes, flip over, and cook for another 1½ minutes. Remove to a plate. Repeat until all of the chicken pieces are fried.

In a small bowl, add the remaining ¼ teaspoon cornstarch along with a splash of water to make a second slurry. Stir in one direction to combine.

Heat the oil once more over medium heat until just below smoking point (about 400°F/200°C, or when you see it start to shimmer). Return the chicken to the pan, working in batches if necessary, and cook until golden brown, 1 to 2 minutes.

In another large skillet that can hold all of the ingredients comfortably, heat the remaining 1 tablespoon vegetable oil over high heat. Add the ginger and garlic and cook for 1 minute, or until tender. Add the sweet-and-sour sauce and cook until slightly thickened, about 2 minutes.

Add the bell peppers and cook for about 2 minutes. Add the pineapple, green onion, and fried chicken and stir-fry for 1 minute. Add the second slurry you made and stir to combine. Cook for an additional 1 minute, then serve.

Note: If you have a pineapple shell, spoon the chicken into the hollowed-out shell for a fun—if kitschy—presentation. Moms love that stuff.

This dish is a perfect example of how immigration and location can transform cultural flavors.

Hong Shao "Red Braised" Spareribs
红烧排骨

This was one of the few dishes my mom made during our time in Michigan that was truly authentic, and it's partially due to the simplicity of the ingredients. Any dish that starts with "hong shao" is typically stewed in a soy sauce and spice combo, infusing the meat with its flavor while rendering it tender. Some families prefer beef in this, others will slow-cook pork belly until the fat is as soft as Jell-O, but my mom always went for pork spareribs, a cut more easily accessible at the time. She'd chop up the ribs, stew them with Sichuan peppercorns (her version has an extra tingle to it), and serve the lean, tender meat with rice. As a kid, I wasn't allowed to leave the table until the bones were sucked dry—and I wasn't mad about it.

Serves
2 to 4

page 60

¾ cup (180 ml) vegetable oil, divided

¼ cup (56 g) sugar

2 pounds (910 g) pork spareribs (ask your butcher to chop these up into 3-inch/7.5 cm long segments)

4-inch (10 cm) cinnamon stick, broken in half

4 bay leaves

4 cloves

2 star anise pods

20 Sichuan peppercorns

2 green onions, trimmed and cut into 1-inch (2.5 cm) segments

2-inch (5 cm) piece fresh ginger, peeled and sliced

6 tablespoons (90 ml) Shaoxing cooking wine

6 tablespoons (90 ml) soy sauce

In a large, heavy-bottomed pot or Dutch oven, heat ¼ cup (60 ml) of the vegetable oil over medium heat.

When the oil just begins to ripple, add the sugar and stir to combine. Keep stirring, being careful not to let the mixture burn. Cook until the sugar is caramel brown, about 2 minutes.

Add the ribs and cook until they just begin to brown, 1 to 2 minutes per side. Remove and set aside.

Clean out the pot and dry it thoroughly. Add the remaining ½ cup (120 ml) vegetable oil to the pot and turn the heat up to high. Add the cinnamon sticks, bay leaves, cloves, star anise, and Sichuan peppercorns and fry, stirring constantly, for about 1 minute. You want to bring out the flavor without letting the spices burn.

Carefully remove the bay leaves from the pot, then add the ribs and stir. Add the green onions, ginger, cooking wine, and soy sauce. Stir, and cook for 2 to 3 minutes. Add 2 cups (480 ml) water and bring to a boil. Cover the pot and turn down the heat to low.

After 30 minutes, uncover the pot and turn the heat up to high. Reduce the sauce as desired (10 to 15 minutes for saucy ribs, or 20 to 25 minutes for a thicker reduction) and serve.

Beef Stew with Potatoes
土豆烧牛肉

Lamb was a rare commodity in our town in Michigan, so my mother often-times would make do with beef. This dish—think American beef stew with Chinese seasonings—would show up on our dinner table at least once a week, steaming up the kitchen with the smell of fennel, star anise, and soy. It's simple and homey, a salty and spicy accompaniment to rice, perfect for cold Michigan winter suppers, and even more tender and flavorful after a day of sitting. You wouldn't necessarily find this dish in restaurants (it isn't sexy enough), but it's what I consider comfort food.

Serves
2

page 60

11-ounce (310 g) beef chuck tender

1 tablespoon soy sauce

1 tablespoon Shaoxing cooking wine

1 tablespoon oyster sauce

¼ teaspoon sugar

2 tablespoons vegetable oil

2 star anise pods

1 teaspoon Sichuan peppercorns

2 bay leaves

3-inch (7.5 cm) cinnamon stick

1½-inch (4 cm) square dried orange peel

½ teaspoon fennel seeds

2 white cardamom pods

1 black cardamom pod

1 garlic clove, peeled and sliced

1-inch (2.5 cm) piece fresh ginger, peeled and sliced

2 green onions, trimmed and cut into 2-inch (5 cm) segments

½ medium white onion, sliced

¼ teaspoon sweet flour sauce

½ teaspoon chili garlic sauce

¼ teaspoon Pixian bean sauce

1 large yellow potato, peeled and cut into cubes, reserved in water until use

½ medium tomato, cut into cubes

In a large pot, add the beef and cover with water. Cover the pot and bring to a boil over high heat. Boil for 10 minutes, uncovered, then take out the beef and discard the water. Once the beef is cool enough to handle, cut into 1-inch (2.5 cm) cubes.

In a small bowl, combine the soy sauce, cooking wine, oyster sauce, sugar, and 1½ cups (360 ml) water. Set aside.

In a clean pot, add the vegetable oil and set over medium heat. Once the oil is hot, add the star anise, Sichuan peppercorns, bay leaves, cinnamon stick, orange peel, fennel seeds, white and black cardamom, garlic, ginger, green onions, and onion and stir-fry until fragrant, about 3 minutes. Add the sweet flour sauce, chili garlic sauce, and Pixian bean sauce and stir to combine for 1 minute.

Add the beef and stir-fry for 2 minutes. Add the prepared sauce, bring to a boil over high heat, and cook for 5 minutes. Turn the heat down to medium-low and cook for 10 more minutes, stirring frequently.

Drain the potatoes and add them to the pot, raising the heat to high. Bring to a boil, then turn the heat down to low. Cover the pot and simmer for 30 minutes.

Add the tomatoes and turn the heat up to high. Let the sauce from the stew reduce for 10 to 20 minutes, until it reaches your desired consistency, before serving. Leftovers can be stored refrigerated in an airtight container for 2 to 3 days.

Pork Zha Jiang
炸酱

I got fat off this dish in middle school. I mean, how could you not? This sweet-savory meat sauce is a staple over noodles, universally beloved across eastern Asia; both Korean and Japanese cuisines have variations of this funky black-brown sauce.

The most important ingredient required for our version of zha jiang mian is the sweet flour sauce (or tian mian jiang), a thick, salty condiment with a roasty backbone, usually served with Peking duck. In Michigan, we could only occasionally find sweet flour sauce in a rare haul from the big city, and I'd savor each bite of these noodles. Fast forward to our Flushing years and there, in our local grocery store, was the coveted sauce. We could have zha jiang mian for *days*. And trust me, I did.

Serves
4

*page 61
(or as a dip for
vegetables)*

6 tablespoons (90 ml) sweet flour sauce

¼ cup (60 ml) Shaoxing cooking wine

3 tablespoons (45 ml) vegetable oil, divided

10 ounces (280 g) ground pork belly, or ground pork with 30% fat

4 green onions, trimmed and sliced

1-inch (2.5 cm) piece fresh ginger, peeled and finely chopped

1 teaspoon sugar

1 Persian cucumber, cut into thin matchsticks (optional)

In a small bowl, add the sweet flour sauce, cooking wine, and 6 tablespoons (90 ml) water and stir in one direction to form a sauce. Set aside for later.

In a large pan, heat 2 tablespoons of the vegetable oil over medium heat. Add the pork belly and cook until no longer pink, about 2 minutes. Remove from the pan and set aside. Clean and dry the pan.

Add the remaining 1 tablespoon vegetable oil to the pan and heat over medium heat. Add the green onions and ginger and cook until the green onions are just wilted, about 1 minute.

Add the meat back to the pan and stir. Then add the reserved sauce and the sugar and cook for 3 more minutes, stirring in one direction to combine; the sauce should be thick. Top with cucumbers if desired.

Zha Jiang Noodles with Wasabi
芥末炸酱面

When we moved to the States and my dad started working in Chinese restaurants, my family discovered the beauty and horror of the Chinese takeout industry. These joints are never just one thing; they serve the classic kung pao chicken and beef and broccoli stir-fry, but also amp up their menu with fried chicken and fries, pad Thai, and California rolls. You have to hand it to them—it's entrepreneurship at its finest.

My dad rolled with it.[7] When I was in middle school, he started working at a Chinese/Japanese restaurant, and there he experimented with the wasabi he saw on a daily basis. He'd put it on everything, including cold noodles, and one day discovered this combination: a refreshing, summery take on our classic zha jiang mian.

This became my go-to snack. I'd come home from school, grab some precooked noodles from the fridge, a dollop of zha jiang, and mix it all up with a hunk of wasabi paste. It was better than instant noodles and didn't even require boiling water.

2 pieces Biang-Biang (or Hand-Ripped) Noodle Dough (page 55), or 1 coil Longevity Noodle (page 49), or store-bought *you mian* 幼面, long thin wheat noodles found in the refrigerated section of a Chinese grocery store

1 serving (4¼ ounces/120 ml) Pork Zha Jiang (page 91)

1 teaspoon wasabi paste, or to taste

2 tablespoons XFF Noodle Sauce (page 43)

1 Persian cucumber, cut into thin matchsticks (optional)

Bring a pot of water to a boil. If using homemade noodles, pull and cook the noodles following the recipe instructions. If you're using store-bought noodles, cook the noodles following the instructions on the package.

Transfer the noodles to cold water to cool down. Strain out and set aside.

Heat up the pork zha jiang if you're grabbing it straight from the fridge (like I often do).

Combine the noodles with the zha jiang, wasabi paste, and XFF noodle sauce. Mix with the cucumbers, if using, and serve.

7   Or you could say he *"California"* rolled with it.

3 THE THROWBACK

Finding a New Place to Call Home

The only time I ever felt like I was just
trips to Flushing, a neighborhood in

BY THE TIME I HIT MIDDLE SCHOOL, I THOUGHT I HAD AMERICAN CULTURE DOWN. I was caught up in class, knew the slang (or, rather, the curse words), and even had a pair of Jordans that made me instantly "cool."[1] But, of course, my parents had to throw me another curve ball: We were moving, again. Some family friends had a connection that would get me into a private Catholic school in Connecticut, which was, in theory, great. We'd be close to our friends, I'd get a "better" education, and my dad would be able to work in the booming industry that is the East Coast Chinese restaurant scene. Wins all around.

But Connecticut was a whole different beast. In Michigan, I was an outsider, but I was never overtly bullied. I was used to getting a few snickers here and there, some kid making fun of the fact that I couldn't differentiate between *th* and *st*, but at least I was left alone. All I did was study, anyway.

My new school, though, was both racially and culturally homogenous. These kids had been together since kindergarten and had probably never had to interact with a Chinese kid like me in real life. And the media wasn't kind to Asians back then—it was either Long Duck Dong in *Sixteen Candles* or nothing at all. My new classmates made it clear to me from day one that I didn't belong. I was constantly made fun of for my accent and was called a "chink" for the first time. When I tagged along to see *The Fast and the Furious*, one kid came up to me and said, "Yo, that chick that was in the movie is Asian like you! And she's actually pretty hot . . . for an Asian."

Still, I did my best to fit in. I ditched the Beethoven I grew up listening to and downloaded what my classmates considered "cool" off Napster. I learned who Eminem was (not a candy, apparently), and felt weird listening to him with my mom around.[2] And at school, I learned how to talk about drugs and sex, even though I'd never done any drugs and hadn't even kissed a girl.

Mostly, though, I learned to never talk about my home life. I was embarrassed by it back then—a fact I'm not proud of today. My classmates had houses with porches and backyards and parents who worked white collar nine-to-five jobs. But my family was in an entirely different universe, living in a dingy two-bedroom apartment. My parents slept on a mattress on the floor. Most, if not all, of our furniture was secondhand or found on the curb, including my twin bed frame (the fact that I even had a frame meant I was lucky). Our coffee table was a round plastic

1 I had no idea what these were; they were a gift from some relatives. When I got actual positive attention for them at school, I realized, *Oh, clothes make you cool.* So I tried to get some JNCO jeans to become even more popular. My mom refused to buy them for me, saying they would make me a bad student.
2 Although it's his "fuck you, I do what I want" attitude that later fueled me as an adult.

another kid was during our monthly
Queens, New York City.

lawn table, its cracks covered with a cheap tablecloth.

And my dad? Instead of putting on a suit and tie like the other kids' parents, he was buying one-way bus tickets to cities all around the East Coast, chasing the next money-making scheme at whatever Chinese restaurant would hire him.[3] One week he'd be in Delaware lugging crates of soy sauce up and down stairs at a giant buffet; the next he's doing prep work in Maryland.

But these gigs never lasted long. My dad's a hothead, and he'd either get fired for talking back, or he'd leave out of anger and pride and book a last-minute bus ticket back to our suburban town. I'd come home from school and find my dad sitting on the floor in his underwear, scouring the Chinese papers for his next job.

Now, of course, I want to tell my younger self to shut up, respect his parents, and be thankful for their hustle. But back when I was twelve, my tumultuous home life was just another way that I was different from my classmates. I wanted nothing more than to be seen as normal.

The only time I ever felt like I was just another kid was during our monthly trips to Flushing, a neighborhood in Queens, New York City. For the uninitiated, Flushing is like Manhattan's Chinatown but bigger, crazier, with more of everything—more supermarkets, more restaurants, more Chinese bakeries with egg tarts and milk bread and pork steamed buns. All around the East Coast, immigrant families would make a monthly or weekly pilgrimage to Flushing to stock up on groceries, eat the food they grew up with, and feel at home for a day.

These treks to New York became our ritual as well. Every month, we'd brave the traffic and drive three hours to the crowded blocks surrounding Main Street. We'd park the car in the cheaper municipal parking lot (or circle around for thirty minutes to snag free parking if it was a Sunday), go get a six-dollar haircut,[4] grab some Sichuan food, and then battle other shoppers to stock up on the necessities. My family would load up the car with jugs of good soy sauce, pounds of rice, and boxes of black vinegar. We'd grab Pixian bean sauce, dried red chile peppers, lamb, chicken feet, pork belly, the works. Then we'd drive back to our apartment and cook it all up, freeze it, and survive off those dishes for the next four weeks.

Flushing was a reminder that there were other people out there like me. There were kids who knew more about Chinese pop music than they did the Beatles because that's what they grew up with; kids who others said spoke with

---

3   The East Coast Chinese restaurant scene is a complex, interconnected system. The big bosses of restaurants all over New Jersey, Connecticut, and NYC put listings in the Chinese newspaper stating a monthly salary (in cash, obviously). Most of the time, these gigs were for giant Chinese food buffets, with the bonus of free housing—a shared room or sometimes the floor in a house with other employees. My dad would pick up these gigs, pack a bag, and move to a different state for weeks at a time, washing dishes or cooking vats of General Tso's chicken.

4   It's gone up to eight dollars, but I still go there.

a slight accent[5] (although I maintain I don't have one); kids who had straight black hair that never seemed to work with Supercuts styles. When I walked the streets, I blended in. I was normal.

The neighborhood was also a promise that certain aspects of my life would gradually become accepted, that I wouldn't always be made fun of for being different. It was an oasis, a sense of belonging. Back then, you could already see it with the food. The area's restaurant scene proved to me that what people saw as "Chinese food" wasn't just the stuff my dad was cooking at his day job; no one in Flushing ever dared to order sweet-and-sour pork and deep-fried orange chicken—and if they did, everyone would not-so-subtly roll their eyes. Instead, we were getting fiery hot pot in the winter (page 139), cool, crunchy cucumbers in the summer (page 108), and juicy, spicy chicken that made our mouths tingly all year round (page 130).

Eventually, I would move to Queens for high school, and I'd learn even more about the neighborhood, grilling barbecue on the Korean side of town, singing at the all-night KTV, shooting pool with Chinese and Korean pop music on in the background. I spent a lot of those years hanging out with groups of teens who, like me, had to figure out their own Asian American identities. And even today, when I return to my old stomping grounds in Flushing, I find that it's always changing. New families are moving in from different regions in China, with another rush of flavors and specialties. More people are learning to call

this place home and finding their own space among the Sichuan spots, the KTV bars, and the numerous noodle houses.

This chapter pays homage to Flushing and its mom-and-pop shops that helped feed my family. It's a collection of the simple home cooking that hit the table when my parents and I were actually able to eat together, with food we actually loved, because of our monthly trips to Flushing. There are definite XFF favorites that came from this time period (our spicy cucumbers and lamb dumplings, for example), but there are also many dishes that aren't specific to Xi'an, combinations and techniques that have traveled from one region to the next. You'll find bright starter salads, salty and spicy pork belly, dumplings that benefit from an assembly crew, and so much more. And if you look at the dinner spreads of Chinese families all around the world, you might see variations of the recipes that follow—moms picking the juiciest piece of dark meat chicken to give to their youngest child, dads teaching their kids how to fold dumplings, or a group of friends gathering around a boiling pot of stock, mixing egg yolks into soy sauce and sesame paste for a leisurely night of hot pot. These are the meals I turn to when I want a simple night in, bringing together my family or my friends, and they're just the right balance of homey, comforting, and memorably delicious.

---

5 What I call the NYC ABC accent—a little more rounded, thicker, slightly more musical.

MY DAD AND ME GROCERY SHOPPING AROUND FLUSHING. AS YOU CAN SEE, IT GETS CROWDED.

A Brief Guide to NYC's Various Chinatowns

WITH THE LARGEST CHINESE POPULATION IN ANY CITY OUTSIDE OF ASIA, NEW YORK CITY IS HOME TO MULTIPLE CHINATOWNS. There's the original one in Manhattan, Flushing in Queens, and Sunset Park in Brooklyn. And more hubs are growing—Flushing has bled into Elmhurst, and Sunset Park paved the way for Bay Ridge and Bensonhurst. To me, Flushing will always be superior. But I'm biased, so in the name of objectivity, I enlisted a few friends to help guide you through three of NYC's many hubs.

FLUSHING

Flushing is so much more than Chinatown, which is probably why it will always be king to me. You have the Korean side, which has been mostly east Flushing, and then you have the Chinese side along Main Street.

In recent years, Flushing has become more of a gaudy tourist destination, where restaurateurs serve up whatever they think is popular at the time, and the neighborhood is expanding outward, growing toward College Point Boulevard with new developments that make Flushing feel like Los Angeles. Nevertheless, a few old go-tos are still hanging around.

What to eat: Hot Space for spicy fish casserole; the latest frog specialty and anything with pickled peppers at Hunan Cafe; and solo hot pot at Fukuoka ShaBu ShaBu, especially for late-night no-frills last-minute meals. And if you're up for exploring, new developments are always popping up around Prince Street and 37th Avenue.

What to do: Drop by a KTV bar, like The Real KTV and SOHO KTV, for a few songs. Get a haircut at Five Star Beauty Salon. Ask for Mr. Zhao.

SUNSET PARK

Being a Queens resident, I rarely venture to Brooklyn. But if I'm on my way to the beach, I might swing by Sunset Park for some spicy and sour rice noodles. Since I'm no Brooklyn boy, though, my friend, food writer, and Brooklyn native Patty Lee is going to give you the lay of the land.

"I grew up along 8th Ave (as we called it) in the 1990s and early 2000s, and a lot of the immigrant families there were from 台山 (Toi San or Tai Shan), my own family included. The whole place felt like one giant extended family. My brother and I are two years apart, so we would end up in classes with other sets of siblings or cousins from the neighborhood who were sons and daughters of our parents' friends. We'd see each other at school on the weekdays, but also at dim sum on Sunday mornings.

"The Chinatown has grown significantly since then. It used to stretch from 50th Street to 62nd, but now it goes farther into the 40s and 60s, towards Fort Hamilton. A lot of the Cantonese families I grew up with moved into other neighborhoods like Bensonhurst and Bay Ridge, and more immigrants from Fujian started moving into Sunset Park. Still, I

have yet to find anything similar to the dumplings in hot-and-sour sauce from Yun Nan Flavour Garden anywhere else."

What to eat: Dim sum at East Harbor; the roast pork (char siu) at Lucky Eight; the No. 1 Banh Mi at Thanh Da; Portuguese egg tarts at Lily Bloom; the aforementioned rice noodles and dumplings from Yun Nan Flavour Garden.

What to do: Shop for fresh produce, meat, and seafood at Fei Long Market, which stretches for a full city block. Then check out the spectacular view of Manhattan from the actual Sunset Park (not technically part of the Chinatown, but worth it).

CHINATOWN

OG Chinatown has had a little renaissance lately, with hip new restaurants popping up on its old-timey streets. Some of these places, though, have been around for a hundred years, like Nom Wah Tea Parlor. Originally a bakery, this dim sum joint was sold to my friend Wilson Tang's uncle in the '70s, and now Wilson runs the place (plus its sister restaurants and offshoots). Here, he shares *his* Chinatown, and what to know about it.

"I actually spent grade school and high school in Queens, because my parents were afraid I would follow the wrong crowd in Chinatown in the '80s. Luckily, I spent most of my weekends and summers in the neighborhood, and I remember having to speak Cantonese everywhere I went. I would literally get laughed at if English came out of my mouth.

"Lunar New Year growing up was a big deal. You could still light real fireworks, so the firecrackers following the lion dancing were a real treat. Over the years, Chinatown has spread to other areas and into other boroughs, so what remains of Manhattan's Chinatown is less vibrant than before, with fewer Chinese immigrants. Still, the tradition of Lunar New Year lion dancing continues—minus the firecrackers."

What to eat: Dim sum at Nom Wah Tea Parlor; Chinese BBQ hanging in the windows of restaurants like Big Wong; beef jerky from Jung's on Mulberry; wonton noodle soup from Great NY Noodletown.

What to do: Visit the Museum of Chinese in America, see the Word War II memorial at Chatham Square, and watch people sing and play cards at Columbus Park.

LEFT: SOME PRETTY CUTE PANDA DEPICTIONS IN MANHATTAN'S CHINATOWN.

MANHATTAN'S CHINATOWN, ON THE ICONIC PELL STREET.

Starter Salads

HERE'S SOMETHING MOST PEOPLE DON'T KNOW ABOUT ME: I HATE CARROTS. The only time I'll eat carrots is if they're overpowered by cumin, like the roasted carrot at ABC Kitchen, or vinegar, like in this salad.

This starter was a constant presence in my childhood. When I was a kid, I'd wake up from my afternoon nap to a pungent, funky smell—the vinegar. From that first whiff, I'd know my mom was home and making dinner. One of these salads would be the first dish to hit the table, something to munch on while my mom finished up the hot dishes and rice.

There are two options, but both are variations on the same theme: a bright vinegar-y slaw, with a tingle of Sichuan peppercorn and a dash of salt. Simple, clean, and quick. The cold version, with julienned carrots, has a slightly sharper garlic kick balanced with the sweetness of sesame oil. The warm rendition, with blanched strips of potatoes, is homier and has a little more heat thanks to the extra step of roasting the chiles in vegetable oil.

Spicy and Sour Carrot Salad
凉拌胡罗卜丝

Serves
2 to 4
as an
appetizer

2 carrots (about 8 ounces/225 g)

4 teaspoons Garlic Puree (page 37)

30 Sichuan peppercorns

4 dried red chile peppers (such as Tianjin), sliced into thin slivers

¼ cup (60 ml) vegetable oil

½ teaspoon salt

½ teaspoon sugar

4 teaspoons (20 ml) toasted sesame oil

¼ cup (60 ml) white vinegar

Handful chopped cilantro (optional)

Peel and slice the carrots into ⅛-inch (3 mm) matchsticks.

Place the carrots in a large bowl. Set the garlic, Sichuan peppercorns, and dried red chile peppers on top of the carrots in a small pile.

In a small skillet, heat the vegetable oil over medium heat until the oil starts to shimmer (or just until the smoking point, about 6 minutes). Remove from the heat and carefully pour the hot oil over the aromatics on top of the carrots.

Add the salt, sugar, sesame oil, and white vinegar to the bowl of carrots and toss to mix evenly. Top with the cilantro, if using, and serve.

Julienned Potato Salad
炝土豆丝

2 yellow potatoes (about 7 ounces/200 g each), peeled

2½ teaspoons salt, divided

½ teaspoon sugar

¼ cup (60 ml) white vinegar

4 teaspoons toasted sesame oil

2 green onions, white part only, chopped

2 tablespoons vegetable oil

4 dried red chile peppers (such as Tianjin), cut into ½-inch (12 mm) segments

30 Sichuan peppercorns

2 sprigs cilantro (optional)

1 longhorn red pepper, seeded and diagonally sliced (optional)

Cut the potato into ⅛-inch (3 mm) thick slices. Then cut the slices into thin matchsticks.

In a large pot, add the potatoes and 2 teaspoons of the salt. Submerge the potatoes with cold water.

Cover the pot and set over high heat. Bring to a boil.

Cook for about 4 minutes, until the potatoes are translucent and tender but not mushy, stirring them every so often to prevent them from sticking.

Drain the potatoes in a colander and shock with cold water to stop the cooking process. Dry the potatoes thoroughly using a kitchen towel or paper towels.

Place the potatoes in a large bowl and add the remaining ½ teaspoon salt, along with the sugar, white vinegar, and sesame oil. Stir to combine, then place the green onions on top of the potatoes in a little pile.

In a small skillet, heat the vegetable oil over medium heat and add the chiles and Sichuan peppercorns. Roast the spices in the oil for about 30 seconds, until the spices turn dark in color and fragrant. Carefully strain the spices out from the oil and discard.

Carefully pour the hot, spice-infused oil on top of the green onions and potatoes. Mix everything together and serve, topped with cilantro and red pepper, if desired.

Spicy Asian Cucumber Salad
凉拌小黄瓜

As a kid, if I wanted a snack, a grown-up would simply pick a crisp, spiny Chinese cucumber off a vine in my grandmother's yard and hand it to me. It was the perfect thirst-quencher for a hot summer day and required no prep whatsoever.

As a grown-up, though, I like to dress up the raw cucumber with our signature sauces, plus an entire clove of garlic and as much chili oil as my taste buds crave. You could go ahead and slice your cucumbers like a regular civilian, but here at XFF we like things a little bit rough—food-wise, I mean. So instead of neat little cucumber spears, we use a cleaver to smash the gourds open, breaking out the juicy, meaty bits for the sauce and spice to cling to.

Serves
2 as an
appetizer

4 Persian or another variety of small, spiny cucumber, about 7 inches (17 cm) long each (Don't go for anything larger—we want small and crisp for this recipe)

2 green or red longhorn peppers, or jalapeños, seeded and diagonally sliced

2 teaspoons Garlic Puree (page 37)

½ teaspoon salt

½ teaspoon sugar

2 tablespoons soy sauce

2 teaspoons black vinegar

1 tablespoon XFF Chili Oil with seeds (page 40), or to taste

Dash of toasted sesame oil

TOOL:
Butcher knife, cleaver, or mallet for smashing the cucumbers

Wash the cucumbers in cold water and dry them with paper towels.

Lay the cucumbers on a cutting board and cut away the tips. Discard the tips.

Using the side of a wide knife or a mallet, carefully apply pressure to the cucumbers, smashing them lengthwise, so there are a few crack lines running along the sides.

Cut the cucumbers into 1½-inch (4 cm) segments and place into a large bowl.

Add as many slices of the longhorn or jalapeño pepper to the bowl as you can handle. This gives the salad an extra kick, but also adds a nice visual flourish, especially if you're using a red pepper.

Combine the remaining ingredients in a separate bowl. Pour over the cucumbers and toss to serve. The cucumbers can sit for up to 10 minutes before eating, allowing the flavors to meld, but any longer and the gourds will lose their satisfying crunch.

Seitan Salad
凉拌面筋

People might not know this, but the by-product of liang pi (page 51) is seitan, a spongy vegetarian protein. When you remove the starch from the original dough, the remaining mass is all the protein—and when cooked, it turns into seitan.

While liang pi is hard to master, seitan is comparatively easy. Consequently, when my family was experimenting with getting the right ratio of water to starch for liang pi, we ended up with a lot of perfectly edible seitan left around from failed liang pi experiments. It worked out for me; seitan was the ultimate vehicle for my favorite dressing: vinegar. I'd toss the springy cubes onto a bed of the vegetables of the moment, mix it up with some black vinegar and soy, and have at it—which is how this salad came about. Here, we use cucumbers for some extra crunch and texture, but you could easily add arugula, butter lettuce, or spinach for a more traditional salad.

4 as an
appetizer

1 batch Seitan from the Liang Pi "Cold Skin Noodles" and Seitan recipe (page 51), cooled and cut into slices, roughly 1½ inch (4 cm) wide, ⅜ inch (1 cm) thick

1 Persian cucumber, cut into thin slivers

1 sprig cilantro, coarsely chopped

¼ cup (60 ml) toasted sesame oil

3 tablespoons (45 ml) soy sauce

6 tablespoons (90 ml) black vinegar

Dash of XFF Liang Pi Sauce (page 44)

XFF Chili Oil (page 40)

Garlic Puree (page 37)

Note: Yes, theoretically, you could use store-bought seitan, but our homemade version is undeniably springier, fresher, tastier, and just better all around.

In a large bowl, toss the seitan with the cucumber, cilantro, sesame oil, soy sauce, vinegar, and liang pi sauce. Add chili oil and garlic puree to taste and serve.

Dumplings

BACK IN CHINA, DUMPLINGS WERE A FAMILY ACTIVITY. YOU'D GATHER AROUND DURING HOLIDAYS, DIVVY UP THE TASKS (SKINS ON ONE SIDE, FOLDING ON THE OTHER, ASSEMBLY-LINE STYLE), AND MAKE BATCHES AND BATCHES. We'd cook them up (saving a few for the freezer) and eat until we were bursting. The next day, we'd take out the frozen dumplings to turn into pot stickers or boil up for last-minute dinners (see Pot Stickers, page 124, or How to Boil Frozen Dumplings, page 123).

When we left China, we also left behind some of that magic. We didn't have family members to share the work with, so we made dumplings less and less often. But when we moved to New York, we ran across another tradition: dollar dumplings.

One of my first memories in New York City was taking the Chinatown bus, which carried hordes of workers and families from Flushing to Manhattan's Chinatown. Right off the Flushing stop, behind the now-closed Red Bowl restaurant, was a hole-in-the-wall dumpling joint selling five fried dumplings for a buck. These suckers were good—fat little pork and chive pot stickers with as much sriracha sauce as you wanted—and man, they were popular. So popular, in fact, the bus company had to ban customers from bringing them on the ride. The first five minutes would be heaven; the last twenty-five minutes would be stuffy, stinky, Chinese-chives-and-stale-oil hell. Let's not even talk about what happened when people started burping.

Those dumplings were my first exposure to Chinese fast food in New York, and it opened my eyes to the fact that people were willing—eager, in fact—to wait in line and spend money on the foods of my childhood. It was the first inkling that something like XFF could really take off.

Even in Flushing, though, it was rare to see lamb, not to mention lamb dumplings. So we made our own at home, perfecting what would become the XFF dumplings. In the pages that follow, you'll find recipes for making the skins, the fillings, and then instructions for rolling out, folding, and finally cooking the dumplings. Our spicy and sour lamb dumplings lean on the licorice-like notes of star anise and the numbing sensations of Sichuan peppercorns, delivering on the "tingly" promise of "spicy and tingly." (The "spicy" comes later from our XFF Chili Oil, page 40.) Spinach dumplings add in hearty tofu and vermicelli, letting the fruitiness of Sichuan peppercorns become brighter, more distinct. And, of course, we have our version of the classic pork and chive dumplings. They're not sold in our stores, but they're better than dollar dumplings, we promise.

Note: I recommend making dumplings with friends on winter solstice, since superstition says it'll help ward off the cold. Cook as many as your heart desires. Freeze the rest for a lazy day.

Dumpling Skin Dough
饺子皮

Dumpling-making was always a group activity in our household, typically reserved for big holidays when we could rope other family members into helping out. My mom and aunties would first prep the filling and the dumpling skin dough. Then the family would divvy up the rolling and folding. Younger kids got folding, the easiest part of the process, but since rolling out the skins is the trickiest skill to master, only the most experienced dumpling makers (mostly adults, some teens) could man that station.

The key here is to get the right kind of rolling pin. Forget about the giant baker's pins you see people work pie crusts with. Those will pinch your fingers if you're not careful. What you want is a skinny roller from an Asian grocery store, essentially a broom handle about a foot (30.5 cm) long, 1 to 1½ inches (2.5 to 4 cm) in diameter. Work the roller with one hand, the dumpling skins with the other, and practice, practice, practice.

Makes
60
skins

4 cups (500 g) all-purpose flour or high-gluten flour, plus more for dusting

¼ teaspoon salt

1½ cups (360 ml) cold water, divided

TOOL:
A thin, evenly cylindrical rolling pin, roughly 1½ inches (4 cm) in diameter

In a large bowl, add the flour and salt and stir to combine.

Add 1 cup (240 ml) of the cold water slowly while mixing with your hands. Then add the remaining water a little at a time, using both hands to knead for about 5 minutes, until it all comes together and forms a smooth dough. You may not use all the water.

Wrap the dough with plastic wrap and let it rest at room temperature for 10 minutes.

After resting, remove the plastic wrap and knead the dough in the bowl a few more times. Wrap again with plastic wrap and let rest for another 10 minutes. You may repeat this process one more time if you wish, for a chewier dough, but the chewier the dough is, the stickier and trickier it will be to work with.

Cover with a damp cloth or plastic wrap while you prep your fillings.

The dumpling skins are best used day of, but if you can't make the dumplings right away, it's best to store the dough in unrolled pieces, generously dusted on all sides with flour to prevent sticking. Cover with plastic or place in a covered container and store for up to 2 days in the refrigerator.

See page 121 for instructions on how to roll out the dough to make the skins.

Spinach Dumpling Skin Dough
菠菜饺子皮

I'm not going to lie—these skins are a pain to make. You have to grab a bunch of spinach, puree it, and then squeeze all the juice out just to dye a small batch of dumpling skins green. But if you're going for show-stopping presentation, it's worth it. Be forewarned, though: You will also be tempted to spend some time getting creative with the leftover spinach. Some options: Spinach Dumpling Filling (page 118), Spinach Cakes (page 235), or even green smoothies.

Makes
60
skins

10 ounces (280 g) spinach

¼ teaspoon salt

4 cups (500 g) all-purpose flour or high-gluten flour, plus more for dusting

TOOLS:
Cheesecloth

Thin, evenly cylindrical rolling pin, roughly 1½ inches (4 cm) in diameter

Wash the spinach well. Drain and pat dry. Add the spinach, salt, and 1 cup (240 ml) water to a blender or food processor and blend until it forms a smooth puree. Strain the mixture through a cheesecloth, reserving the liquid in a measuring cup, which should yield at least 1½ cups (360 ml). Put aside the drained spinach for another use.

In a large bowl, add the flour and gradually stream in 1 cup (240 ml) of the reserved spinach liquid, using one hand to mix. Then gradually add the remaining spinach liquid a little at a time, using both hands to knead for about 5 minutes, until it all comes together and forms a smooth dough. You may not use all the liquid. Cover the dough with plastic wrap and let rest at room temperature for 10 minutes.

After resting, remove the plastic wrap and knead the dough in the bowl a few more times. Cover again with plastic wrap and let rest for another 10 minutes. You may repeat this process one more time for a chewier dough, but the chewier the dough is, the stickier and trickier it will be to work with.

Cover with a damp cloth or plastic wrap while you prep your fillings.

The dumpling skins are best used day of, but if you can't make the dumplings right away, it's best to store the dough in unrolled pieces, generously dusted on all sides with flour to prevent sticking. Cover with plastic or place in a covered container and store for up to 2 days in the refrigerator.

See page 121 for instructions on how to roll out the dough to make the skins.

Spinach Dumpling Filling
菠菜饺子馅

Makes
enough
for 60
dumplings

½ carrot, peeled and sliced lengthwise into ½-inch (12 mm) thick strips, about 2 ounces (60 g)

1 green onion, trimmed and finely chopped

3 tablespoons (45 ml) toasted sesame oil

4 Shanghai baby bok choy, root ends removed, about 3 ounces (90 g)

10 ounces (280 g) fresh spinach, finely chopped, mixed with ¼ teaspoon salt, or the spinach left over from making Spinach Dumpling Skins (page 117)

2 ounces (60 g) rice vermicelli noodles, soaked in hot water for 5 minutes, drained, and coarsely chopped

2 ounces (60 g) fried tofu, finely chopped

1-inch (2.5 cm) piece fresh ginger, peeled and finely chopped

1 teaspoon salt

¼ teaspoon white pepper powder

1 tablespoon vegetable oil

½ teaspoon Sichuan peppercorns

1 egg

Prep a bowl of ice water. Bring a medium pot of water to a boil over medium heat and add the carrot. Cook for about 5 minutes, then immediately remove the carrot to the bowl of ice water to shock them and stop the cooking process. Meanwhile, marinate the green onion in the sesame oil for 5 minutes.

Add the bok choy to the boiling water and cook for about 1 minute, then remove and add to the ice water. Once cooled, squeeze the bok choy between your hands or in a dishcloth to drain it of all water.

Finely chop the carrot and bok choy, then add them to a bowl and combine with the spinach.

Add the vermicelli noodles, fried tofu, ginger, green onion in sesame oil, salt, and white pepper powder to the bowl of vegetables and mix to combine by stirring in one direction to promote better cohesion of the filling.

Set a small pan over low heat and add the vegetable oil. Add the Sichuan peppercorns and fry until fragrant, about 8 minutes. Carefully strain and discard the peppercorns and pour the infused oil into the bowl of dumpling filling. Stir to combine.

Allow the filling to cool slightly, then crack in the egg and mix in one direction to combine. Store in an airtight container in the fridge until ready to use, up to 3 days, or freeze for up to 3 months.

Lamb Dumpling Filling
羊肉饺子馅

11 ounces (300 g) ground lamb (preferably a 70% lean, 30% fatty mix)

¾-inch (2 cm) piece fresh ginger, peeled and finely chopped

1 teaspoon oyster sauce

2 teaspoons soy sauce

2 teaspoons Shaoxing cooking wine

½ teaspoon white pepper powder

½ teaspoon sugar

1 teaspoon salt, divided

2 ounces (60 g) bok choy, finely chopped

2 ounces (60 g) green cabbage, finely chopped

2 green onions, trimmed and finely chopped

3 tablespoons (45 ml) toasted sesame oil

1 tablespoon vegetable oil

2 star anise pods

½ teaspoon Sichuan peppercorns

1 egg

TOOL:
Cheesecloth

Add the lamb to a large bowl.

In a blender, combine the ginger with ¼ cup (60 ml) water. Pulse until it becomes a smooth mixture.

Add the ginger to the lamb, along with the oyster sauce, soy sauce, cooking wine, white pepper powder, sugar, and ½ teaspoon of the salt. To combine, stir in one direction, as it promotes better cohesion of the filling.

In a separate bowl, combine the bok choy, green cabbage, and remaining ½ teaspoon salt. Let sit for 5 minutes.

In the meantime, combine the green onions and sesame oil in a small bowl and let marinate for 5 minutes.

Wrap the bok choy and cabbage in cheesecloth and squeeze any excess liquid through it into the sink. Set the vegetables aside in a bowl, since you're going to pour infused oil over them.

Add the vegetable oil to a small skillet and set over medium heat. Add the star anise and Sichuan peppercorns and fry until fragrant (but not burnt), about 5 minutes. Discard the spices, let cool, then pour the infused oil over the vegetables and stir to combine.

Add the vegetable mixture and green onions in sesame oil to the lamb mixture and combine well. Crack in the egg and stir in one direction to combine. Store in an airtight container in the fridge until ready to use, up to 3 days, or freeze for up to 3 months.

Pork and Chives Dumpling Filling
猪肉韭菜饺子馅

11 ounces (300 g) ground pork (preferably a 70% lean, 30% fatty mix)

¾-inch (2 cm) piece fresh ginger, peeled and finely chopped

½ teaspoon salt

1 teaspoon oyster sauce

2 teaspoons soy sauce

2 teaspoons Shaoxing cooking wine

½ teaspoon white pepper powder

2 ounces (60 g) lotus root or water chestnuts, finely chopped

2 green onions, trimmed and finely chopped

3 tablespoons (45 ml) toasted sesame oil

2 ounces (60 g) Chinese chives, chopped into ⅛-inch (3 mm) segments

1 egg

Add the ground pork to a large bowl.

In a blender, combine the ginger with ¼ cup (60 ml) water. Pulse until it becomes a smooth mixture.

Mix the ginger mixture into the pork. Add the salt, oyster sauce, soy sauce, cooking wine, white pepper powder, and lotus root or water chestnuts. To combine, stir with chopsticks in only one direction to promote better cohesion of the filling.

In a small bowl, combine the green onions with the sesame oil. Let marinate for 5 minutes. Add to the pork filling and mix.

Add the chives. Then crack the egg into the mixture and mix thoroughly. Store in an airtight container in the fridge until ready to use, up to 3 days, or freeze for up to 3 months.

How to Roll Out Your Dumpling Skins

Using your hands, roll the dough into a long and even snake-like cylindrical shape until it is about 1 inch (2.5 cm) in diameter.

On a large wooden board or a clean work counter, use a knife to cut even, 1-inch (2.5-cm) segments of the dough.

Note: You can also rip pieces off by hand, but it requires a certain experience, accuracy, and speed. Cutting with a knife is definitely easier.

Sprinkle a little flour on the board or work surface to prevent sticking (but don't go overboard). Place each segment on the board with the cut part facing up (like a little stubby piece of firewood), and use the heel of your palm to flatten it slightly on the board.

Hold a small cylindrical roller with your dominant hand. With your other hand, hold the piece of dough by the edge. From the opposite edge, gently roll the piece of dough with your roller toward the center and then back, then turn the dough slightly and roll again toward the center and back. Repeat this several times until the dough becomes an almost-perfect circle, 2½ to 3 inches (6 to 7.5 cm) in diameter. The idea is to roll the dough out evenly from the sides so it is smooth and round, with the center slightly thicker than the edges (around ⅛ inch/3 mm thick overall).

Repeat this process for all pieces of dough and use immediately in folding dumplings as instructed on the following page.

How to Wrap the Dumplings

Every family has a different tactic and aesthetic to folding dumplings, but this is one I've found to be the most efficient. Pack your dumplings full, and I promise they'll keep their shape once cooked, too.

Makes 60 dumplings

All-purpose flour

1 recipe Dumpling Skin Dough (page 115) or Spinach Dumpling Skin Dough (page 117) (You could use store-bought dumpling skins, too)

1 recipe dumpling filling (pages 118, 119, or 120)

Prep a tray or a plate by sprinkling flour on the bottom to prevent sticking.

Put a dumpling skin on the palm of your hand.

Use a spoon (or chopsticks) to scoop 1 to 2 tablespoons of your filling mixture into the middle of the skin (see illustration step 1, below). Fold the skin in half so the two sides meet and can be pressed into each other to bind (step 2). Squeeze the rest of the sides together as well (step 3). Make sure the sides are pressed fully into each other to avoid the dumplings breaking, and avoid any filling touching the edges, as the oil in the filling could prevent the sides from sticking properly (step 4).

Note: If you're using store-bought skins, wet the rim of the wrapper with a little bit of water to help the edges seal. The goal is to maximize the amount of filling in your dumpling, but not put so much that the dumpling breaks or cannot be pressed together.

Place the finished dumplings in your prepared tray or plate, being careful to space them apart so they don't stick. These are best cooked and eaten fresh, but you can also place the entire tray of folded dumplings in the freezer, covered carefully with plastic wrap. Once the dumplings are frozen solid, transfer them to an airtight zip-top bag and freeze for up to 3 months.

1

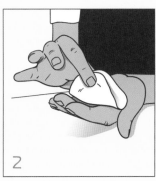

2

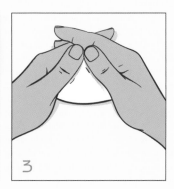

3

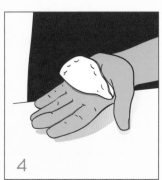

4

How to Boil Frozen Dumplings

Every proper Chinese household will have a bag of dumplings in the freezer. They might be from an evening when you or your family spent hours folding them and stowing them away, or they could be from the Chinatown cash-only shops, where a bag of fifty can go for ten dollars. Regardless, frozen dumplings are the perfect rainy-day food fund. Boil them up when it's too late to go to the grocery store, when you need a snack at 3 p.m., or, if you're like me, when you're a little tipsy from a night out and need something to soak up the booze while mindlessly watching Netflix.

Bring a large pot of water to a simmer, with the water on the verge of boiling. Right before the water boils, gently add the frozen dumplings—this timing is crucial to prevent cracking. Keep the dumplings moving so they don't stick. When the water comes up to a boil again, add ½ cup (120 ml) cold water and stir. Repeat two more times. Once it comes up to a boil the fourth time, the dumplings should be floating and ready to eat, but if you're nervous, go ahead and cut one open to check. The entire process should take 10 minutes, just enough time to chug some water and queue up your show. Fish out the dumplings with a slotted spoon and serve with XFF Dumpling Sauce (page 44), XFF Chili Oil (page 40), sesame oil, and Roasted Sesame Seeds (page 34).

XFF

Pot Stickers
煎饺

Pot stickers, or pan-fried dumplings, are what I like to think of as the bar version of dumplings, best paired with a bottle of Tsingtao beer. First seared until browned on the bottom, then steamed with water, the resulting dumplings are crispy on the outside and juicy on the inside. These are the versions I used to buy five for a dollar in Chinatown, since they could be held at temperature for longer, and I have fond memories of scarfing them down on the side of the road as I walked to the bus.

You could make pot stickers from cooked leftover dumplings if you really wanted to, but the tastiest (and most presentable) method would be to start with frozen. Not only do the packets tend to keep their shape better, they're also less likely to be overcooked. It's just another reason to keep a bag of frozen dumplings in your freezer at all times.

**Serves
1 or 2**

2 teaspoons vegetable oil, divided

10 uncooked frozen dumplings (pages 115 to 122)

½ green onion, trimmed and chopped

½ teaspoon Roasted Sesame Seeds (page 34)

XFF Dumpling Sauce (page 44)

XFF Chili Oil (page 40)

Heat a small skillet over medium heat for 1 to 2 minutes. Turn the heat down to low, then add 1 teaspoon of the vegetable oil, tilting the pan to allow the oil to evenly coat the bottom.

Turn the heat back up to medium and, using tongs, carefully place the dumplings into the pan with the folded section pointing up, spacing them out evenly. After a few seconds, move each dumpling to a slightly different spot in the pan to prevent sticking—don't flip them, just shift them around.

After 1 minute, pour 1 cup (240 ml) water into the pan, which should submerge the dumplings halfway. Cover the pan with a lid and cook for 6 to 8 minutes, until the water evaporates.

Turn the heat down to low and remove the lid. Pour the remaining 1 teaspoon vegetable oil into the pan, tilting the pan slightly to allow the oil to coat the bottom of the dumplings. Turn the heat up to high and cook for 1 to 2 minutes.

Use tongs to carefully but forcefully scrape the dumplings off the bottom of the pan. You don't want to break any, but you need to make sure the bottoms continue to brown without burning.

Once the bottoms of the dumplings are a golden brown, remove from the pan and garnish with green onion and roasted sesame seeds. Serve with sides of dumpling sauce and chili oil.

XFF Spicy and Sour Dumplings

The trick to boiling dumplings is to shock them with cold water once or twice during the cooking process, bringing the external temperature down so the insides and the outsides are done cooking at the same time. (For how to boil frozen dumplings, see page 123.) To be honest, though, it sounds harder than it is. And while we go all out at the stores with the works (chili oil, dumpling sauce, sesame seeds, and a handful of cilantro), you could make it easier on yourself and just top them with a mix of soy sauce and vinegar in a pinch.

Serves
1

8 dumplings (pages 115 to 122)

2 cups (480 ml) cold water, divided

XFF Dumpling Sauce (page 44)

XFF Chili Oil (page 40)

Garlic Puree (page 37)

Roasted Sesame Seeds (page 34)

Cilantro sprig, trimmed and cut into ½-inch (12 mm) segments

Bring a pot of water to a boil over high heat.

Drop in as many dumplings as you would like to eat without overfilling the pot. The dumplings should have enough room to be able to swim around freely. Carefully stir the dumplings right after dropping them into the pot to prevent them from sticking to the bottom and sides, but be careful not to break them.

Once the water comes back to a rapid boil and the dumplings float to the top (1 to 2 minutes), add 1 cup (240 ml) cold water. Wait for the water to come to a rapid boil again, then add 1 more cup (240 ml) cold water. Bring to a boil once more, then remove the dumplings from the pot. The whole process should take 5 to 6 minutes.

Top your dumplings with dumpling sauce, chili oil, garlic puree, sesame seeds, and cilantro to taste.

XFF Spicy and Sour Dumplings in Soup

If you're in the mood for something homier, you can serve your dumplings in soup, using either the water you cooked the dumplings in or bone
broth, if you have it. Eat these up fast, though; if they stand too long, the
dumplings could get soggy.

Serves
1

8 cooked dumplings (pages 115 to 122)

2½ cups (600 ml) dumpling cooking
water or Bone Broth (page 42)

¼ cup (60 ml) XFF Dumpling Sauce (page
44)

¼ teaspoon salt

Pinch of white pepper powder

XFF Chili Oil (page 40)

Toasted sesame oil

Roasted Sesame Seeds (page 34)

1 sprig cilantro

Garlic Puree (page 37)

Place the dumplings in your serving bowl and cover with the hot
cooking water or broth.

Mix in the dumpling sauce, salt, and white pepper powder.

Drizzle with chili oil and sesame oil to taste. Sprinkle on the
roasted sesame seeds, top with the cilantro and garlic puree,
and serve.

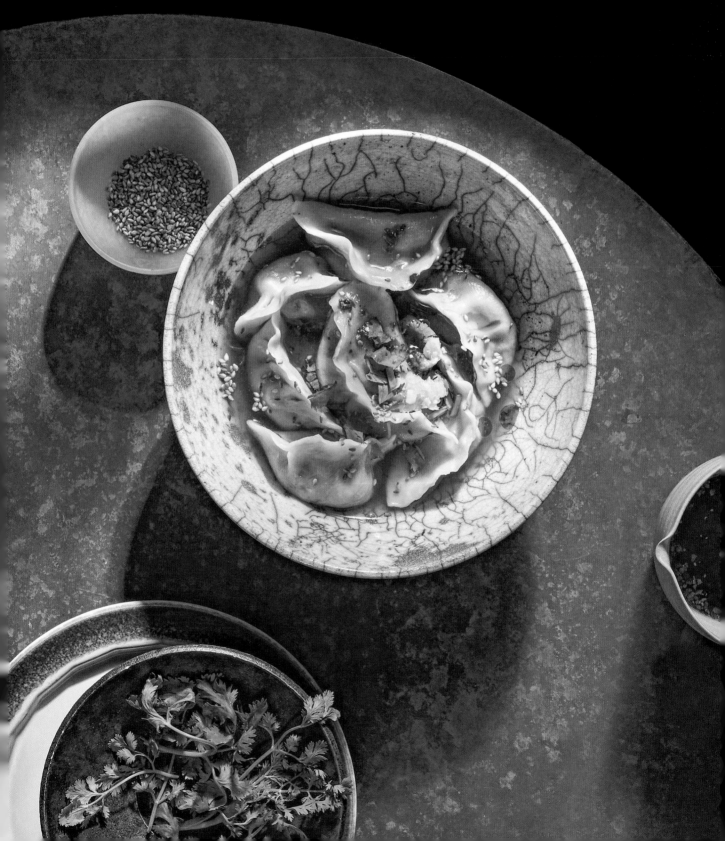

Eggs and Tomatoes
西红柿炒鸡蛋

Eggs and tomatoes are a common combination in many Chinese house-holds; some people I know put ketchup on their eggs or in their fried rice specifically because it mimics this flavor pairing. I don't cook at home often—I don't really have time—but this is something I'll actually make. It's what my friends call "bachelor cooking," because it's fast, simple, filling, and protein-packed.

It's also incredibly versatile. Everyone has their own preferred method for eggs and tomatoes, based on their family's style of cooking. Some families use just salt, others toss in soy sauce. Some people put tomatoes in first, then add the eggs; others scramble it all together. I've had bowls of noodles with egg drop tomato soup for breakfast in Xi'an, while lunch or dinner might be this thick stew of the two ingredients served over rice.

My version is all about capturing the unique flavors of the individual elements, only letting it all meld together in the end. I like to scramble the eggs first, set those aside, and then cook the tomatoes to make the most out of the juice. It's a little bit more work, but this way, you won't end up with a watery, bland mess. This dish might not impress your friends, but do it right and you might impress your mom.[1]

Serves
1 or 2

pages 60–61

2 tablespoons vegetable oil, divided

2 large eggs, beaten

2 green onions, trimmed and chopped

1 medium tomato, roughly sliced into odd-sized pieces

½ teaspoon salt

1 tablespoon soy sauce

½ teaspoon sugar

Heat 1 tablespoon of the vegetable oil in a skillet over low heat.

Add the beaten eggs to the pan and stir until you have a soft scramble but before they get browned, about 3 minutes. Remove to a plate and set aside.

Turn the heat up to high and add the remaining 1 tablespoon oil. Add the green onions and stir-fry for 15 seconds.

Add the tomatoes, stir to combine, and cook for another 15 seconds. Add the salt, stir, and cook for 30 seconds.

Add the soy sauce and sugar and stir to combine. Add the reserved eggs, stir to combine, and cook for another 30 seconds. Serve immediately.

1 Or at least, my mom.

Dry Pot Chicken
干锅鸡

If you've never cooked with freshly killed chicken, do yourself a favor and scout out a quality live poultry shop. The fresher the kill, the better the texture. In Xi'an, you could just go to the street vendors and buy any chicken of your choice. At my grandmother's house, we'd eat the chickens that were too old to lay eggs anymore.[6] And in Flushing, there was a shop with everything: live rabbits, geese, ducks, pigeons, quail, the works. You'd go in, pick out the animal that looks the fattest, juiciest to you, and wait as they butcher it in the back. The blatant carnivorism of choosing your dinner while it's still breathing might make some feel queasy, but the way I see it, if you're going to eat meat, you better face it, and you better make it worth it.

When my dad had time off from work, he'd go out of his way to visit the live poultry shop and make this dish for a family meal. The chicken, roughly chopped, would arrive on the table steaming, fragrant with five spice and ginger and sharp Sichuan peppercorns. We'd attack it while hot, being careful not to burn our tongues, balancing the salty-sweet-spicy sauce with a bite of plain white rice every now and then. The first few minutes would be completely silent, save for the sounds of bones clanking into bowls, teeth biting into tender, juicy chicken, as the family savored this rare treat. This isn't a difficult dish to make, but it does rely heavily on how good your ingredients are. So hunt down a good poultry purveyor, grab some chiles, and make it worth it.

Serves
6 to 8

page 60

1 whole chicken, about 1½ pounds (680 g), cut roughly into 2-inch (5 cm) pieces (Ask your butcher to do this for you, or if you're scared of getting side-eye, carefully chop up the chicken yourself using a butcher knife.)

1 tablespoon Shaoxing cooking wine

2 teaspoons salt, divided

5 cups (1.2 L) plus 2 tablespoons vegetable oil, divided

1 teaspoon Sichuan peppercorns

1 tablespoon Pixian bean sauce

3 garlic cloves, peeled and sliced

1-inch (2.5 cm) piece fresh ginger, peeled and sliced

2 green onions, trimmed and cut into 2-inch (5 cm) segments

½ green or red bell pepper, cut into 1-inch (2.5 cm) squares

2 longhorn peppers, cut into 1-inch (2.5 cm) segments

½ red onion, peeled and cut into 1-inch (2.5 cm) wedges

½ teaspoon sugar

1 teaspoon aged soy sauce

1 teaspoon Chinese five-spice powder

1 tablespoon Roasted Sesame Seeds (page 34)

Note: A young chicken was used here, typically preferred for this dish. However, for those with no access to young chickens, use a mix of thighs and breast to preference

6 A sad but inevitable fate in those days.

Mix the chicken pieces with the cooking wine and 1 teaspoon of the salt using your hands and let marinate for 20 minutes in the refrigerator.

Bring a large pot of water to a boil over high heat. Working in batches so as not to crowd the pot, blanch the chicken pieces in the water for up to 1 minute. Remove with a slotted spoon to a bowl or plate and set aside.

Clean and dry the pot thoroughly. Prepare a plate by covering it with a paper towel.

Pour 5 cups (1.2 L) of the vegetable oil into the pot, or enough to fill it halfway. Heat over medium heat until the oil just begins to shimmer (or registers 350 to 375°F or 175 to 190°C with a thermometer). Working in batches, use a metal slotted spoon with a long handle to transfer the chicken pieces to the oil to fry, using the spoon to move the chicken continuously around to encourage even cooking and browning. Fry until golden all over, about 4 minutes, then transfer the chicken to the paper towel–covered plate. Repeat as necessary until all the chicken pieces are fried to a golden brown.

In a large skillet or wok, heat the remaining 2 tablespoons vegetable oil over high heat. Add the Sichuan peppercorns and fry for 30 seconds, then add the Pixian bean sauce and cook for another 30 seconds. Add the garlic, ginger, and green onions and cook for up to 1 minute.

Add the chicken and stir-fry for 1 minute.

Add the bell pepper, longhorn peppers, onion, sugar, soy sauce, and the rest of the salt and stir to combine.

Add the Chinese five-spice powder and roasted sesame seeds and stir to combine, then turn off the heat.

Place the dry pot chicken into a cast-iron pot that can be served at the table, over sterno, if possible, so the dish can stay elevated and hot.

Twice-Cooked Pork Belly
回锅肉

I would apologize for including such a common dish in this book, but honestly, how could I not? Twice-cooked pork belly is a classic, common in most parts of China (although I believe it originated in Sichuan). It's one of those go-to dishes on every table, and once you try it you'll understand why it's such a crowd-pleaser.

The point here is to solidify the flavor. Cook it once with seasoning to infuse the pork with ginger, green onions, and peppercorns. Cook it again with two types of bean sauces for extra umami, tossing in a handful of green garlic or leeks while you're at it. And, of course, make sure to use the fattiest pork belly you can find—this dish is meant to be a treat.

Serves
2

page 60

TO COOK THE PORK BELLY:
(1st time)

10 ounces (280 g) pork belly

2 green onions, trimmed and cut into 1½-inch (4 cm) segments

1½-inch (4 cm) piece fresh ginger, peeled and sliced

20 Sichuan peppercorns

2 tablespoons Shaoxing cooking wine

(2nd time)

1 teaspoon sweet flour sauce

¼ teaspoon soy sauce

1 tablespoon vegetable oil

1 teaspoon fermented black soybeans (douchi)

2 teaspoons Pixian bean sauce

3 green onions, white part only, chopped

1-inch (2.5 cm) piece fresh ginger, peeled and sliced

2 garlic cloves, peeled and sliced

½ teaspoon sugar

3 stalks green garlic or ½ leek (for leek, use only the white section, diagonally sliced into 1-inch/2.5 cm segments and broken apart)

To cook the pork belly for the first time: Place the pork belly into a medium pot and cover with water, about 6 cups (1.4 L).

Add the green onions, ginger, Sichuan peppercorns, and cooking wine. Cover the pot and bring to a boil over high heat.

Turn the heat down to a simmer and cook for about 30 minutes. The pork is done when chopsticks can poke through the meat easily.

Carefully remove the pork to a colander set in the sink and shock with cold water to halt the cooking process. Let drain and cool to room temperature.

To cook the pork belly for the second time: Cut the pork belly into 2-inch (5 cm) slabs, then into ¼-inch (6 mm) thick slices. Set aside.

In a small bowl, combine the sweet flour sauce and soy sauce. Set aside.

In a medium skillet, add the vegetable oil and heat for 1 minute over high heat. Add the pork belly and cook, stirring with a spatula so it doesn't stick. Cook until the fat begins releasing from the meat and it starts to curl.

Add the douchi and cook until fragrant. Add the Pixian bean sauce and cook until red oil is released. Add the green onions, ginger, and garlic and stir. Add the reserved sweet flour and soy sauce mixture as well as the sugar and cook for 1 more minute. Add the green garlic or leeks, stir to combine, and serve.

Beef and Ginkgo Congee
牛肉白果蔬菜粥

Think of this as a savory oatmeal. Congee has been touted as a "cool new thing," and there are a lot of fancy versions out there with poached eggs or abalone. Traditionally, though, it's actually pretty plain—a budget-friendly breakfast made from rice and water. The flavors and seasonings come in through the toppings: super salty pork floss, slightly funky thousand-year egg, umami-packed fish flakes, you name it.

Our version is sort of a compromise between highbrow and lowbrow congee. We start with a really plain base but add in cooking wine, ginkgo seeds, and green onions for a bit of flavor, plus some fresh ginger. For my bowl, I'll mix in pickled mustard marinated with vinegar to soften the salty kick. And, of course, I like to put a few spoonfuls of chili oil into my congee; it's not traditional, but sometimes you have to break the rules.

Serves 2

1 ounce (28 g) ground beef chuck

½ teaspoon Shaoxing cooking wine

⅛ teaspoon cornstarch

¼ cup (45 g) jasmine rice

1 green onion, trimmed and cut into 2-inch (5 cm) segments

8 ginkgo seeds

1 broccoli floret, cut into small pieces

1 walnut-sized piece red carrot, peeled and cut into small, flat coins

1 baby bok choy, leaves separated

½-inch (12 mm) piece fresh ginger, peeled and finely chopped

½ teaspoon salt

¼ teaspoon white pepper powder

Pickled mustard marinated in black vinegar (optional)

XFF Chili Oil (page 40; optional)

In a small bowl, add the beef, cooking wine, and cornstarch. Mix well to combine. Set aside.

In a medium pot, add the rice, green onion, and 4 cups (960 ml) water.

Cover the pot and bring to a boil over high heat. Boil for 4 to 5 minutes, then turn the heat down to low and simmer for 20 minutes.

Add the ginkgo seeds and simmer, covered, for 20 more minutes.

Remove the green onion and discard. Stir in the beef and simmer, covered, for 2 more minutes. Add the broccoli, carrot, and baby bok choy.

Note: The vegetables will cook very quickly in hot congee, and since they are cut into such small pieces, they will cook fast. You could also add them at the table, serving them mostly raw for texture, instead.

Add the ginger, salt, and white pepper powder. Stir to mix, then serve. For a thicker congee, simmer, uncovered, until it reaches your desired consistency (up to 1 hour). Top with pickled mustard and chili oil, if desired, to taste.

The Hot Pot

IN THE FALL OF 2018, "HOT DUCK" MANIA TOOK OVER CENTRAL PARK, WITH HORDES OF PEOPLE CROWDING THE LAKE TO PHOTOGRAPH A PARTICULARLY STRIKING BIRD COVERED IN PURPLE, BLUE, AND ORANGE FEATHERS. The mandarin duck, typically found in East Asia, became *the* attraction in New York City for a surprising period of time.

It's important to note (and you'll see why soon) that the "hot" mandarin duck is only the male duck of this species. The female mandarin duck is actually pretty plain, with brown and white plumage. Visually, the two genders are completely different, but they're complementary, like yin and yang.

With hot pot, you're going to need both a hot side and a plain side, your male and female duck, so to speak. So you're also going to need a mandarin duck pot, a pot with a handy divider that lets you heat two separate broths at once. One broth might be the spicy side, a colorful vibrant red (the "hot" male duck); the other, a more herbaceous and subtle soup (the female side).

With this meal, variety is the name of the game. The rules are: There aren't a lot of them. You boil whatever foods you like in a broth, dip it into whatever sauces you feel like, and then eat immediately. Because it's so easy, this has become my go-to. I'll go get solo hot pot in Flushing on late nights after work (see my Flushing guide, page 101), but also pull it together if I want to have friends over for a casual hang. So heat up your two broths (or

just one, that's totally fine!), and start assembling the accoutrements: the sauces, the aromatics, and the dipping sauces. Here are a bunch of options for your hot pot spread—just pick and choose the ones that speak to you the most.

Spicy and Tingly Hot Pot Broth
麻辣火锅

FOR THE SPICE MIX:

²/₃ cup (165 ml) vegetable oil

3 tablespoons unsalted butter

2 green onions, trimmed and cut into 4-inch (10 cm) segments

1-inch (2.5 cm) piece fresh ginger, peeled and sliced

3 garlic cloves, peeled and sliced

1 teaspoon soybean paste
黄豆酱

1 tablespoon Pixian bean sauce

1 teaspoon chili garlic sauce

2 black cardamom pods

15 white cardamom pods

1½-inch (4 cm) square dried orange peel

2 cloves

½ teaspoon black peppercorns

1 small piece dried galangal, enough to make two ³/₈-inch (1 cm) slices

10 to 15 dried red chile peppers, cracked

3-inch (7.5 cm) cinnamon stick

4 star anise pods

3 bay leaves

2 slices dried Chinese licorice root (gan cao)

1 tablespoon fennel seeds

5 tablespoons (20 g) Sichuan peppercorns

2 tablespoons liquid from fermented sweet rice (you can buy this in a mason jar in the refrigerated aisle of Chinese or Korean grocery stores)

1 teaspoon sugar

FOR SERVING:

4 cups (1 L) Bone Broth (page 42) or chicken broth

2 green onions, white part only, cut into 4-inch (10 cm) segments

3 garlic cloves, peeled and sliced

3 dried red jujubes

1 star anise pod

6 white cardamom pods

TOOL:
Portable butane burner stove

To make the spice mix: In a large skillet, heat the vegetable oil over medium heat. Add the butter and melt it into the oil. Add the green onions, ginger, and garlic to the pan and sweat for 1 to 2 minutes, until fragrant. Add the soybean paste, Pixian bean sauce, and chili garlic sauce and cook until fragrant, 1 to 2 minutes.

Add all of the dry spices to the pan, turn the heat down to low, and cook for 15 minutes, stirring constantly to avoid burning. Add the fermented sweet rice liquid and sugar and cook for 1 to 2 minutes.

Note: You can store this spice mix in the freezer in an airtight container for up to 1 month.

To serve: In a hot pot, add the bone broth and set over high heat until boiling.

Add half of the spice mix along with the green onions, garlic, jujubes, star anise pod, and cardamom pods and bring to a boil. Add more spice mix as desired.

Serve over a portable butane burner stove to cook on the tabletop.

Herbal Hot Pot Broth
药膳火锅

FOR THE HERBAL WATER:

2 slices dried ginseng

3 dried red jujubes

2 slices dried Chinese licorice root (gan cao)

3 slices dried female ginseng (dang gui)

1 teaspoon goji berries

5 slices milkvetch (huang qi)

FOR THE SOUP:

2 tablespoons vegetable oil

1½-inch (4 cm) piece fresh ginger, peeled and sliced

1 teaspoon Sichuan peppercorns

2 garlic cloves, peeled and sliced

1 tablespoon liquid from fermented sweet rice (you can use store-bought)

4 cups (1 L) Bone Broth (page 42) or chicken broth

⅛ teaspoon sugar

1 green onion, trimmed and cut into 2-inch (5 cm) segments

TO SERVE:

2 green onions, white part only, cut into 4-inch (10 cm) segments

2 dried red jujubes

10 dried goji berries

2 white cardamom pods

TOOL:

Portable butane burner stove

To make the herbal water: Fill a pot with 4 cups (960 ml) water. Add all of the ingredients and bring to boil over high heat. Turn the heat down to low and cook for 40 minutes. You can store this herbal water in an airtight container in the freezer for up to 1 month.

To make the soup: In a hot pot, heat the vegetable oil over medium-high heat.

Add the ginger, Sichuan peppercorns, and garlic and fry for 1 to 2 minutes, until fragrant. Add the fermented sweet rice liquid and bone broth and bring to a boil. Add the sugar and green onion and cook for 2 minutes.

Turn off the heat. Strain out the ginger, peppercorns, and garlic.

To serve: Add half of the herbal water to the soup, along with the green onions, red jujubes, goji berries, and cardamom pods, and bring to a boil. Add more of the herbal water if you'd like, to taste.

Serve over a portable butane burner stove to cook on the tabletop.

For Your Dipping Sauce and Other Additions

For the most basic of offerings, make a dipping sauce consisting of equal parts black vinegar, Garlic Puree (page 37), and sesame oil and double parts of soy sauce. You could take it one step further, though, and provide a whole spread of sauces.

Traditionally, northwestern Chinese diners will use a dipping sauce that is a mix of vinegar, soy sauce, sesame oil, and garlic—plus some buttery fermented bean curd for a salty kick. I don't actually adhere to that. I have friends who are American-born Chinese, or from Guangzhou, plus a few Japanese buddies who introduced me to shabu-shabu, so my dipping sauce of choice is a little more eclectic. Typically I'll start off with some Chinese barbecue sauce (popular in the south), black vinegar, and a dash of Japanese shabu-shabu sesame sauce for a little sweetness. I'll sprinkle in chopped cilantro and pour in our XFF Chili Oil (of course). For the final flourish, I'll crack an egg, stirring the egg yolk into the sauce for texture and dumping the egg white into the boiling broth.

In addition to dipping sauces, serve the hot pot with a collection of your favorite seasonings and aromatics. Have some fun tasting all these different sauces, then mix them together based on your preference and top with your desired aromatics.

SEASONINGS:

Black vinegar (obviously)

Soy sauce

Toasted sesame oil

XFF Chili Oil (page 40)

Leek paste: People either love or hate this condiment, which is made with Chinese leek flowers and has a salty, garlicky kick.

Fermented bean curd: Some people say this smells a little cheesy, and it makes sense; it's fermented, after all. This pasty, buttery spread is amplified by spices like red chile, star anise, and more, and comes in red or white versions. I prefer the red, but either is fine.

Barbecue sauce or shacha sauce: Not the barbecue sauce you're thinking of. This paste is garlicky, a little spicy, a little fishy, and so, so good.

Japanese shabu-shabu sesame sauce (*goma dare*): You could make this at home with some ground sesame seeds, garlic, and more, but the bottled stuff works just fine. This thick sauce is both sweet and savory, with a creamy consistency that clings onto your hot pot meats.

AROMATICS:

Chopped garlic

Chopped green onions

Chopped cilantro

Chopped green chile peppers

For the Meal

THERE'S A CERTAIN ORDER TO HOW YOU BUILD UP YOUR HOT POT. YOU START WITH THE THINGS THAT ADD FLAVOR—HEARTY MUSHROOMS, TOMATOES, THICKER-CUT VEGETABLES. Then you go with meat, since you'll probably be hungry. Once you get more comfortable, toss in the leafy veggies. And as you start getting full, make yourself some noodles and crack an egg into the flavorful broth for a bowl of noodles before you roll yourself to bed.

ROUND ONE:

Mushrooms: You want to start with heartier mushrooms like shiitake or oyster. Save the thin, stringy mushrooms like enoki mushrooms for later (as we like to say, you'll see those tomorrow, too[7]).

Tomatoes: I like putting in whole tomatoes to help build up flavor, but slices work as well.

Firm tofu: These cubes will take a while to cook (and are annoying to fish out) but will soak up all of the flavors over time.

ROUND TWO:

Sliced beef, lamb, or pork: I like to get fatty beef, lean lamb, and pork belly. You want these sliced as thinly as possible, so make an extra run to a Chinese or Japanese grocery store, where they sell these meats pre-sliced. The thinner the meat, the faster it will cook; really, each slice should only take one or two swishes in the boiling soup. Try holding on to them with your chopsticks, only letting go for a second to cook thoroughly, but avoid losing them in the bubbling pot. If you must, you can also get those little nets for hot pot noobs.

Sliced fish: Sea bass, if you're feeling fancy; carp, if you're willing to deal with the bones. Fish breaks up easily, so this is a good place to use a slotted spoon or a hot pot net.

Clams: Toss them in, wait for them to open up, devour. Trash the ones that are wide open before cooking or stay closed after cooking. Mussels, octopus, shrimp, and calamari all work, too.

Fish balls: Some people love these, and I'm cool with the ones that are solid. The ones with fillings can get way too hot and burn your tongue. Those tend to surprise me in a negative way.

Meatballs: Unlike Western meatballs, these have a bit of bounce and bite to them. You'll find these next to the fish balls in the freezer section of most Chinese grocery stores.

Spam: If you haven't had Spam in hot pot, you're missing out. The fatty, sweet meat concoction is the perfect pairing for our spicy and tingly soup (page 139).

ROUND THREE:

Cabbage: Heartier cuts with thicker cores will last longer in the soup, so give it some more time to cook. The leafy sections, though, tend to get coated with too much chili oil, so I prefer to leave them for the end. The trick is to first bring your pot to a rapid boil, and then rinse the greens off at the point of the boil (since the oil, being thicker, will move away from the bubbles) before putting the greens on your plate.

Spinach/watercress: Toss these in too soon and you risk having them soak up all your spice mix, turning them into an oily vehicle for chile pepper. Instead, wait to add them and then treat them like your sliced meat: quickly blanch, rinse off the oil at the point of the boil, and then eat.

ROUND FOUR:

Noodles: You could use fresh noodles, but store-bought will do just fine. Vermicelli also works. Hell, even instant ramen noodles will work here.

Egg: Crack an egg in, let it cook for about 2 minutes in the broth, and you'll find yourself with the best possible ending to hot pot: a spoonful or two of soup, a serving of noodles, and a perfectly runny egg yolk to bind it all together.

7   Sorry, it's a poop joke.

The Official Xi'an Famous Foods Story

IN CHINA, FRIENDS GREET EACH OTHER WITH "CHI FAN LE MA?" *Have you eaten?* **Or, quite literally,** *Have you eaten rice?* **My dad, though, says, "Yao bu yao chi mian?"** *Do you want to eat some noodles?*

My dad's dream was always to open up a restaurant of his own to serve *mian*, noodles of all kinds in all forms, soupy or saucy, hot or cold. It's his comfort food. I'd come home from school and find him with chopsticks in one hand, a pot in the other, stirring vigorously as droplets of soy sauce stained his shirt. "Yao bu yao mian?" he'd ask, before putting a stainless steel mixing bowl of the day's experiment in front of me.

Finally, he decided to make his dream a reality. Here's how it all went down:

I graduate high school with an acceptance letter to a pretty good college with scholarships and financial aid in place. My dad breathes a sigh of relief; I'm on track to working the white-collar life that he's been planning for me.

FALL 2005

I go off to Washington University in St. Louis and my dad suffers a bout of empty nest syndrome. He decides to set off on his own journey and lands on bubble tea, which is having a moment. He snags a franchise license to a bubble tea brand and the lease to a spot in Flushing's Main Plaza. It's low cost, high margin, and a way to guarantee profit (albeit very little) while he futzes around with his recipes.

WINTER 2005

When I return home for winter break, I find a slew of surprises. First, I discover that we've downgraded from our one-bedroom basement apartment to a single room on the second floor of a house, sharing a bathroom and kitchen with other tenants. In an effort to cut down on living expenses to fuel the business, my dad has crammed our family and our belongings into a 300-square-foot (28 sq m) room. The only upside: There's sunlight and cell-phone signal.

The second surprise is the bubble tea shop. Never in any of my phone calls home did he bother to mention that he opened up the shop, that I was expected to help out over the break, and that he had started selling food, too. Which brings us to the most important surprise: the shop's liang pi. It's still experimental, still not quite there yet, but still good. It's my first taste of authentic liang pi in ten years.

EARLY 2006

My dad decides to go where the real action is: the Golden Shopping Mall, the hottest food court in Flushing at the time. But competition is so fierce, he can't get into the actual basement food court. Instead, he's relegated to a street stand in an alcove along the building's exterior, a literal hole in the wall next to the Q58 bus stop. He spends the winter making food at home, carting it over to his stall, freezing in the cold until he sells out, and starting all over again.

OUR FOUNDER, DAVID SHI, IN ONE OF THE EARLIER XI'AN FAMOUS FOODS KITCHENS.

SPRING 2006

Finally, a spot opens up in the Golden Shopping Mall's main food court. Stall number 36. My dad snags it and expands his menu. Word spreads fast; people start coming in from out of state to try our liang pi, a formerly elusive dish that few have been able to master. I return home on breaks and help cashier, watching the lines grow longer and longer.

SPRING 2007

Food forums like Chowhound are buzzing with talk about the Golden Shopping Mall, and commenters start posting translated menus and recommendations. Our stall number keeps popping up. I put up a website with English menus. More people come, traffic spikes, and I get used to the lines snaking up from the basement stall, out into the street, and around the corner. I start to realize this isn't just a livelihood for my dad. This is a phenomenon.

FALL 2007

We get even more press. After the food blogs, the *New York Times* comes. Every time an article is published, I translate it for my dad. Finally, a giant camera crew shows up. A tall white dude is the star of the show. My dad snaps a picture (with flash, pissing off the producer), sends it to me, and I show it to my friends. My roommate's girlfriend immediately freaks out. It's Anthony Bourdain, and apparently he's kind of a big deal.

A YOUNG ADULT JASON WITH THE LEGENDARY ANTHONY BOURDAIN CIRCA 2011.

Things move quickly from there. We tape up photos of Bourdain around the stall, and I add a section about him to our website. Our lines get longer and more diverse. We aren't just catering to Flushing locals anymore, or even just the Chinese community; we're representing our food to people everywhere.

SUMMER 2009

Four years after my dad first had his idea to start selling noodles, things finally settle down. The basement stall is stable in its own chaotic way, and I get a corporate merchandising job at a big company in Minneapolis post-graduation. Honestly, the story could end here, with me sticking with my white-collar gig. But, as you may have guessed, things don't really go according to plan.

4 | THE GRIND

Making It in NYC

"I've been thinking about it, too, and
and expand the business,"

YOUNG ADULT JASON SHOWING OFF HIS FRESH NOODLE-PULLING SKILLS.

FUCK IT, I GOT FIRED.

After three months of putting on a tie, keying things into a system I didn't fully understand, and schmoozing with managers and directors at company happy hours, I started to realize that maybe the corporate life wasn't for me. At school I was enticed by the idea of owning my own business, but working at a big conglomerate wasn't teaching me anything about that. Instead, I was a tiny little cog in a giant machine. I wasn't learning anything about building a company, let alone being a leader.

So I started slacking off, showing up late, ditching company happy hours, and half-assing my projects. Meanwhile, the restaurant plateaued. Yes, the customers were steady, but it felt stuck, stranded in that basement stall while opportunists were jumping on the bandwagon and imitating our brand. I knew we could go bigger, and during my off time I started scheming of ways to expand, thinking about what neighborhoods we should hit first. Chinatown, obviously. East Village? Maybe.

And then one slow, boring Friday afternoon, a meeting invite popped up in my email. I walked into the room and saw my boss with someone from HR. The only words that mattered from that meeting: "Your relationship with the company has been terminated."[1]

That night, I got back to my apartment and crammed all my belongings into my car. I called up my dad and broke the news. Surprisingly, he wasn't mad. "I've been

---

1 And now I know: Friday afternoon meetings with HR are usually bad.

I think you should come back he told me (in Chinese, obviously).

thinking about it, too, and I think you should come back and expand the business," he told me (in Chinese, obviously). "But you're going to have to work from the bottom up. It's not going to be easy."

In my naïveté, I thought, *How hard can it be?*

I got in my car and drove, stopping for a night to party in St. Louis and drink away my insecurities, my termination still fresh and raw. Then, onward to New York. After fourteen hours of driving, napping at rest stops, and eating junk food in my car, I moved all my belongings into a tiny studio in Flushing, Queens. The next morning, I started working.

Let me tell you, my fresh-out-of-college, cocky twenty-one-year-old self was not ready for this shit.

At this point, the basement stall was fairly established in its own way. I was on my feet at least twelve hours a day, helping out where I could, but I still wasn't trusted to do anything related to the food. So, I was given tasks that I presumably could not fuck up: computer stuff, marketing, and taking out the trash. After the first month, my coworkers noticed. "This boss's son is pretty useless," my dad overheard one of them say. It was the sign that I needed to step it up.

Meanwhile, I soon discovered that while I was driving from Minneapolis to New York, my dad was busy signing papers for not one, but two new locations: a second Flushing spot plus a 100-square-foot (9 sq m) space right under the Manhattan Bridge in Chinatown. So, while I was learning the ropes in our first store, I was also immediately tasked with all of the random shit you have to deal with when you open a restaurant in NYC.

Those first three months felt like an entire year. In the restaurants, I graduated from trash takeout to cashiering, food prep and storage, and cleaning. I mastered (and then taught my coworkers) the POS system, since my dad never used it. I started pulling noodles, first making them for myself and then finally for our customers.

And on the business side of things, I was doing shit like restaurant design (thank goodness for those CAD classes in high school) and sorting through piles of paperwork for the various city departments (hat-tip to those high school law classes). I learned the art of dealing with contractors and cockroaches and how to mercy kill unlucky mice stuck in our traps during construction. Mostly, though, I learned how to work nonstop, morning to night, seven days a week.

THE ENTRANCE TO OUR ORIGINAL ST. MARK'S LOCATION, WHERE LINES WOULD OFTEN REACH THE DOOR.

The East Village location would be my version of XFF . . . It would be my vision, and it would put XFF on the map like never before.

Our first Chinatown store on East Broadway opened in December 2009, and my dad and I spent our days running the kitchen side by side. He manned the stoves while I cashiered, cooking when necessary. We got to a point where he stopped being completely disappointed in what I was doing, and I started itching for more, driving around Manhattan looking at For Rent signs. One day, I was coasting around the East Village, where my high school friends and I used to blow off steam, and I saw those two lucky words right on bustling St. Mark's Place, where all of the NYU students hang out. *We're in business.*

The East Village location would be *my* version of XFF, I decided, the first store I would launch, design, and operate all on my own. It would be my vision, and it would put XFF on the map like never before. I could do it. I had manned the original location solo on slow days in Flushing, cashiering *and* cooking. I knew the prices, the ingredients, the timing to the dishes like clockwork. Opening a fourth store would be fine. Or so I thought.

Instead, I found myself pulled in multiple directions, working the two Flushing stores and the East Broadway location while negotiating with our first non-Chinese landlord in the East Village and building out a completely new staff. Once we opened, I was in the store every day from 10 a.m. to 10 p.m., teaching and training and never once trusting

the newbies to not fuck it up. When I wasn't manning the kitchen, I was changing light bulbs in Chinatown, dropping off change and fixing sinks in Flushing, or talking my dad out of firing one of my hires because he didn't like the way they dressed the noodles.

This did not bode well for my personal life. I rarely saw my family outside of work, never saw my friends, and my girlfriend at the time was not happy. We never went out, barely texted. Finally, she demanded dinner—and I decided to try leaving the store for one evening. It would be my first night away in the three months since opening.

That night, we went to an Ethiopian eatery two blocks away from the restaurant. We ordered food, sat down, got some drinks . . . and I proceeded to spend the entirety of dinner staring at my phone, refreshing the live sales data. The night ended with us yelling at each other on the street, my girlfriend storming off to the subway, and me returning to the store to find an abnormally large crowd of impatient diners waiting for their orders, the kitchen a chaotic mess. There was chili oil in the Tiger Vegetable Salads (which is just incorrect) and noodles being served soggy and bland (an unforgivable affront to me). It was a shitshow, and I was the only person who could fix it. Needless to say, I did not leave the store again for a long time after that.

Shit No One Tells You About Running a Restaurant

IT FEELS LIKE EVERY DAY, SOMEONE CHATS ME UP ABOUT OPENING A RESTAURANT OF THEIR OWN. Typically, these are cool, fashionable people with really elaborate and interesting ideas but zero restaurant experience. So for all of you with restaurant dreams, here are five very important things to know before diving in:

1 Your body will hate you. You should know every little detail of how your business runs, and be able to do it, too, which means you'll be working harder and longer than any of your employees. Your feet will hurt and your back will be sore, your joints will be achy and creaky, and you'll feel ten years older when you wake up in the morning. Slowly, the pain will become your new norm. Enjoy.

2 You will probably get into a fight. I've been spit on, yelled at, cursed out, and once even got into a fistfight with a drunk dude and three of his boys who were pissing on my storefront at closing time. Luckily, a worker at the Japanese restaurant next door intervened. (Shout out to Hiro.)

3 Money will not always solve the problem—unlike in many other industries.

4 It's dirty. Think you have what it takes to open a restaurant? Go try to unclog a filled grease trap box with your hands. Hell, go open and just look at a grease trap. Take a whiff. Then come back and we'll talk.

5 Look, things are going to get repetitive. A lot of people think they'll be creating new dishes every week, but the reality is that consistency is key in restaurants. You'll be making the same thing the exact same way over and over again. So the dishes in this following section? These are the core recipes seared into my memory, each extra tablespoon of soy sauce or spice adding to the map to create our original XFF flavors.

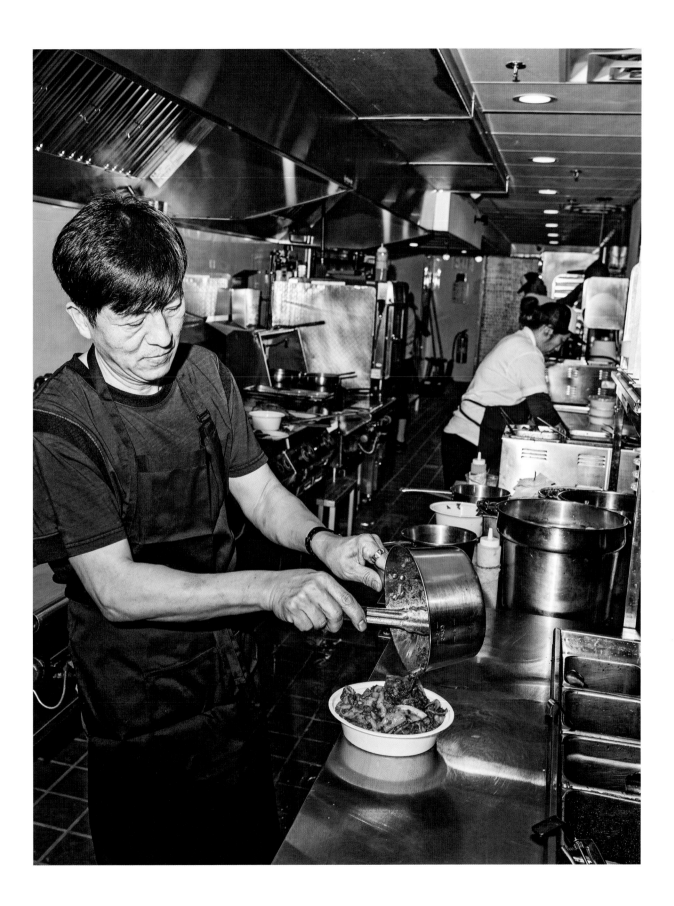

Tiger Vegetables Salad
老虎菜

This salad's name doesn't come from the colors of the salad (tigers aren't green), but from the essence. This is a fiery, sinus-clearing, aggressively herbaceous mixture that packs a wallop with cilantro, celery, green onions, and longhorn pepper slivers. Contrary to popular belief, the heat doesn't come from chili oil, but from the raw peppers. The idea is that once you eat this, you'll roar like a tiger . . . because you're in so much pain.

Of course, you can make this as spicy or as mild as you want, and luckily the sesame and vinegar dressing adds a touch of sweetness to balance it all out. I like to have this at the beginning of the meal to whet my appetite, but it's also good in between meat dishes, since it doesn't just cleanse your palate—it straight-up obliterates it.

Serves
2 as an
appetizer

2 small handfuls (about 2 ounces/54 g) cilantro sprigs, coarsely chopped

2 Chinese celery stalks, diagonally sliced into long segments

4 green onions, white part only, halved and then cut vertically into matchsticks

2-inch (5 cm) piece red longhorn pepper, thinly sliced

2-inch (5 cm) piece green longhorn pepper, thinly sliced

½ teaspoon salt

1 teaspoon sugar

1 tablespoon white vinegar

½ teaspoon toasted sesame oil

Note: Leafy Chinese celery, which is skinnier, not as watery, and twice as flavorful, is preferred here, but you can use conventional celery if you can't get your hands on it.

Add the cilantro, celery, green onions, and peppers to a bowl and toss to combine. In a small bowl, whisk together the salt, sugar, vinegar, and sesame oil to create the dressing. Pour the dressing over the vegetables. Toss to combine and serve.

Lamb Meat Soup
水盆羊肉

The concept of soup in the States was a shock to me as a kid. Here, it's hearty, with chunks of potato, or pureed into a smooth, viscous consistency. It's almost a meal in and of itself. In China, though, the soups my family loved were clean, broth-forward. While lamb meat soup was never a best-seller in our stores, this humble dish was a staple in my household, slurped up for breakfast and lunch or a pre-dinner snack. We start with a classic, clean lamb broth, add in lamb meat and some mung bean noodles, and then dress it up with a little cilantro or chili oil. It's not super flashy, but one bowl of this will warm you up real good on a cold winter day.

Serves
6 as an
appetizer

FOR THE BROTH:

1 pound (455 g) lamb leg meat, cut into 2 pieces

4 ounces (115 g) lamb leg bone, cracked or cut in half to expose the marrow

1 teaspoon Sichuan peppercorns

2 star anise pods, broken

1 teaspoon fennel seeds

4 white cardamom pods

1½-inch (4 cm) piece cinnamon stick

1 black cardamom pod, cracked or smashed to release the flavor

2 green onions, trimmed and cut into 2-inch (5 cm) segments

1-inch (2.5 cm) piece fresh ginger, peeled and thickly sliced

1 garlic clove, peeled and sliced

1 teaspoon Shaoxing cooking wine

FOR SERVING (per individual serving):

1 ounce (28 g) thin dry mung bean noodles, hydrated in warm water for 10 minutes

½ teaspoon salt

⅛ teaspoon white pepper powder

½ green onion, trimmed and thinly sliced

1 cilantro sprig, chopped

¼ teaspoon toasted sesame oil

1 Daily Bread bun (page 46)

XFF Chili Oil (page 40; optional)

For the broth: In a large pot, add the lamb meat and bone and submerge in water. Cover the pot, set over high heat, and bring to a boil. Boil for 2 minutes. Remove the meat and bone to a colander to drain. Discard the boiled water and set aside the meat and bone. This process removes impurities and creates a cleaner broth.

In a large pot, add the remaining ingredients along with the lamb meat and bone, plus 14 cups (3.4 L) water. Cover and bring to a boil over high heat. Once boiling, turn the heat down to low and simmer, covered, for 2 hours. Turn off the heat and let sit, covered, for 20 minutes.

Remove the lamb meat and let it cool in the fridge for 3 to 4 hours, then cut into ¼-inch (6 mm) thick slices. The meat can be stored in the fridge for up to 3 days, covered, or frozen for up to 1 month.

Strain the broth, discarding the bone and aromatics. Store the broth in an airtight container until ready to use, for up to 3 days in the fridge or 1 month, frozen.

To serve: To make one serving, in a small pot, add 2 cups (480 ml) of the lamb broth. Bring to a boil, uncovered, over high heat.

Add approximately 2½ ounces (40 g) of the sliced lamb meat, along with the hydrated mung bean noodles. Bring to a boil and cook for 1 minute.

Pour the contents into a bowl, along with the salt, white pepper powder, green onion, cilantro, and sesame oil.

Serve with the bread, broken into large pieces to soak up the broth. For spice fiends, chili oil may be added to taste.

Lamb Pao-Mo Soup
羊肉泡馍

According to legend, pao-mo soup came to be in the aftermath of a major battle during the Tang dynasty. One defeated general found himself AWOL, traveling around on foot and searching for home, subsisting only off his ration of dried bread. As luck would have it, he stumbled upon a butcher shop making broth with scraps of lamb. The starving general begged for a little bit of broth to boil his bread in, hoping to soften the hard-as-a-rock loaves. The resulting soup was so nutritious and fulfilling, it gave him the fortitude to find his way back home.

My dad used to tell me this story when I was a kid, so it's probably full of crap. But it's a good story, and once you have this soup in all its lamb-y, gamey, bread-y glory, you'll understand why it's so believable.

Serves 4

FOR THE PAO-MO BREAD:

3 cups (375 g) all-purpose flour

¼ teaspoon active dry yeast

1 cup (240 ml) cold water

FOR SERVING:

8 cups (2 L) lamb broth (from Lamb Meat Soup, page 159)

10 ounces (280 g) sliced lamb meat (from Lamb Meat Soup, page 159)

4 ounces (115 g) thin dry mung bean noodles, hydrated in warm water for 10 minutes

16 wood ear mushrooms, hydrated in warm water for 30 minutes and coarsely chopped

1 teaspoon salt

½ teaspoon white pepper powder

2 green onions, trimmed and thinly sliced

4 cilantro sprigs, chopped

1 teaspoon toasted sesame oil

12 pickled garlic cloves (found in Chinese and Korean supermarkets, usually sold in bags or containers)

2 teaspoons chili garlic sauce

For the pao-mo bread: In a large bowl, add the flour and yeast and stir to combine. Slowly add the cold water, using your hands to mix. Once the dough forms a smooth ball, cover with plastic wrap and let it rest at room temperature for 10 minutes.

Knead the dough for 1 minute, then cover in plastic and let it rest for another 10 minutes. Uncooked dough can be stored, covered in plastic wrap, for up to 1 day refrigerated, or 1 week in the freezer, but it's best to use it right away.

Divide the dough into 4 evenly sized pieces and use your hands or a roller to flatten into pancakes, about ½ inch (12 mm) thick.

Heat a dry, ungreased skillet over high heat, then turn the heat down to low. Add as many pancakes as will fit in the pan and toast until golden, about 3 minutes on the first side.

Flip and toast for approximately 1 minute on the other side.

Set aside. Cooked bread can be stored in a zip-top bag for up to 2 days, refrigerated, or 2 weeks frozen.

To serve: Use your hands to break the pao-mo bread into bite-sized pieces.

In a medium pot, add the broth, followed by the lamb meat, broken bread, and mung bean noodles. Bring to a boil over high heat and boil for 3 minutes. Skim off any foam on top.

Divide the mushrooms, salt, white pepper powder, green onions, cilantro, and sesame oil among four bowls, and evenly distribute the contents of the pot into the bowls. Stir each bowl to combine.

Serve with pickled garlic and chili garlic sauce on the side.

Liang Pi "Cold Skin Noodles"
凉皮

True XFF fans, I know this is what you're here for. This is the dish that put us on the map. Before us, liang pi was rare—hard to come by, even harder to make. When my father managed to perfect this recipe and repeat it, over and over, it blew the minds of Flushing folk and beyond. Part of the magic was the noodle itself, but the second part was the dressing and preparations. The slick, bouncy noodles are a perfect complement to crisp, delicate bean sprouts and cucumbers, all tossed in a seemingly simple blend of tangy vinegar and soy sauce.

By now, you've hopefully mastered how to make liang pi (if not, go to page 51). And if you haven't mastered it yet, go try and try again. Once you've got the noodles down, though, the rest is easy—just add some chopped vegetables, a dash of our XFF Chili Oil (page 40), and our Liang Pi Sauce (page 44). And if you fail at making the tricky ribbons? Go ahead and try the Seitan Salad (page 111) instead. You can always get the liang pi at our stores, anyway.

Serves 2

4 sheets Liang Pi (page 51)

2 (4-inch/10 cm cubes) Seitan (page 51)

5 ounces (140 g) blanched bean sprouts

½ Persian cucumber, cut into matchsticks

4 sprigs cilantro, chopped

½ cup (120 ml) XFF Liang Pi Sauce (page 44)

1 teaspoon Garlic Puree (page 37)

XFF Chili Oil (page 40)

Take two sheets of liang pi and fold each into thirds. Stack them on top of each other and cut them from one side to the other. You should end up with ⅜-inch (1 cm) thick liang pi ribbons. Repeat with remaining liang pi sheets.

Cut the seitan into 1-inch (2.5 cm) slices and add to your portions of liang pi. Toss in the bean sprouts, cucumber, cilantro, liang pi sauce, garlic puree, and as much chili oil as you want. Mix to combine and serve.

Stir-Fried Liang Pi "Cold Skin Noodles"
热炒凉皮

How to save leftovers, step one: Grab a frying pan. This method works for day-old rice, dumplings, even cold pizza. And, as it turns out, liang pi, too. Just like fried rice, the addition of green onions makes a day-two rendition even better. This works if you couldn't eat your liang pi fresh when you made it (and you stored it in the fridge), but if you have a bowl of already dressed noodles, you can just start by sautéing the green onion, adding the leftover liang pi, and topping with fresh cucumbers and cilantro. Warning: The extra heat softens the texture of the liang pi, so be wary of overcooking.

Serves
2

4 sheets Liang Pi (page 51)

2 (4-inch/10 cm) cubes Seitan (page 51)

5 ounces (140 g) blanched bean sprouts

½ cup (120 ml) XFF Liang Pi Sauce (page 44)

1 teaspoon Garlic Puree (page 37)

XFF Chili Oil (page 40)

2 tablespoons vegetable oil

1 green onion, trimmed and diced

½ Persian cucumber, cut into matchsticks

4 sprigs cilantro, chopped

Take two sheets of liang pi and fold each into thirds. Stack them on top of each other and cut them from one side to the other. You should end up with ⅜-inch (1 cm) thick ribbons of liang pi. Repeat with remaining liang pi sheets.

Cut the seitan into 1-inch (2.5 cm) slices and add to your portions of liang pi. Toss in the bean sprouts, liang pi sauce, garlic puree, and chili oil.

In a medium skillet, heat the vegetable oil over medium-high heat for 1 minute. Toss in the green onion and sauté for 30 seconds.

Add the prepared liang pi, raise the heat to high, and stir-fry for 1 minute, or until the noodles are translucent. Plate, top with the cucumber and cilantro, and serve.

Concubine's Chicken
贵妃鸡

Back in the Tang dynasty, there was a famous voluptuous concubine named Yang Guifei 杨贵妃. She was considered one of the great beauties of ancient China, and her influence over the emperor in Chang-an (ancient Xi'an) brought music, art, dance, and food to the forefront of high culture. Bonus: She was from the nearby Shanxi province. We named this dish after her not just because she was from our region, but also because she was a little hedonistic, a woman who knew what she liked and ate what she wanted. We like to think she would've loved this dish of juicy dark-meat chicken, with every flavor you could possible crave: sweet, sour, and just a little spicy. A perfectly hedonistic meal.

Serves
2

pages 60–61

10 ounces (280 g) boneless chicken thighs

¼ teaspoon plus 1 tablespoon Shaoxing cooking wine, divided

¼ teaspoon cornstarch

½ teaspoon white pepper powder, divided

2 tablespoons vegetable oil

1 dried red chile pepper (I use Tianjin chiles), soaked for 1 minute in warm water

2 star anise pods

½ tablespoon Sichuan peppercorns

2 teaspoons Pixian bean sauce

1 green onion, trimmed and cut into 2-inch (5 cm) segments

1-inch (2.5 cm) piece fresh ginger, peeled and sliced

½ longhorn pepper (or another thin, fresh, moderately hot chile pepper), sliced

½ red bell pepper, cubed

½ teaspoon soy sauce

½ yellow potato, peeled and cubed

⅛ teaspoon sugar

2 large garlic cloves, peeled and sliced

½ red onion, chopped

With a sharp cleaver or chef's knife, chop the chicken thighs into 2-inch (5 cm) cubes. You may remove the skin if you wish. Dab off excess liquid with paper towels.

In a large bowl, add the chicken, ¼ teaspoon of the cooking wine, the cornstarch, and ¼ teaspoon of the white pepper powder. Mix together with your hands.

In a large pot or wok, heat the vegetable oil over high heat. Dry off the soaked chile and add it to the pan, along with the star anise and Sichuan peppercorns. Fry until fragrant, up to 30 seconds. Strain out from oil and discard.

Turn the heat down to medium and add the Pixian bean sauce, green onion, and ginger. Stir to combine. Turn the heat up to high before adding the chicken, longhorn pepper, bell pepper, and the remaining 1 tablespoon cooking wine. Stir-fry for 2 minutes. Add the soy sauce and 1 cup (240 ml) water. Stir and cook for 10 minutes.

Add the potatoes. Stir and cook for 5 more minutes. Add the sugar, the remaining ¼ teaspoon white pepper powder, and the garlic. Stir and cook for 2 minutes. Add the onion, stir to combine, and serve.

Spicy and Tingly Beef
麻辣牛肉臊子

I like to think of this pairing as China's version of burgers and fries, a common, simple beef dish that everyone has had in their life. The depth of flavor is first developed from the red meat and the funky, soy-like Pixian bean sauce, but this dish's calling card is the ma la, or spicy and tingly qualities thanks to both heady chile peppers and fruity Sichuan peppercorns. And unlike many other dishes in this book, this recipe comes with a wallop of Sichuan peppercorn powder, rather than an infused oil.

Which is all to say, be careful when consuming this dish. At first, the heat might feel manageable, an undercurrent to the tender braised beef and fragrant garlic-onion mix, but several bites in and the pepper spice begins to build, your mouth starts to subtly vibrate, your tongue feels a familiar tingle, and soon enough you're experiencing the almost-euphoric brain-clearing high of a powerful *ma la* kick. While you can serve this beef in a lot of ways, my favorite is with biang-biang noodles (as shown on page 167 and as directed on page 61).

Serves
2

pages 60–61

---

11 ounces (310 g) beef shank

1½ tablespoons vegetable oil

2 green onions, trimmed and sliced

1½-inch (4 cm) piece fresh ginger, peeled and finely chopped

1 garlic clove, peeled and sliced

¼ medium red onion, diced

1 star anise pod, broken

2 dried red chile peppers, cut into ¼-inch (6 mm) segments

1½ teaspoons Pixian bean sauce

1 tablespoon soy sauce

2 tablespoons Shaoxing cooking wine

¼ teaspoon sugar

¼ large tomato, diced

1 tablespoon Sichuan peppercorn powder

1 teaspoon Red Chili Powder (page 35)

In a large pot, submerge the beef in water. Set over high heat, cover the pot, and bring to a boil. Boil for 3 minutes, then turn off the heat.

Remove the meat to a cutting board to cool and discard the water. Once cool enough to handle, cut into 1-inch (2.5 cm) cubes.

In a large pot, heat the vegetable oil over medium heat for 1 minute. Add the green onion, ginger, garlic, onion, star anise, and dried red chiles and sauté for 30 seconds, or until fragrant.

Reduce heat to medium, add the Pixian bean sauce, stir, and cook for 30 seconds, or until red oil is released and fragrant. Add beef and mix. Add the soy sauce, cooking wine, sugar, and 2 cups (480 ml) water. Cover the pot, turn the heat up to high, and bring to a boil. Once boiling, turn the heat down to medium. Simmer for 30 minutes covered, then uncover the pot and cook at a low boil for an additional 20 minutes, or until the meat is tender and the sauce is reduced.

Add the tomatoes, Sichuan peppercorn powder, and red chili powder and stir to combine. Turn off the heat and let sit, covered, for 5 minutes before serving.

Stewed Pork
腊汁猪肉

Pork belly has only recently become fetishized in the Western world, but for me it's always been a highly desirable cut, because: A) It's got the perfect mix of fat and lean meat, B) it's relatively easy to cook, and C) it's fucking delicious.

Point A is important because this dish leans on the decadent fattiness of pork belly, and getting a good fat-to-meat ratio is key. For burgers, I'll chop up the final product to coat each and every bit in pork fat, creating a succulent mouthfeel to balance out the bread. For noodles, though, I might add into the stew some leaner cuts like pork butt or pork ham with the fat trimmed off.

In either situation, you'll be using a ton of spices that will perfume the air for hours, since the longer you cook it, the juicier and more tender the meat will be. It's common in Chinese cooking to see pork belly stewed in soy sauce and spices until the fat is practically Jell-O, delicate enough to be cut through with a spoon. Our version adds extra sugar for caramelization, browning the meat to impart even more flavor, resulting in the mildest of all our meat sauces. In fact, there isn't a single pepper or Sichuan peppercorn in this recipe. Rather, the stew is infused with the same warming spices you might find in hot apple cider: heavy on the cinnamon and cloves for a savory-sweet base. Your home will smell so good, you'll be dreaming of this dish in your sleep.

Serves
2

pages 60–61

---

1 pound (450 g) pork belly

1 tablespoon sugar

1 tablespoon vegetable oil

5 tablespoons (75 ml) soy sauce

1 cup (240 ml) Shaoxing cooking wine

3 green onions, trimmed and cut into 3-inch (7.5 cm) segments

1½-inch (4 cm) piece fresh ginger, peeled and sliced

FOR THE SPICE BAG:
3 star anise pods

1 teaspoon Sichuan peppercorns

1½-inch (4 cm) cinnamon stick

1 tablespoon fennel seeds

2 black cardamom pods, cracked

3 bay leaves

1½-inch (4 cm) square dried orange peel

3 cloves

8 white cardamom pods

2 slices dried Chinese licorice root (gan cao)

6 black peppercorns

TOOLS:
Cheesecloth or coffee filter

Twine

Bundle the spices together in a cheesecloth or coffee filter to create a spice bag.

Cut the pork belly into 4-inch (10 cm) cubes.

In a medium pot, add the pork belly and submerge in water. Cover the pot and bring to a boil over high heat. Boil for 5 minutes. Remove the pork and drain the water from the pot.

Clean and thoroughly dry the pot. Add the sugar along with the vegetable oil. Place over medium heat and vigorously stir for 1 minute, or until the sugar is completely melted and just turning golden brown.

Add the pork to the pot and cover with water (about 4 cups/ 960 ml). Stir to dissolve the syrup on the bottom.

Add the remaining ingredients, including your spice bag. Cover and bring to a boil over high heat. Once boiling, turn the heat down to low. Maintain a gentle boil at low heat and cook for 1 hour, covered, stirring occasionally to prevent sticking and burning. The leaner the pork, the longer it needs to cook, so check to make sure the meat is tender; you should be able to easily poke into the pork belly using chopsticks.

Turn the heat off and allow the pork belly to sit, covered, for 20 minutes. This ensures that the flavor sinks in.

Slice the pork into ¼-inch (6 mm) pieces and serve with some of its stew.

Spicy Cumin Lamb
孜然炒羊肉

If there's anything you need to know about this dish, it's this: Bourdain loved it. Of course, the customers chose it as our knockout dish before he did. When we first started, we would sell the lamb on its own, but it would sell out so quickly, we couldn't even make noodles with it. It didn't help that this has to be cooked in small batches with the strongest fire possible, evenly browning the small, manageable pieces of lamb so every morsel of meat is properly seasoned, every bite a punch of spice, fire, and onion seasoning. Think the lamb pieces are too small? Think again: The increased surface area helps the meat absorb the spices and flavor, making the extra effort well worth it. Once you cook a batch, you'll see why N1, our spicy cumin lamb with noodles, is one of our most copied dishes.

In fact, I'd say we put lamb noodles and lamb burgers on the culinary map. While cumin lamb is commonly found in many parts of northern and western China, this dish is rarely served with biang-biang noodles or in a bun in Xi'an. So if someone is serving lamb noodles or burgers without shouting out XFF, you know who they were inspired by.

Serves
2

pages 60–61

10 ounces (280 g) boneless lamb leg (ideally partially frozen)

1½ teaspoons cornstarch

2 teaspoons plus 2 tablespoons vegetable oil, divided

1 green onion, trimmed and chopped

1-inch (2.5 cm) piece fresh ginger, peeled and finely chopped

1 garlic clove, peeled and sliced

1½ tablespoons ground cumin

1 teaspoon salt

1½ teaspoons Red Chili Powder (page 35)

½ medium red onion, sliced

1 longhorn pepper, diagonally sliced

Carefully slice the lamb into ⅛-inch (3 mm) thick pieces (note: it's easier to cut when partially frozen).

Place the sliced lamb into a large bowl along with the cornstarch and 2 teaspoons of the vegetable oil. Mix together with your hands.

In a large skillet or wok, heat the remaining 2 tablespoons vegetable oil over high heat for 1 minute. Add the green onions, ginger, and garlic and sauté for 30 seconds. Add the lamb and stir-fry for about 5 minutes.

When the meat turns an even brown color, turn the heat down to low, add the cumin, salt, and chili powder, and stir to combine. Add the onions and longhorn pepper, stir to combine, and serve.

Mt. Qi Pork
岐山臊子

According to legend (aka my dad), there once was a king in Shaanxi who wanted to hold a feast for his subjects. The problem: He didn't have enough pigs to slaughter to feed everyone. His solution: Cut the meat up into very small pieces and serve it over noodles so everyone in the village could enjoy it.

As with the rest of my father's stories, I don't know if this story is B.S. or not, but this dish does have a historical association with large group meals. For us, Mt. Qi refers not to one mountain, but the region of Qishan in the Shaanxi province. The area, near the city of Baoji, served as the center of the ancient Zhou dynasty, and as the story goes, Mt. Qi soup noodles were oftentimes at the heart of festivities. To kick off the meal, before anyone could even lift their chopsticks, a scoop of the soup would be spilled outside the residence gate for the deities. A second scoop would be divvied among memorial tablets for ancestors. Then the eldest and most respected family member would begin eating, prompting the next tier of the family, and so on and so forth until the kids were finally able to pick up their chopsticks.

For me, the interesting part of this story has to do with what happens after the first bowl is finished. Because the stew is so savory, with meaty bits of pork and a heavy hit of mouth-puckering vinegar, diners would only eat the noodles, refraining from eating the resulting broth. That leftover soup would go back into a big pot to be reheated and scooped onto fresh noodles for seconds. It was a sign of how flavorful the meat was as well as the scarcity of the times.

Nowadays, this is more of a common meal, and it's definitely not served with leftover secondhand soup. So in our modernized recipe, we decided to create a version for meat lovers and add in more pork belly for a touch more decadence (traditionally, there were more vegetables in the stew, as you'll see in Mt. Qi Vegetables, page 177). And if you do find yourself in the Mt. Qi region of Shaanxi province, you might see giant porcelain jars of this stuff in many houses and restaurants, sealed and preserved in a thick layer of fat and chili oil. I wouldn't recommend preserving it like that yourself, but chances are, you'll eat it so quickly you won't need to.

Serves
2

pages 60–61

X
F
F

1 tablespoon vegetable oil

1 star anise pod, broken

1 teaspoon whole Sichuan peppercorns

1 green onion, trimmed and cut into 3-inch (7.5 cm) segments

1½-inch (4 cm) piece fresh ginger, peeled and sliced

10 ounces (280 g) pork belly, cut into ½-inch (12 mm) pieces

¼ cup (60 ml) Shaoxing cooking wine

¼ cup (60 ml) black vinegar

1 teaspoon soy sauce

1 teaspoon salt

1 tablespoon Red Chili Powder (page 35)

⅛ teaspoon white pepper powder

½ teaspoon Sichuan peppercorn powder

In a large pot, heat the vegetable oil over high heat for about 1 minute. Add the star anise and Sichuan peppercorns and fry for about 30 seconds.

Add the green onion and ginger and then the pork and stir-fry for about 2 minutes, until the meat evenly browns on the outside. Add the cooking wine, vinegar, soy sauce, salt, and ⅓ cup (80 ml) water and continue to stir-fry, tossing to mix.

Once thoroughly combined, cook for 2 minutes at a boil. Turn the heat down to low and cook for 5 minutes, stirring often. Add the red chili powder and cook for 1 minute, stirring frequently. Cook more to reduce the sauce as desired.

Turn off the heat. Sprinkle the white pepper and Sichuan peppercorn powders over the top, mix to combine, and serve.

Mt. Qi Vegetables
素菜臊子

We added this dish to the menu because my dad decided he wanted to create a vegetable-forward option, something where we can use seasonal produce, which tends to be tastier (and as an economic benefit, cheaper, too). So while Mt. Qi Vegetables isn't exactly a traditional dish, it does draw on the classic flavors of Mt. Qi Pork (page 175). The main vegetables here are carrots and potatoes, which add heartiness to the stew. Without the pork, though, the sauce needed some tweaking. So we toned down the sour flavors and amped up the savory to create a vegetarian-friendly version that's still fucking delicious.

Serves
2

pages 60–61

2 tablespoons soy sauce

½ teaspoon salt

⅛ teaspoon sugar

1 tablespoon Shaoxing cooking wine

1 tablespoon vegetable oil

1 star anise pod, broken

10 Sichuan peppercorns

1 green onion, trimmed and chopped

1½-inch (4 cm) piece fresh ginger, peeled and sliced

1 garlic clove, finely chopped

½ carrot, peeled and cut into ⅜-inch (1 cm) cubes

½ yellow potato, peeled and cut into ⅜-inch (1 cm) cubes

5 wood ear mushrooms, hydrated in warm water for 30 minutes and coarsely chopped

3 ounces (85 g) firm tofu, cut into ⅜-inch (1 cm) cubes

1 celery stalk, preferably Chinese celery, cut into ⅜-inch (1 cm) pieces, leaves removed

4 string beans, cut into ⅜-inch (1cm) pieces

2 Chinese long beans, or cowpeas (long, string-shaped beans commonly found in Chinese grocery stores), cut into ⅜-inch (1 cm) pieces

¼ large tomato, diced

¼ green bell pepper, cut into ⅜-inch (1 cm) pieces

¼ red bell pepper, cut into ⅜-inch (1 cm) pieces

¼ teaspoon white pepper powder

In a small bowl, mix together the soy sauce, salt, sugar, cooking wine, and 2 tablespoons water. Set aside.

In a large pan, heat the vegetable oil over medium heat for 1 minute. Add the star anise and Sichuan peppercorns and sauté for 30 seconds, or until fragrant. Add the green onion, ginger, and garlic and sauté for 1 minute.

Add the carrot, potato, and reserved sauce from the first step. Stir to combine and cook for 1 minute. Add the mushrooms, tofu, celery, string beans, cowpeas, tomato, and bell peppers, and sauté for 2 minutes.

Add 2 tablespoons water along with the white pepper powder. Cook for 1 minute and serve.

Stewed Oxtail
腊汁牛尾

The classic Chinese tradition is to use every part of an animal. We use the lamb face for our salads (page 189), the hearts and the offal in soups, and the spines and tails in stews. Our oxtail dish was actually inspired by a stewed lamb spine my family used to make (page 191), slowly cooked and softened in soy sauce and spices until tender. But in the States, lamb spine was hard to come by, so we tried it with oxtail instead. It stuck for good reason. Try this on top of some noodles; you'll thank me come winter.

Serves
2

pages 60–61

1 pound (450 g) oxtails, cut into 1-inch (2.5 cm) thick segments

1 tablespoon sugar

1 tablespoon vegetable oil

1 teaspoon Sichuan peppercorns

¼ teaspoon black peppercorns

5 star anise pods

8 white cardamom pods

2 black cardamom pods, cracked

1 slice dried Chinese licorice root (gan cao)

1½-inch (4 cm) square dried orange peel

1½-inch (4 cm) cinnamon stick

3 bay leaves

3 cloves

3 green onions, trimmed and cut into 3-inch (7.5 cm) segments

1½-inch (4 cm) piece fresh ginger, peeled and sliced

1 teaspoon sweet flour sauce

5 tablespoons (75 ml) soy sauce

¼ cup (60 ml) Shaoxing cooking wine

In a large pot, add the oxtails and submerge in water. Let sit for 1 hour to remove blood, changing out the water if it becomes cloudy before the hour is up. Discard the water after soaking.

Submerge the oxtails with a fresh batch of water and bring to a boil over high heat. Cook for 5 minutes. Remove the oxtails and set aside to drain.

Clean and thoroughly dry the pot. Add the sugar along with the vegetable oil. Place over medium heat and vigorously stir for 1 to 2 minutes, until the sugar is completely melted and just turning golden brown.

Add the oxtails to the pot along with 4 cups (960 ml) water, making sure the oxtail is submerged. Stir to dissolve the syrup on the bottom. Add the remaining ingredients. Cover and bring to boil over high heat.

Once boiling, turn the heat down to medium-low but maintain a gentle boil and cook for 20 minutes, covered, stirring occasionally to prevent sticking and burning. Uncover and cook for an additional 30 minutes, stirring occasionally. The leaner the oxtails, the longer it has to cook.

When you can easily poke into the meat with chopsticks, turn off the heat and cover the pot. Let the meat sit in the sauce for 20 minutes, covered, to allow the flavor to fully set in.

5 | THE PARTY

Work Hard, Play Hard

Work hard, play hard *had been my motto since college, and I finally felt it was time for me to go in on the play hard side of things.*

IT'S 10:30 P.M. AND I'M JUST CLOSING UP SHOP IN CHINATOWN. THE STOOLS ARE UP ON THE COUNTERS, FLOORS WIPED, BURNERS OFF AND SCRUBBED, CASH COUNTED AND BALANCED. I step out into the dimly lit New York night and get a text from a certain friend we'll call "Kyle."[1] "Circle?"

Back in 2011, Circle was *the* Asian club in town, where girls showed up in heels and glitzy dresses, pulling out IDs of questionable validity, and guys in suits and nice shoes splurged on bottle service. It was the usual endgame of a typical night out in K-town, Manhattan's neighborhood filled with Korean BBQ joints and karaoke. My friends and I would pre-game at Third Floor (a soju-centric lounge fittingly on the third floor of an office building), head over to Circle to pay twenty dollars at the door (or, better yet, blow a thousand dollars on a bottle and a tiny table), before finally stumbling out (maybe with someone new, maybe with your original crew), and ordering up some bulgogi and galbi at Miss Korea.

So how did I get from having no time for my girlfriend to partying 'til 3 a.m.? Well, first, that girlfriend became an ex-girlfriend.[2] Second, I was given a sign that I should loosen up a

bit, and that sign came in the form of swollen lymph nodes that scared the shit out of me.

See, even after East Village settled down, we didn't stop. Expansion had to keep going; we opened up a second Chinatown spot on Bayard Street and started scheming up what was to be Biang!, our first sit-down spot, in Flushing.[3] I kept working nonstop, barely having enough time to eat most days. I spent mornings talking to contractors, days at the store, and nights sending emails and scheduling the staff. And then one morning, while rushing through a shower to get to the stores on time, I felt something strange on my neck. *What the hell are these bumps?!*

Several Google searches later, I was convinced I had cancer. I got myself to the first doctor I could find in Flushing (I didn't have health insurance at that time), and the man gave me two options: Wait to go to a hospital for a biopsy, or let him cut into me right then and there. I went for the latter. He gave me a shot of local anesthesia, cut into my neck, pulled out a piece of the tissue, and screamed at his assistant to grab the gauze and stop the blood. It was the first time I actually considered my health above the business, and it was pretty damn scary.

---

1 At first, I wrote "friends," but let's be real, it was just one friend in particular.

2 I was busy as hell! But I'm sure you saw that coming.

3 Biang! served not just our XFF dishes but also many of the dishes in this book, including the skewers as well as some of the desserts. It was open for a good four years, and we even expanded into the East Village, but in the end we decided to focus on the main XFF dishes. The Flushing space that was formerly Biang! is now the only Xi'an Famous Foods that serves a few of the skewers in this chapter.

Those bumps ended up just being a symptom from a cold virus (whew), but after that, I was determined to at least try to have a work-life balance. In my mind, that meant blowing off some steam and having some fun the minute I clocked out. I was young, newly single, and flush with cash. *Work hard, play hard* had been my motto since college, and I finally felt it was time for me to go in on the *play hard* side of things. I was going to catch up on all those hours spent working at St. Mark's, saying no to hanging out with friends and missing out on parties and concerts. If I wasn't working, I was going to be out, and I was going to be going hard.

Once or twice a month, when I felt overworked and almost burnt out, I'd feel an itch to blow off some steam. If it was a weekday, I'd finish up my shift, pack a bag with a laptop, and hop on a bus to Mohegan Sun or Foxwoods in Connecticut. I'd spend the three-hour bus ride sleeping or binge-watching *24*, get to the casino at 1 a.m., and play poker with all sorts of people until 6. Then it was back on the bus for a quick nap, home for a shower, and two more hours of sleep before yet another twelve-hour shift.[4]

The weekends were another story. If my high school and local friends were around, we'd kick it in Flushing and go out for KTV or karaoke. We'd book a private room with one giant TV, order some green tea and Hennessy (page 216), play some drinking game,[5] and sing some Nelly or Jay Chou until the early morning. Overall, a wholesome night compared to the craziness that was Circle.

My college friend "Kyle" was the first person to tell me about the club. While the clientele may have been primarily Asian, the purpose of the club was the same as every other hotspot in the city: get a little tipsy, meet some girls, flex a little. There was plenty of dick measuring going on, guys bragging about buying more bottles or getting a bigger table (which came with a mandatory fruit plate, like on page 217). By the time I hit twenty-four, I was fully buying into the scene. I bought myself my first nice ride (an Audi R8 with the plates "WANGJA"), and felt like Ironman in that car.[6] I'd drive up to Circle, park in front (they only let the nice cars park at the door), tip the bouncer, and stroll right in.

What can I say? I felt I deserved it. It wasn't even about getting wasted—I never drank that much to begin with. It was about the respect. It felt good to get doors opened for me, to be recognized every now and then as "the guy who owns Xi'an Famous Foods," just like it felt good to have people stop and stare at me in my car, ask to take photos with it. Because while all my friends were getting salaries and benefits and a 401(k)—a path I was on track for throughout college—I had none of that. No stability, no healthcare, no step-by-step path to promotion, no fucking vacation days. I was constantly humbled in the restaurants, getting yelled at by patrons, having soup thrown at me by grannies, and having people spit on my face, all while doing everything from cleaning the bathroom to balancing the cash register, long after everyone else had gone home. It didn't help that half of my days were spent fighting with

---

4 This work-casino-sleep-work cycle is almost a rite of passage for the restaurant industry in Flushing. The Chinatown buses used to give a coupon for a free meal and some gambling chips, so people would just go, grab some food, gamble one or two hands to maybe make some money, and then wait around for the next bus back. I once saw my contractor on the bus—it was pretty awkward.

5 I think the game was called Liar's Dice, which is basically Bullshit but with dice.

6 I later upgraded to a white Lambo and then to a white Aston Martin (no vanity plates this time; I grew up a little).

my dad, telling him he can't just add a tasting menu without telling me,[7] or change up a central kitchen process without thinking about how it affects the rest of the business. If he didn't agree with something I said, or if I offended him, he'd refuse to talk to me and turn employees against me. Every day, I felt like I was proving my worth over and over to him—and to the company.

A few songs in, though, I could forget all of that, feel like I was a part of the corporate, money-centric world that I left. I could kick it with the consultants and bankers, meet some girls on the dance floor. When the club's fog machine would come on, just as the beat dropped and the strobe lights hit, flooding the room with light and mist and sound, I could feel removed from the real world, removed from the restaurant, and feel like just another twentysomething kid making mistakes and fucking shit up.

This chapter is dedicated to that escape—those hazy, neon-tinged nights dancing to EDM at Circle or singing loudly off-key in KTV rooms with disco balls and all the golden toilets in the private restrooms, leaving the to-do list for tomorrow. And it's also dedicated to those meals right after, the feasts we'd forage for to soak up the booze. My friends and I would order sizzling bowls of spicy stews and barbecue at Miss Korea, or giant hot pots of bright red soup brimming with ramen, Spam, bowtie pasta, and cheese at Pocha 32, washed down with gulps of watermelon soju (page 215). Or, if we cabbed it back to Flushing, we'd congregate outside the old Fat Ni BBQ street cart on 39th Avenue and scarf down the classic meat sticks of my childhood: lamb skewers, beef skewers, even on occasion a whole frog or a quail.

The party dishes and drinks in this chapter are meant to be shared, inspired by the foods of Xi'an and the post-party meals of my twenties. I don't really go out to clubs anymore (Circle closed in 2018, and I'm too old for that anyway), but I do miss those 2 a.m. meals with friends, the hours spent eating, drinking a little more soju, and rehashing the misadventures of the night. Good times, man.

---

7   This really happened. One time when I was out of town, my friends sent me a text with a picture of a "teating menu" offering at Biang!

A TYPICAL TABLE AT A KTV PARTY, RIGHT WHEN PEOPLE HAVE LOOSENED UP ENOUGH TO SING.

CLOCKWISE FROM TOP:
GREEN TEA AND HENNESSY (PAGE 216); YOGURT-FLAVORED SOJU COCKTAIL (PAGE 216); AND FRESH WATERMELON SOJU COCKTAIL (PAGE 215). THESE DRINKS ARE DECEPTIVELY STRONG, SO MAKE SURE YOU GRAB A CAB BACK HOME.

A Brief History of Circle

CIRCLE WAS THE CLUB OF MY TWENTIES—AND FOR A LOT OF MY FRIENDS, TOO. Because unlike every other club queue in the borough of Manhattan, this one was overwhelmingly Asian. It got a bit of a bad rap through the years, but the megaclub remained true to its mission from day one: providing a place for young Asians and Asian Americans in NYC to get a little crazy. Here, a brief history of the infamous club—from inception to its closing in 2018—the owners, the regulars, and the regulars who would never admit to being regulars.

"I was working in corporate in Manhattan, and my friend and I started throwing birthday parties by reserving lounges. This was in 1998, and it was all done through emails, just plain text, no HTML. An email would go out with a time and a place, and then people would just show up. Sooner or later, a twenty-person gathering turned into a fifty-person gathering, and then we started hosting multiple birthday parties the same night, so they turned into one hundred–person gatherings. The next thing you know, it doubled into two hundred–person gatherings. Instead of reserving a spot in a lounge, we're reserving entire venues. We started throwing young Asian American professional happy hour events, and all of a sudden five hundred people were showing up. Some of our events would draw over a thousand people. That's when we knew that a standalone Asian American nightclub could work. When we had the opportunity to purchase a venue space in February 2008, that's when Circle nightclub was born."
Bobby Kwak, owner

"I started going to Circle around 2013. When I walked in, I would head straight up to the top bar, where it overlooked the whole club. To find so many Asians in one place . . . you don't really get that in other clubs in New York. I met a lot of good friends, a lot of business acquaintances. On any given night I could drop by and I'd bump into a friend."
Perry Shum, 29, regular

"When we first opened, we thought, *How do we make this place hot?* So we got a lot of Korean celebrities and K-pop stars; that's how we got people excited at first. We got Big Bang to show up, CL of 2NE1. Right when 'Gangnam Style' was number one, boom, we had Psy show up with Usher. The crazy thing is, we also had American pop stars show up. Diplo showed up, Rihanna showed up."
Bobby

"There were a good two years when I would go religiously. I knew everyone from the bouncers to the bathroom attendant, Amina. It was just my usual spot. The whole ambience was the reason why I kept going. For me, I knew I could walk in there and I wouldn't experience racism. I remember going into one of the other clubs, and we walked up as a group of Asians and they sort of looked at us like, *You're not going to get in.* But at Circle, I felt safer going there. Society was not kind to me when I was growing up. I would get groped on the street on the way to a nightclub, and what are you going to do? But I knew the people that worked at Circle, and I knew that if anything went down they would have my back."
Amy,[8] 39, regular

"I was born and raised in New Jersey, but I worked in Manhattan. I would go out with my Caucasian friends, and I would be one of the token Asians inside the club. Then I would go out with my Asian American friends, and the experience would be very, very different. We didn't get a welcoming vibe, had to wait in line for much longer, we'd have to get bottle service, and the minimums would be much, much higher. We weren't part of the brand. We weren't welcome. For Circle, ultimately, I personally welcomed anybody and everybody. It was a business. But we wanted to model it after nightlife in Asia, and we also wanted to create a hub, a platform for Asians and Asian Americans to just feel comfortable. To have something they could call their own. A place where they didn't have to feel discriminated against. They could go and when they went, they'd be treated right."

Bobby

"There was a point when I would go almost every weekend. At the time I was really into K-pop and they would play K-pop for one or two songs. But I definitely felt like it was created for Asians and Asian Americans especially. There weren't that many non-Asians, me being one, and there were a couple stories about how Circle was notorious for not letting people in. I definitely felt that a little bit. There was one time a guy actually grabbed my ass in there and I couldn't figure out who it was, and I didn't feel comfortable starting something because I felt like maybe *I'd* be the one to get kicked out."

Naja, 29, model

"The funny thing is, everyone felt entitled. Have you been to Marquee? Or Lavo? Clubs like that. You have to wait in line. People would show up to Circle, and everyone felt privileged and entitled, whether they were the Asian customers or non-Asian customers, because everyone saw it as a minority nightclub. They automatically had this sense of entitlement. So we might say, 'Hey, you're not dressed appropriately; you can't wear baseball caps, boots, a sweatshirt,' or 'I'm sorry, you're too intoxicated,' or 'I'm sorry, we're at max capacity.' And sometimes the people would act in a way, where if they acted this way in front of Marquee or Lavo, they would be banned. But at Circle? It was weird. These people acted as if they owned the club, and that's what we had to deal with every weekend."

Bobby

"I've had friends celebrate their thirtieth birthday there, and then they celebrated their fortieth, too. As we got older, nobody would talk about going to Circle, but the minute someone brought it up . . . they'd be unwilling to go at first, but they always had a good time. But people definitely tapered off. A lot can happen in ten years. Like, if you were there at the beginning, and you're still going at the end, you could've gone from being single to being married with kids."

Amy

"I was actually there for the closing party. Everyone came out. Everyone wanted one last time at Circle. Everyone wanted to relive the memories they had when they were younger. I miss not being able to go there. Even at their new place, Mission, I see some of the same faces, but it's not the same. When you go somewhere for long enough, you just become used to everything, and it feels like home."

Perry

IXFFI

A SNAPSHOT OF WHAT A NIGHT OUT MIGHT LOOK LIKE, THIS TIME AT MISSION (THE LATEST ITERATION OF CIRCLE).

Spicy and Tingly Lamb Face Salad
麻辣羊脸肉

Walk into any butcher shop in Xi'an and chances are you're going to see a few animal heads strung up, all full of different muscles and tendons. This salad was inspired by the ubiquity of these heads, another home experiment from my dad, who likes to utilize every part of the animal. The adventure-seeking food world took to it, if not for its shock value then for its textures and flavors. A single plate would always hold a surprise: You would get some muscles and tendons and some meat, but if you were truly lucky, you'd also get a cut of the tongue, lips, or an eyeball (which is chewier than you might expect). Every bite would be a different experience, mixed with crispy vegetables and our spicy house dressing. I personally enjoy the chewier sections of the face, like the tongue or cheeks, but if you find the lamb's palate on your plate, you're in for a crunchy treat.

Note: You'll have to make friends with your local butcher to get a whole lamb's head, but butchers are really good friends to have. If you don't manage to score a head, you can always make it with a lamb leg instead.

Serves
2

- X
F
F
-

FOR THE LAMB'S HEAD:

1 whole lamb's head, about 4½ pounds (2 kg), or 1 pound (455 g) boneless lamb leg meat

5 star anise pods

3-inch (7.5 cm) cinnamon stick

2 teaspoons Sichuan peppercorns

1 teaspoon fennel seeds

1 black cardamom pod, cracked

10 bay leaves (for lamb leg, 8 bay leaves)

1 green onion, trimmed and cut into 2-inch (5 cm) segments

1½-inch (4 cm) piece fresh ginger, peeled and sliced (for lamb leg, a 1-inch, or 2.5 cm piece)

1 teaspoon salt

FOR THE SAUCE:

2 tablespoons XFF Noodle Sauce (page 43)

1 tablespoon Garlic Puree (page 37) (for lamb leg, reduce to 2 teaspoons)

½ longhorn pepper, seeded and cut into slivers

1½ teaspoons Sichuan peppercorn powder (for lamb leg, reduce to 1 teaspoon)

1 tablespoon toasted sesame oil

2 tablespoons XFF Chili Oil (page 40)

1 teaspoon XFF Chili Oil seeds (page 40)

FOR SERVING:

1 green onion, trimmed and cut into slivers

½ sprig cilantro, cut into ½-inch (12 mm) segments

1 Chinese or Persian cucumber, thinly sliced into slivers (optional)

To make the lamb's head: In a large pot, submerge the lamb's head in cold water. Soak for 1 hour, then discard the water and wash off any blood or other debris. If you're using the lamb leg, skip the soaking and simply wash off any blood.

Clean the pot. Place the lamb's head back inside and submerge in a new batch of cold water. Add all of the aromatics and spices, cover the pot, and bring to a boil over high heat. Turn the heat down to a simmer and cook uncovered for 2 hours. For lamb leg, reduce the cooking time by 20 minutes. When chopsticks can easily poke through the lamb, it is done.

Remove the meat to a colander to drain, then cover and refrigerate for 1 to 2 hours, until completely cooled.

Note: The broth created from the boiled lamb leg (the broth from the head will be too gamey and funky) can be served with ⅛ teaspoon white pepper powder, 1 teaspoon chopped green onions, 1 teaspoon chopped cilantro, and salt to taste for a light soup.

Remove the head from the fridge. With disposable food prep gloves on, start peeling the cheek meat from the thickest parts of the head, trying to remove the largest pieces possible. Open the lamb's mouth and pull out the tongue, eyeballs, and palate cartilage. Slice the various parts into ¼-inch-wide (6 mm) strips and set aside to be dressed. The cooked lamb head can be refrigerated, undressed, for up to half a day, while cooked lamb leg can be stored in the refrigerator, undressed and wrapped in plastic wrap, for up to 3 days, or frozen for up to 1 month.

To make the sauce: In a small bowl, add the sauce ingredients. Mix to combine and set aside.

To serve: Put the cut face parts in a container. If you're using lamb leg, remove the meat from the refrigerator and cut the lamb leg meat into slices that are ⅛ inch (3 mm) thick, 1½ inches (4 cm) long, and 1 inch (2.5 cm) wide.

Add the sauce (or as much as desired) and mix to combine.

Top with green onion, cilantro, and cucumber and serve cold.

Stewed Lamb Spine
羊蝎子

Lamb spine was a common dish around Xi'an when I was a kid, but in the States we really had to hustle for these. We'd buy them off the meat stick stands around Flushing for cheap, or make the rounds with our go-to lamb butchers to see if we could get enough for a day. Because of the supply's irregularity, though, we eventually had to take this dish off our menu, which is a shame because it's really fucking delicious. This dish balances the sweetness of caramelization with the savory lamb, funky sweet flour sauce, red chile pepper, Sichuan peppercorns, and fennel seeds. My favorite way to eat this is with my hands like eating chicken feet, ripping off pieces as I work around the spine, then sucking the juice and sauce off the bones (and my fingers).

Note: You could substitute in pork ribs here, but what's the point then?

**Serves
2**

*pages 60–61
(or on its own as a
drinking snack)*

1 pound (450 g) whole lamb spine, cut into 4- to 5-inch (10 to 12 cm) pieces

1 tablespoon sugar

1 tablespoon vegetable oil

1 teaspoon Sichuan peppercorns

3 star anise pods

8 white cardamom pods

2 black cardamom pods, cracked

3 bay leaves

1 tablespoon fennel seeds

1½-inch (4 cm) cinnamon stick

6 black peppercorns

3 cloves

1 whole dried red chile pepper

1½-inch (4 cm) piece fresh ginger, peeled and sliced

2 green onions, trimmed and cut into 2-inch (5 cm) segments

1 garlic clove, peeled and sliced

1 teaspoon sweet flour sauce

½ teaspoon salt

2 tablespoons soy sauce

1 tablespoon Shaoxing cooking wine

In a medium pot, add the lamb spine and submerge in cold water. Set over high heat, cover the pot, and bring to a boil. Boil for 5 minutes, then turn off the heat. Remove the lamb spine to a plate and set aside.

Clean and thoroughly dry the pot. Add the sugar along with the vegetable oil. Heat over medium heat and vigorously stir for 1 to 2 minutes, until the sugar is completely melted and is just turning golden brown.

Add the lamb spine to the pot and cover with water (roughly 4 cups/960 ml). Stir to dissolve the syrup on the bottom.

Add the Sichuan peppercorns, star anise, white and black cardamom, bay leaves, fennel seeds, cinnamon, black peppercorns, cloves, red chile pepper, ginger, green onions, and garlic.

Add the sweet flour sauce, salt, soy sauce, and cooking wine. Cover and bring to a boil over high heat.

Once boiling, turn the heat down to low but maintain a low boil. Cook for 1 hour, covered, stirring occasionally to prevent sticking and burning. When you can easily poke into the meat with chopsticks, turn off the heat and cover the pot. Allow the meat to sit for 20 minutes, covered, for the flavor to set in before serving.

XFF

Skewers

WHEN I WAS A KID, I ASSOCIATED SKEWERS WITH THE MUSLIM QUARTER IN XI'AN, WHERE SKEWER STANDS WOULD SET UP ON SMALLER STREETS, BLOWING SMOKE IN THE AIR AND PERFUMING THE BLOCK WITH THE SMELL OF GRILLED MEAT. As a twentysomething, though, I started to associate skewers (or "meat sticks," as my friends and I called them) with food carts. In Flushing, you might be able to find Fat Ni BBQ Cart next to a parking lot, serving everything from chicken heart to quail on sticks. We used to serve these skewers at our (now closed) sit-down restaurant Biang!, but they're much better enjoyed out in the open, with friends, after a beer (or, if it's late at night, a few shots). The key here is the seasoning: Almost anything will taste delicious when grilled, topped with red chili powder, and slathered with the right sauce. But while the prep might look similar for all the skewers, watch out for the differences in marination, cooking time, and sauces—each recipe is perfectly tailored for maximum flavor. So master these sauces, grab some cumin, and plan for a party.

XFF Spicy and Tingly Sauce
秘制麻辣酱

Seeing as this is street food, efficiency is key. This one sauce, which is typically used on boiled skewers (page 197), condenses every flavor you'd possibly want when you're a little tipsy: nutty, spicy, roasted, salty, and funky. It's got the pungent kick of Pixian bean sauce, the sweet-salty maltiness of sweet flour sauce, and that iconic *ma la* tingle. Needless to say, it's *good*.

Note: If you have some of this sauce lying around and you just so happen to be making dumplings, mix a spoonful with your dumpling sauce (page 44). It's so good, I almost want to be like my dad and impulsively add it to the menu.

Makes
4 cups
(960 ml)

1⅓ cups (320 ml) vegetable oil

1 star anise pod

1½-inch (4 cm) cinnamon stick

2 bay leaves

⅓ cup (80 ml) Pixian bean sauce

2 teaspoons sweet flour sauce

⅓ cup (80 ml) sesame paste

2 teaspoons sugar

½ teaspoon white pepper powder

6 tablespoons (38 g) Red Chili Powder (page 35)

¼ cup (25 g) Sichuan peppercorn powder

TOOL:
Digital instant-read thermometer

In a small pot set over medium-low heat, heat the vegetable oil to 300°F (150°C). Add the star anise, cinnamon stick, and bay leaves and cook until fragrant, about 5 minutes. Carefully remove the spices from the oil and discard them.

Turn the heat down to low and carefully add the Pixian bean sauce, stirring immediately. Cook for 8 minutes, stirring frequently to prevent the sauce from burning and sticking to the sides of the pot. The sauce should become roasted and fragrant but not burnt.

Add the sweet flour sauce and continue to cook for 1 more minute, stirring frequently.

Add the sesame paste and sugar and cook for 2 minutes, stirring frequently.

Add the white pepper powder, red chili powder, and Sichuan peppercorn powder and stir to combine evenly. Immediately turn off the heat, cover the pot, and let sit for at least 15 minutes before using. Cool the sauce completely at room temperature before storing in the refrigerator in a closed container for up to 2 weeks. When using, be sure to mix the sauce up, as the seasoning tends to settle to the bottom.

Homemade Green Onion Oil
自制香葱油

If you were someone who had some time on your hands, you might pound all these ingredients together, toss it in a bag with some meat, and let that meat marinate for several hours. But I rarely have time for a half-day marinade, so having something like this infused oil in my fridge is a lifesaver. Made with fresh green onions, ginger, and cilantro, this oil is your ten-minute cheat for food that tastes like you planned the party days in advance. Just brush it onto your skewers over the grill to impart some extra oil (aka fat, aka flavor), or you could also use this to kick up any weekday stir-fry dinner.

Makes
4 cups
(960 ml)

4 cups (960 ml) vegetable oil

3 green onions, trimmed and cut into 1-inch (2.5 cm) segments

1½-inch (4 cm) piece fresh ginger, peeled and sliced

¼ medium red onion, sliced

1 sprig cilantro, cut into 1-inch (2.5 cm) segments

TOOL:
Digital instant-read thermometer

In a medium saucepan, heat the vegetable oil over medium heat to 320°F (160°C).

Carefully add the green onions, ginger, red onion, and cilantro. Turn the heat down slightly and fry until golden, about 10 minutes.

Turn off the heat. Carefully remove the aromatics from the oil and discard. Let the oil cool down to room temperature and keep refrigerated until ready to use. The oil can be stored refrigerated in an airtight container for up to 1 month.

XFF

Spicy and Tingly Boiled Skewers

THINK OF THIS AS A FAST-FOOD COUSIN OF HOT POT (PAGE 138). Instead of sitting down to platters of meat and a giant bubbling pot of broth, you're ordering three to five sticks from a street vendor and watching as these suckers get flash-boiled in front of you. The cooked skewers then get slathered with a spicy and tingly sauce, plopped into a cup, and served. It's genius—you get all the fun of walking and eating without dribbling sauce down your shirt.

As for what's actually on the skewers, the same rules for hot pot hold true here: What you're looking for is a flat, thin, textured surface that can both cook quickly and grip onto the sauce, making beef tripe and bean curd sheets the perfect candidates. When done right, these skewers veer on the good side of chewy without being rubbery. And at the end of the day, the key here is the sauce. We say 2 tablespoons, but you can use as much as you want.

Spicy and Tingly Boiled Bean Curd Sheet Skewers
麻辣涮豆腐皮

Makes
10 skewers

1 (17.6 oz/500 g) package bean curd sheets

2 tablespoons XFF Spicy and Tingly Sauce (page 194)

1 tablespoon XFF Chili Oil (page 40)

½ tablespoon Roasted Sesame Seeds (page 34)

TOOLS:
10 bamboo skewers

1½-inch (4 cm) brush

Cut the bean curd sheets into 1½-inch (4 cm) square pieces.

Skewer about 6 pieces on each of the skewers without overlapping them, making sure to leave at least 2 inches (5 cm) of empty space on one side of the skewer. These can be refrigerated, covered, for up to 3 hours before cooking, or frozen for 1 week.

Fill a large pot with enough water to submerge the bean curd, cover, and set over high heat to bring to a boil. Once boiling, add the skewers and boil for 3 to 4 minutes. Remove from the water and place on a plate.

To serve, brush the bean curd with the spicy and tingly sauce, along with the chili oil, if desired. Sprinkle with the sesame seeds and serve immediately.

Spicy and Tingly
Boiled Beef Tripe Skewers
麻辣涮牛肚

FOR THE SKEWERS:

1 pound (455 g) honeycomb beef tripe

2 teaspoons Sichuan peppercorns

6 star anise pods

2-inch (5 cm) cinnamon stick

2 green onions, trimmed and cut into 2-inch (5 cm) segments

1½-inch (4 cm) piece fresh ginger, peeled and sliced

2 dried red chile peppers

2 tablespoons Shaoxing cooking wine

1 teaspoon salt

FOR SERVING:

2 tablespoons XFF Spicy and Tingly Sauce (page 194)

1 tablespoon XFF Chili Oil (optional, page 40)

½ tablespoon Roasted Sesame Seeds (page 34)

TOOLS:

10 bamboo skewers

1½-inch (4 cm) brush

Clean the beef tripe under cool running water. Add it to a large pot along with 10 cups (2½ quarts/2.4 L) water and all of the seasonings. Cover and bring to a boil over high heat.

When the water starts boiling, turn the heat down to low and simmer for 1 hour, making sure all the tripe remains submerged in the water. You may need to weigh it down with a heat-safe plate. When a chopstick can easily poke through the beef tripe, it's done. Transfer it to a colander to drain and cool.

Once cool enough to handle, cut the cooked beef tripe into 1½-inch (4 cm) square pieces. Evenly divide the pieces among the skewers without overlapping, leaving at least 2 inches (5 cm) of empty space at the end of each skewer. The skewers should fit 4 or 5 pieces of beef tripe each. These can be refrigerated, covered, for up to 3 hours before cooking, or frozen for 1 week.

Fill a large pot with enough water to submerge the beef tripe. Cover the pot and bring the water to a boil over high heat. Once boiling, add the skewers and boil for 3 to 4 minutes. Remove from the water and place on a plate.

To serve, brush the skewers with the spicy and tingly sauce, along with the chili oil, if desired.

Sprinkle with the sesame seeds and serve immediately.

X
F
F

Spicy Grilled Cumin Skewers

THE FIRST STEP OF THESE SKEWERS: GET A GRILL. Make sure it's charcoal (the wood kind). Then put your favorite things onto a skewer and grill both sides, sprinkling on a handful of cumin while you're at it. The best things in life are simple, right?

Some proteins are trickier than others to skewer, some require a little dab of oil, so watch out for those minor differences. Once you get the general gist down, though, you can turn pretty much anything into a spicy cumin skewer.

Spicy Cumin Fish Tofu Skewers
孜然烤鱼豆腐

Let's start easy, with these pre-cooked "tofu" cakes made out of pureed fish—very similar to the fish balls you might see in any hot pot spread (page 142), but even tastier when grilled and smoky.

Makes
6 skewers

8½ ounces (240 g) fish tofu pieces

1 tablespoon Homemade Green Onion Oil (page 195)

1 tablespoon XFF Spicy and Tingly Sauce (page 194)

½ tablespoon coarsely ground cumin

2 teaspoons Red Chili Powder (page 35)

Salt

TOOLS:

6 bamboo skewers

Robata grill or barbecue

1½-inch (4 cm) brush

Cut each of the fish tofu pieces in half.

Thread 4 pieces of the fish tofu onto each skewer, skewering them lengthwise. These can be refrigerated, covered, for up to 1 day.

Prepare a robata or other grill with charcoal that has turned ashy gray and is smoldering hot but not actively emitting flames.

Cook the skewers by rotating them constantly on the grill to prevent burning, 3 to 5 minutes.

When the tofu pieces are golden along the edges, brush each side with the green onion oil, then the spicy and tingly sauce, and then sprinkle each side with the cumin, red chili powder, and salt to taste. Some seasoning will fall into the grill; that is fine. Serve immediately.

Note: When brushing oil and sauce on the fish tofu while over the fire, do so sparingly, dabbing off any excess oil so it doesn't drip onto the flames. If at any point the flames flare up, remove the skewers from the grill until the flames die down.

Spicy Cumin Buns
孜然烤馍

I almost laughed when I first saw these in Xi'an. Imagine: You're going out to eat some skewers, and you order some lamb, some beef, and then . . . some bread buns on a stick. They look pretty damn ridiculous. But somehow, it works, especially if you have some of our leftover bread. You could, in a pinch, even use pita bread. Slathered in oil and sprinkled with our signature spices, it's like our version of garlic bread—a spiced-up crispy carb that is just as good as the meat sticks (and also slightly more filling).

**Makes
2 skewers**

2 Daily Bread buns (page 46)

1 tablespoon Homemade Green Onion Oil (page 195)

2 teaspoons XFF Spicy and Tingly Sauce (page 194)

2 teaspoons coarsely ground cumin

2 teaspoons Red Chili Powder (page 35)

⅛ teaspoon salt

TOOLS:
4 bamboo skewers

Robata grill or barbecue

1½-inch (4 cm) brush

Cut cross-hatched lines on the two sides of the buns with a bread knife, about ¼ inch (6 mm) deep, spaced 1½ inches (4 cm) apart. Using two skewer sticks, skewer each bun, one on the left side and one on the right, running parallel to each other. These skewers will serve to hold up the bun over the grill for easy flipping and handling. At this point, the skewers can be refrigerated, wrapped in plastic wrap, for up to 3 days before grilling.

Prepare a robata or other grill with charcoal that has turned ashy gray and is smoldering hot but not actively emitting flames.

Set the buns down on the grill surface and cook for 3 minutes. Flip the skewers over and cook for another 3 minutes.

Once the buns just start to get brown and crisp on each side, lightly brush one side with half of the green onion oil and spicy and tingly sauce. Sprinkle with half of the cumin, red chili powder, and salt.

Flip the buns over and brush the other side with the rest of the oil, sauces, and spices.

Flip the skewers once more and toast the newly seasoned side for 30 seconds. Serve immediately.

Note: When brushing oil and sauce on the bread while over fire, do so sparingly, dabbing off any excess oil, so it doesn't drip onto the flames. If at any point the flames flare up, remove the skewers from the grill until the flames die down.

XFF

Spicy Cumin Chicken Skewers
孜然烤鸡肉串

Chicken is an easy crowd pleaser, and working with boneless chicken thighs means we can maintain the uniformity of the skewers, making cooking a breeze. We amp up the flavors here by marinating the boneless dark meat chicken with some ginger, green onions, and sesame oil. Then these suckers get smoky over a grill, slathered with our green onion oil and topped with an explosive amount of cumin, red chili powder, and just a tiny hit of Sichuan peppercorn powder.

Makes
7 skewers

FOR THE CHICKEN:

3 boneless, skinless chicken thighs

2 teaspoons Sichuan peppercorns

1 star anise pod

1 green onion, trimmed and cut into 2-inch (5 cm) segments

1½-inch (4 cm) piece fresh ginger, peeled and sliced

1 teaspoon white pepper powder

1 teaspoon salt

¼ teaspoon Chinese five-spice powder

2 tablespoons Shaoxing cooking wine

1 teaspoon toasted sesame oil

FOR GRILLING AND SERVING:

1 tablespoon Homemade Green Onion Oil (page 195)

1 tablespoon coarsely ground cumin

2 teaspoons Red Chili Powder (page 35)

1 teaspoon Sichuan peppercorn powder

Salt

½ tablespoon Roasted Sesame Seeds (page 34)

TOOLS:

7 bamboo skewers

Robata grill or barbecue

1½-inch (4 cm) brush

To make the chicken: Cut each chicken thigh into about twelve 1½-inch (4 cm) pieces.

Add the remaining ingredients to a container to make a marinade and mix well to combine.

Add the chicken to the marinade and combine thoroughly. Cover the container with plastic wrap and let marinate in the refrigerator for 1 hour. Any longer and you risk over-marinating.

To grill and serve: Remove the chicken from the refrigerator. Thread 5 chicken pieces onto each skewer. The skewers may be kept refrigerated, covered, before grilling, but for no longer than 2 hours.

Prepare a robata or other grill with charcoal that has turned ashy gray and is smoldering hot but not actively emitting flames.

Set the skewers down on the grill surface and cook for 2 minutes, then flip over and cook for 2 minutes more.

Brush the green onion oil on both sides. Cook for a minute or so more, until the chicken is golden.

Brush another layer of green onion oil on both sides and sprinkle one side with half of the cumin, red chili powder, Sichuan peppercorn powder, and salt, to taste.

Flip and repeat the oil and seasoning on the other side. Then flip back and roast this newly seasoned side for 30 seconds.

Remove the cooked skewers to a plate, sprinkle with the sesame seeds, and serve immediately.

Note: When brushing oil and sauce on the meat while over the fire, do so sparingly, dabbing off any excess, so the oil or sauce doesn't drip onto the flames. If at any point the flames flare up, remove the skewers from the grill until the flames die down.

Spicy Cumin Chicken Wing Skewers
孜然烤鸡翅

You haven't lived until you've eaten an entire crispy chicken wing grilled over smoky charcoal with cumin and chili. The chicken skin's fattiness melds perfectly with the savory spices, leaving you salivating, wanting more. Remember those XFF chicken wings (page 73)? This has the same peppery notes but with the added aroma of smoky charcoal and a heavy dusting of spice.

**Makes
6 skewers**

FOR THE CHICKEN WINGS:

1 green onion, trimmed and cut into slivers

1-inch (2.5 cm) piece fresh ginger, peeled and sliced into slivers

6 whole chicken wings

1 teaspoon salt

1 teaspoon Sichuan peppercorns

3 star anise pods

2 tablespoons Shaoxing cooking wine

FOR COOKING AND SERVING:

1 tablespoon Homemade Green Onion Oil (page 195)

1 tablespoon coarsely ground cumin

2 teaspoons Red Chili Powder (page 35)

1 teaspoon Sichuan peppercorn powder

Salt

½ tablespoon Roasted Sesame Seeds (page 34)

TOOLS:

6 bamboo skewers

Robata grill or barbecue

1½-inch (4 cm) brush

To make the chicken wings: On a cutting board, smash the green onion a bit with the side of a knife. Add the green onion to a small bowl along with the ginger and ¼ cup (60 ml) water. Set aside for 10 minutes.

In a large container, combine the chicken wings, green onion, ginger (and the accompanying water), salt, Sichuan peppercorns, star anise, and cooking wine. Rub the liquid and seasonings of the marinade evenly into the chicken.

Cover the container with plastic wrap and refrigerate for at least 1 hour and up to 2 hours.

To cook and serve: Preheat the oven to 200°F (93°C). Remove any solid spices from the marinade off of the wings.

Place the wings on an ovenproof pan and bake for 20 minutes. Set aside to cool.

Skewer each whole wing with 2 skewers, inserted about 1 inch (2.5 cm) apart. This makes it easier to hold and flip them on the grill. At this point, the skewers can be kept in the refrigerator, covered, for up to 1 day before grilling.

Prepare a robata or other grill with charcoal that has turned ashy gray and is smoldering hot but not actively emitting flames.

Set the skewers down on the grill surface and cook for 2 minutes, then flip over and cook for another 2 minutes.

Brush the green onion oil on both sides. Cook for a minute or so more on both sides, until the chicken is golden.

Brush another layer of green onion oil on both sides and sprinkle one side with half of the cumin, red chili powder, Sichuan peppercorn powder, and salt.

Season the other side, then flip once more and toast the newly seasoned side for about 30 seconds.

Remove the cooked skewers to a plate, sprinkle with the sesame seeds, and serve immediately.

Note: When brushing oil and sauce on the meat while over fire, do so sparingly, dabbing off any excess oil so it doesn't drip onto the flames. If at any point the flames flare up, remove the skewers from the grill until the flames die down.

XFF

Spicy Cumin Chicken Heart Skewers
孜然烤鸡心串

Some people might be afraid of cooking chicken hearts, but they're not that much different from any cut of dark chicken meat. These morsels of muscle are perfect for grilling: lean, flavorful, with a perfect bouncy bite.

Makes
10 skewers

FOR THE CHICKEN HEARTS:

1 pound (455 g) chicken hearts, or about 50 hearts

2 green onions, trimmed and sliced into slivers

1½-inch (4 cm) piece fresh ginger, peeled and sliced

2 teaspoons Sichuan peppercorns

½ teaspoon Chinese five-spice powder

1 tablespoon Shaoxing cooking wine

1 teaspoon salt

FOR GRILLING AND SERVING:

1 tablespoon Homemade Green Onion Oil (page 195)

½ tablespoon coarsely ground cumin

2 teaspoons Red Chili Powder (page 35)

Salt

½ tablespoon Roasted Sesame Seeds (page 34)

TOOLS:

10 bamboo skewers

Robata grill or barbecue

1½-inch (4 cm) brush

To make the chicken hearts: Butterfly the chicken hearts by slicing them lengthwise, cutting deeply without cutting them entirely in half.

Smash the green onions and ginger with clean hands to release their flavors.

Add the smashed green onions and ginger, along with the Sichuan peppercorns, five-spice powder, cooking wine, and salt to a container along with 1 cup (240 ml) water to make a marinade.

Add the chicken hearts to the marinade and stir well to combine. Cover the container with plastic wrap and let marinate in the refrigerator for 1 hour. Any longer and you risk over-marinating.

To grill and serve: Thread 5 chicken hearts onto each skewer. The skewers may be kept refrigerated, covered, before cooking for no longer than 2 hours.

Prepare a robata or other grill with charcoal that has turned ashy gray and is smoldering hot but not actively emitting flames.

Set the skewers down on the grill surface and cook for 2 minutes, then flip over and cook for an additional 2 minutes.

When the meat tightens up and oil begins to seep out, it is almost done. At this point, brush the green onion oil on one side of the meat, then sprinkle half of the cumin, red chili powder, and salt, to taste, on top.

Flip the skewers over and season the other side in the same way. Flip the skewers once more and toast the newly seasoned side for about 30 seconds. Cook for about a minute or so more on each side.

Remove the cooked skewers to a plate, sprinkle with the sesame seeds, and serve immediately.

Note: When brushing oil and sauce on the meat while over the fire, do so sparingly, dabbing off any excess, so it doesn't drip onto the flames. If at any point the flames flare up, remove the skewers from the grill until the flames die down.

A SELECTION
OF SKEWERS
I LIKE TO SERVE AT MY
PARTIES. (CLOCKWISE
FROM TOP):
SPICY CUMIN CHICKEN
WING SKEWERS, SPICY
CUMIN BEEF SKEWERS,
SPICY AND TINGLY
BOILED BEEF TRIPE
SKEWERS, SPICY CUMIN
SQUID SKEWERS, SPICY
AND TINGLY BOILED
BEAN CURD SHEET
SKEWERS, AND SPICY
CUMIN FISH TOFU
SKEWERS

Spicy Cumin Chicken Gizzard Skewers
孜然烤鸡胗

These grisly, crunchy skewers are as fun to eat as they are hard to make. (But did I ever say any of this would be easy?) Every time I think about these skewers, I worry about accidentally stabbing myself as I try to thread the gizzards onto the sticks. But I do it for the crunch, and if you're into that texture, you should, too. (Just be careful not to stab yourself.)

Makes
7 skewers

FOR THE CHICKEN GIZZARDS:

13 ounces (370 g) chicken gizzards

2 teaspoons Sichuan peppercorns

6 bay leaves

6 star anise pods

1 teaspoon fennel seeds

3 dried red chile peppers

1½-inch piece (4 cm) fresh ginger, peeled and sliced

2 tablespoons Shaoxing cooking wine

1 green onion, trimmed and cut into 2-inch (5 cm) pieces

FOR GRILLING AND SERVING:

1 tablespoon Homemade Green Onion Oil (page 195)

½ tablespoon coarsely ground cumin

2 teaspoons Red Chili Powder (page 35)

Salt

½ tablespoon Roasted Sesame Seeds (page 34)

TOOLS:

7 bamboo skewers

Robata grill or barbecue

1½-inch (4 cm) brush

To make the chicken gizzards: Clean the chicken gizzards by running them under cool water. Add to a large pot along with 4 cups (1 L) water and the remaining ingredients.

Cover and bring to a boil over high heat. Once boiling, turn the heat down to low and simmer for 30 minutes. Transfer the gizzards to a colander to drain and cool.

To grill and serve: Butterfly the gizzards by slicing them deeply through their thickest part without cutting all the way through.

Thread 5 gizzards onto each skewer. The skewers may be kept refrigerated, covered, for up to 1 day before grilling.

Prepare a robata or other grill with charcoal that has turned ashy gray and is smoldering hot but not actively emitting flames.

Set the skewers down on the grill surface and cook for 2 minutes. Then flip over and cook for an additional 2 minutes.

When the meat tightens up and oil begins to seep out, it is almost done. At this point, brush the green onion oil on one side of the meat, then sprinkle half of the cumin, red chili powder, and salt, to taste, on top.

Flip the skewers over and season the other side in the same way. Flip the skewers once more and toast the newly seasoned side for about 30 seconds.

Cook for about a minute or so more on each side.

Remove the cooked skewers to a plate, sprinkle with the sesame seeds, and serve immediately.

Note: When brushing oil and sauce on the meat while over the fire, do so sparingly, dabbing off any excess oil so it doesn't drip onto the flames. If at any point the flames flare up, remove the skewers from the grill until the flames die down.

Spicy Cumin Beef Skewers
孜然烤牛肉串

These beef skewers have all the fixings of the legendary lamb skewers, plus some oyster sauce for sweetness and Chinese five-spice for flavor. I tend to prefer lamb, obviously, but if you're not a fan of its gaminess, beef is a good substitute. Or do what the best hosts do and offer both.

Makes
5 skewers

FOR THE BEEF:

1 pound (455 g) beef loin

½ teaspoon salt

1 tablespoon Shaoxing cooking wine

2 teaspoons oyster sauce

1 teaspoon soy sauce

½ teaspoon cornstarch

½ teaspoon Chinese five-spice powder

1 green onion, trimmed and cut into slivers

1½-inch (4 cm) piece fresh ginger, peeled and sliced

¼ medium red onion, sliced

FOR GRILLING AND SERVING:

½ tablespoon coarsely ground cumin

2 teaspoons Red Chili Powder (page 35)

Salt

½ tablespoon Roasted Sesame Seeds (page 34)

TOOLS:

5 bamboo skewers

Robata grill or barbecue

To make the beef: Cut the beef into rectangles that are 1 inch (2.5 cm) long, ½ inch (12 mm) wide, and ½ inch (12 mm) thick.

In a large bowl, combine the remaining ingredients to make a marinade and add the beef. Stir well to combine.

Cover the bowl with plastic wrap and let marinate in the refrigerator for 1 hour. Any longer and you risk over-marinating.

To grill and serve: Skewer the beef lengthwise on the skewers, adding 5 leaner pieces and 2 fattier pieces of beef to each skewer, interspersing the fattier pieces with the leaner pieces to impart some extra flavor. The skewers may be kept refrigerated, covered, before cooking, but for no longer than 2 hours.

Prepare a robata or other grill with charcoal that has turned ashy gray and is smoldering hot but not actively emitting flames.

Set the skewers down on the grill surface and cook for 2 minutes, then flip over and cook for an additional 2 minutes.

When the meat tightens up and oil begins to seep out, it is almost done. At this point, sprinkle half of the cumin, red chili powder, and salt, to taste, on top of the skewers.

Flip the skewers over and season the other side in the same way. Flip the skewers once more and toast the newly seasoned side for about 30 seconds.

Remove the cooked skewers to a plate, sprinkle with the sesame seeds, and serve immediately.

Spicy Cumin Beef Tendon Skewers
孜然麻辣烤牛筋

Like gizzards, this one is a tricky one. Raw tendons are tough and unforgiving, and you practically have to force them onto skewers. Plus, you'll need to simmer them for far longer than you think to tenderize these gelatinous cubes, before dousing them with spices continuously so the cumin and chili powder sticks. But if you do it right, you end up with a burst of flavor, a crunchy, crispy surface, and a tender, gelatinous bite.

**Makes
10 skewers**

FOR THE BEEF TENDONS:

2 pounds (910 g) beef tendon

10 bay leaves

3 cloves

2 slices dried Chinese licorice root (gan cao)

½-inch (12 mm) cinnamon stick

3 black cardamom pods

2 teaspoons Sichuan peppercorns

1½-inch (4 cm) square dried orange peel

15 white cardamom pods

2 green onions, trimmed and cut into 2-inch (5 cm) pieces

1½-inch (4 cm) piece fresh ginger, peeled and sliced

3 tablespoons soy sauce

1 tablespoon Shaoxing cooking wine

FOR GRILLING AND SERVING:

1 tablespoon Homemade Green Onion Oil (page 195)

½ tablespoon coarsely ground cumin

2 teaspoons Red Chili Powder (page 35)

Salt

½ tablespoon Roasted Sesame Seeds (page 34)

TOOLS:

10 bamboo skewers

Robata grill or barbecue

1½-inch (4 cm) brush

To make the beef tendons: Add the tendons to a large pot along with 6 cups (1.4 L) water and all of the seasonings.

Cover and bring to a boil over high heat. Once boiling, turn the heat down to low and simmer for 2½ hours. The tendons should be tender enough to easily poke through with a chopstick.

Turn off the heat and let sit, covered, for 15 minutes. Remove the tendons to a colander to drain and cool.

To grill and serve: Cut the tendons into 1-inch (2.5 cm) squares. Thread 5 pieces of meat onto each skewer. The skewers may be kept refrigerated, covered, for up to 1 day before grilling.

Prepare a robata or other grill with charcoal that has turned ashy gray and is smoldering hot but not actively emitting flames.

Set the skewers down on the grill surface and cook for 2 minutes. Then flip over and cook for an additional 2 minutes.

Brush the green onion oil on one side of the meat, then sprinkle half of the cumin, red chili powder, and salt, to taste, on top.

Flip the skewers over and season the other side in the same way. Flip the skewers once more and toast the newly seasoned side for about 30 seconds.

Cook for about a minute or so more on each side.

Remove the cooked skewers to a plate, sprinkle with the sesame seeds, and serve immediately.

Note: When brushing oil and sauce on the meat while over fire, do so sparingly, dabbing off any excess oil so it doesn't drip onto the flames. If at any point the flames flare up, remove the skewers from the grill until the flames die down.

Spicy Cumin Pig Intestines Skewers
孜然烤猪脆肠

When cooked correctly, the intestines are crisp on the outside and fatty and soft on the inside. Wrong, and you end up with nearly burnt slices. Do yourself a favor and get the timing right.

*Makes
4 skewers*

FOR THE PORK:

10 ounces (280 g) cleaned pig intestines

1 green onion, trimmed and cut into 2-inch (5 cm) pieces

1½-inch (4 cm) piece fresh ginger, peeled and sliced

2 dried red chile peppers

2 teaspoons Sichuan peppercorns

½-inch (12 mm) cinnamon stick

4 star anise pods

1 teaspoon fennel seeds

2 garlic cloves, peeled and smashed

½ teaspoon black peppercorns

½ teaspoon cloves

8 bay leaves

3 black cardamom pods

2 slices dried Chinese licorice root (gan cao)

1½-inch (4 cm) square dried orange peel

1 tablespoon Shaoxing cooking wine

2 tablespoons soy sauce

½ teaspoon sugar

FOR GRILLING AND SERVING:

½ tablespoon coarsely ground cumin

2 teaspoons Red Chili Powder (page 35)

Salt

TOOLS:

4 bamboo skewers

Robata grill or barbecue

To make the pork: Add the intestines and the remaining ingredients to a large pot and submerge with water.

Cover and bring to a boil over high heat. Boil for 5 to 6 minutes, then turn down the heat to low. Simmer for 1½ hours. The intestines should be tender enough to poke through with a pair of chopsticks.

Drain the intestines from the water and set aside to cool. Discard the aromatics and water.

To grill and serve: Cut the intestines into ½-inch (12 mm) thick rings, then thread 5 rings onto each skewer. The skewers may be kept refrigerated, covered, for up to 1 day before grilling.

Prepare a robata or other grill with charcoal that has turned ashy gray and is smoldering hot but not actively emitting flames.

Set the skeweres down on the grill surface and cook for 2 minutes, then flip over and cook for another 2 minutes.

When oil starts coming out of the intestines, they're ready for seasoning. Sprinkle one side of each skewer with half of the cumin powder, red chili powder, and salt, to taste.

Flip and season the other side. Flip once more and toast the newly seasoned side for 30 seconds before removing to a plate. Serve immediately.

Spicy Cumin Lamb Skewers
孜然烤羊肉串

When I was a kid, I didn't really like eating. I preferred playing with my toys in the sunroom or catching crickets. But that changed when I had my first skewer from the Muslim Quarter's street market. These were dangerously easy to eat, made with tiny little morsels of lamb, occasionally interspersed with a fatty, juicy piece for extra flavor, all speared onto a thin needle-like skewer. It was smoky, savory, and spicy all at once, sprinkled with Middle Eastern spices and crunchy, coarsely ground cumin seeds. I used to brag about eating sixty to eighty in one sitting—and for a scrawny kid like me, that was a lot.

This was the dish I missed the most when I first moved to the States, and learning to re-create it took years. When I finally got around to mastering the flavors at a lakeside barbecue one summer day, I was so happy I almost cried.

Note: We use sesame seeds here for the crunch, but if you have whole cumin seeds lying around, feel free to add those in addition to the ground cumin (you can never have too much, in my opinion).

Makes
10 skewers

FOR THE LAMB:
2 pounds (910 g) boneless lamb leg meat

2 tablespoons Shaoxing cooking wine

1 teaspoon salt

½ teaspoon white pepper powder

1 teaspoon Sichuan peppercorns

2 green onions, trimmed and cut into slivers

1½-inch (4 cm) piece fresh ginger, peeled and cut into slivers

¼ medium red onion, sliced

FOR GRILLING AND SERVING:
½ tablespoon coarsely ground cumin

2 teaspoons Red Chili Powder (page 35)

Salt

½ tablespoon Roasted Sesame Seeds (page 34)

TOOLS:
10 bamboo skewers

Robata grill or barbecue

To make the lamb: Cut the lamb into rectangles that are 1 inch (2.5 cm) long and ½ inch (12 mm) thick.

In a large bowl, combine the remaining ingredients to make a marinade and add the lamb. Stir well to combine.

Cover the bowl with plastic wrap and let sit in the refrigerator for 1 hour. Any longer and you risk over-marinating.

To grill and serve: Skewer the lamb lengthwise onto the skewers, making sure to retain the lamb cut's shape and keep the meat long and slender. Add 5 leaner pieces and 2 fattier pieces of lamb to each skewer, interspersing the fattier pieces between the leaner pieces. The skewers may be kept refrigerated, covered, before cooking, but for no longer than 2 hours.

Prepare a robata or other grill with charcoal that has turned ashy gray and is smoldering hot but not actively emitting flames.

Set the skewers down on the grill surface and cook for 2 minutes. Flip over and cook for an additional 2 minutes.

When the meat tightens up and oil begins to seep out, it is almost done. At this point, sprinkle half of the cumin, red chili powder, and salt, to taste, on top. Try to get as much on the meat as possible, but it's okay if a little of the seasoning falls into the grill.

Flip the skewers over and season the other side in the same way. Flip the skewers once more and toast the newly seasoned side for 30 seconds. Cook for about a minute or so more on each side.

Remove the cooked skewers to a plate, sprinkle with the sesame seeds, and serve immediately.

Spicy Cumin Squid Skewers
孜然烤尤鱼

If you typically shy away from squid because the texture can be rubbery, give these a try. In skewer form, the cephalopod is rendered crispy and crunchy. When cut into small, bite-sized pieces for maximum flavor, this dish is also incredibly easy to cook, contrary to popular belief.

Makes
12 skewers

4 squid (approximately 13 ounces/ 370 g), cleaned with heads removed

2 teaspoons XFF Spicy and Tingly Sauce (page 194)

1 tablespoon coarsely ground cumin

2 teaspoons Red Chili Powder (page 35)

Salt

TOOLS:
12 bamboo skewers

Robata grill or barbecue

1½-inch (4 cm) brush

Cut the cleaned squid into roughly 1½-inch (4 cm) squares. Thread about 6 pieces onto each skewer. These skewers may be kept refrigerated, covered, for up to 1 day before grilling.

Prepare a robata or other grill with charcoal that has turned ashy gray and is smoldering hot but not actively emitting flames.

Set the skewers down on the grill surface and cook for 1½ minutes. Flip over and cook the other side for another 1½ minutes. Cook, flipping often, for about 1 minute more.

Once the squid has become white and firm and the flesh is curling, brush the spicy and tingly sauce on one side, then sprinkle with half of the cumin, red chili powder, and salt, to taste.

Repeat seasoning on the other side, then flip again and toast the newly seasoned side for about 30 seconds. Serve immediately.

Note: When brushing sauce on the squid while over the fire, do so sparingly, dabbing off any excess, so the sauce doesn't drip onto the flames. If at any point the flames flare up, remove the skewers from the grill until the flames die down.

Spicy Cumin Whole Fish
孜然烤全鱼

Any flaky white fish will do here, but we tend to go for perch or croaker, choosing a small, whole fish that will cook easily. Deep-fried, the marinated fish will be flaky, fragrant, and practically perfect. But if you deep-fry, *then* grill the fish, you add on an extra smoky kick that makes this irresistible.

**Serves
1 or 2**

FOR THE FISH:

1 whole fresh perch or similar fish, approximately 1½ pounds (680 g) total, scaled and gutted

½ teaspoon white pepper powder

¼ teaspoon salt

2 tablespoons Shaoxing cooking wine

1 green onion, trimmed and cut into slivers

1½-inch (4 cm) piece fresh ginger, peeled and cut into slivers

2 garlic cloves, peeled and smashed

FOR COOKING AND SERVING:

2 tablespoons Red Chili Powder (page 35)

1 tablespoon coarsely ground cumin

1 teaspoon Sichuan peppercorn powder

¼ teaspoon salt

6 cups (1.4 L) vegetable oil for frying

Homemade Green Onion Oil (page 195) for brushing (if grilling)

6 tablespoons (90 ml) XFF Chili Oil without seeds (page 40)

TOOL:

Digital instant-read thermometer

To make the fish: Clean the inside and outside of the gutted fish by running it under cold water and patting it dry with paper towels.

In a large container, combine the remaining ingredients to make a marinade. Add the fish and use your hands to evenly rub the marinade inside the fish as well as on the surface of the skin. Cover the container with plastic wrap and marinate for 30 minutes in the refrigerator. Any longer and you risk over-marinating.

To cook and serve: In a small bowl, stir together the red chili powder, cumin, Sichuan peppercorn powder, and salt.

In a large, deep skillet, heat the vegetable oil over medium heat until an instant-read thermometer registers 350°F (175°C). Carefully place the fish into the pan (it should be submerged in the oil) and fry for 6 to 7 minutes, until golden.

Set a rack over a sheet pan, and remove the fish to the rack to drain.

If grilling, brush some green onion oil on both sides. Cook on both sides, each side up to 10 minutes, to finish the dish.

While hot, brush the chili oil on the outside of the fish. Then sprinkle on the red chili, cumin, peppercorn, and salt mixture. Brush on another layer of chili oil and serve immediately.

XFF

Fresh Watermelon Soju Cocktail
西瓜烧酒

For me and my crew, a late-night meal in K-Town meant one of two places: Miss Korea or Pocha 32.

The latter was always a crowd-pleaser, especially if friends were visiting from out of town. Pocha 32 is a tiny little second-floor restaurant covered in festive string lights and paper notes from customers, known for its extensive menu of Korean drinking foods. The main draw here is their Korean army stew, or *budae jeongol*, a boiling, sizzling hot pot melangerie of everything you can possibly think of: ramen, Spam, bowtie pastas, shredded cheese, hot dogs, rice cakes, and some veggies to make you feel better about yourself.

The second-best order, though, would be their watermelon soju punch, a dangerously refreshing concoction of fresh watermelon juice and a surprising amount of barely detectable booze. Here's one rendition of that classic combo.

Ice cubes

1 large watermelon

12.7-ounce (375 ml) bottle soju (my Korean friends like Chum-Churum)

1 shot Domaine de Canton liqueur (optional)

Slice off a bit of the bottom of the watermelon so it can be set flat on the table without rolling around. Be careful to just cut the rind; you don't want to expose the flesh.

Slice off the top of the watermelon. This time, you want to go just far enough to expose the flesh so you can scoop it all out with a spoon. Place the scooped watermelon flesh in a blender. Set some aside in a bowl if it doesn't all fit. Reserve the scooped-out watermelon shell.

Working in batches if needed, puree the watermelon flesh in a blender until smooth. Pour the puree through a strainer set over a bowl or pitcher and reserve the watermelon juice. Discard the leftover watermelon pulp.

When ready to serve, fill the watermelon shell with a handful of ice. Pour in the bottle of soju.

Fill up the watermelon shell the rest of the way with the reserved watermelon juice and the Domaine de Canton, if desired. The liqueur adds a nice ginger flavor, but it's not worth buying on its own unless you plan to make a lot of this, in my opinion.

Stir to combine. Ladle into small bowls or cups to serve.

Green Tea and Hennessy
绿茶轩尼诗

I grew up surrounded by green-labeled, rectangular bottles of tea—the standard package for many green teas at Chinese supermarkets. It was a staple at family gatherings, something the adults drank as the kids went for the soda and juice. Once I got older, though, the green tea bottle became a staple at KTV, served alongside cheap Hennessy.

The trick here is to get the sweetened green tea, which helps mask any whiskey taste. Grab a pitcher of ice, pour in some Henny, and then dump the entire bottle of tea in. After one or two glasses of this, you might just lose your karaoke stage fright.

Serves 2
if you have high tolerance; serves 4 or more if you're taking it easy

Ice cubes

4 shots Hennessy V.S.O.P.

16-ounce (480 ml) bottle sweet Chinese green tea drink

Fill a pitcher a third of the way up with ice and add the Hennessy. How much you put in really depends on how strong you'd like your drink.

Add the entire bottle of tea to the pitcher and stir with a long spoon or a clean chopstick, if you want to be legit.

Serve in rocks glasses, right when your friend loses at a game of BS with dice.

Yogurt-Flavored Soju Cocktail
养乐多烧酒

I grew up drinking Yakult, a slightly tart yogurt-flavored drink, and to this day, you'll still find a pack in my freezer. When I got older, my friends and I would mix the Yakult with soju, experimenting with the different flavors out there (I always felt lychee was the best). This was our go-to group order when we'd pre-game at Third Floor before heading over to Circle. Once, someone dared me to drink the whole carafe, and while it was easy to gulp down, the brain freeze afterward was not fun. (The morning after wasn't fun, either.)

Serves 2

3 shots soju, chilled

3 (2.7-ounce/80 ml) containers Yakult or another brand of yogurt drink, chilled

Sprite or 7UP, chilled

In a small carafe, add the soju and yogurt drink.

Top with Sprite or 7UP.

Place the carafe in a larger container filled with ice in order to keep it cool. Pour into shot glasses and serve.

Fruit Plate
水果拼盘

In many a Chinese restaurant, especially the ones with a giant round table and a lazy Susan, a meal will always end with dessert and fruit. More often than not, you'll get orange or watermelon slices, which the table finishes off with the last sips of tea. Honestly, this might be why Circle served a fruit plate with every bottle order. When I first went to Circle, I almost laughed when the platter of oranges, strawberries, and melons showed up, complete with toothpicks to help pick up the pieces. But when girls would drop by for a drink, I'd see them nibble at a strawberry or grab an orange slice. And then I realized why the fruit works—sure, it's not as fulfilling as fries, but hey, if something is going to make you feel better about a night out drinking, it's probably going to be something "healthy" like honeydew. So, serve one at your next party, along with alcohol and good drunken times, and think to yourself, *This makes up for my debauchery tonight!*

Serves
2 to 4

1 banana, peeled and cut into ¼-inch (6 mm) thick slices

1 orange, cut into 8 wedges

10 grapes, individually skewered on tasseled toothpicks

1 kiwi, peeled and cut into ¼-inch (6 mm) thick slices

You can arrange your fruit plate whatever way you want, but here's one method:

On a white plate, arrange the banana slices in a circular pyramid.

Place the orange slices flesh side down around the banana pyramid.

Place the grapes in between the gaps of the bananas and oranges, saving one to top off the banana pyramid as a final flourish.

Place the kiwi slices around everything.

Rediscovering
Xi'an

LEFT: A BEDROOM IN MY GRANDMOTHER'S HOME. **ABOVE:** A SPREAD OF FRESH NOODLES, READY TO BE COOKED AT MY GRANDFATHER'S HOME IN XI'AN.

A SELLER OF TCHOTCHKES AT XI CANG MARKET, THE STREET MARKET WHERE MY GRANDFATHER SHOPS FOR GROCERIES AND BARGAINS FOR DEALS.

SEVENTEEN YEARS IS A REALLY LONG TIME, BUT I DIDN'T REALIZE IT UNTIL THE FIRST TIME I RETURNED TO CHINA. The Xi'an I left at eight years old was a barren, dusty place; the Xi'an I found at twenty-five years old was a burgeoning metropolis. While my family and I were busy trying to pay our bills, make progress on my student loans, and build up the XFF empire, the city was also growing and transforming.

Let's just start with the drive from the airport. What I remembered as a boring, flat drive through farmlands (dotted with—exciting!—old ancient graves[1]) has become one filled with skyscrapers, apartment complexes, and cranes on cranes on cranes. The previously empty area surrounding the Giant Wild Goose Pagoda is now filled with Vegas-worthy fountains with nightly light shows and glistening new Tang dynasty–inspired buildings. There's a mall, a Starbucks Reserve, a KFC, and a Burger King. There's even an Aston Martin dealership in one corner of the plaza.

Then, there's the old city center. The buildings still show their age, but what used to be a pedestrian-centric, slightly run-down neighborhood has turned into the Times Square of Xi'an, full of blinking neon lights, tourists crowding the sidewalks, and honking scooters and cars. The old Xi Cang street market my grandfather shops at has become so crowded with visitors, you spend peak hours barely walking, just shuffling by stalls, stuck behind students on scooters who dare to enter the crowd. It's gotten so bad, my grandfather only goes early in the mornings to get his groceries.

When I first went back, I immediately tried to seek out the familiar: lamb skewers. But everywhere I looked, street stands were selling deep-fried scorpions and potato slices, touristy fare popular in any major

1   As a kid, I spent those trips to the airport imagining the lives of the important people buried in those graves.

Chinese city. The burgers, grilled skewers, and liang pi stands were all gone, replaced by stalls with giant hunks of meat forced onto twigs, sold by a man hacking away at a lamb sesame liang pi has been around for a while, but customers seem to be expecting this version more often than the one I love. The toppings can also get suspiciously modern-

I had this image of China, frozen in time for seventeen years, but I've come to terms with the fact that the Xi'an I knew is gone.

carcass strung up for the show of it. Walking down the main drag of the Muslim Quarter, I felt displaced, in a different city altogether.

I had this image of China, frozen in time for seventeen years, but I've come to terms with the fact that the Xi'an I knew is gone. Every trip back, I see a new, more efficient, automated way to make liang pi, another Instagram-friendly shop, another fusion version of a traditional dish. Things are changing and keep changing, so quickly. Just this past trip, I went to a cheese tea[2] place twice in one week—and the second time, there was a brand-new digital screen announcing orders. This was in a span of a few days.

It's not just because of modernization; tastes have changed, too. Take liang pi. When I was younger, liang pi was more commonly dressed with a basic combination of vinegar and salt, served in little street carts in plastic bags meticulously wrapped around bowls. But as time has gone by, more stores around the Muslim Quarter have started serving liang pi in a sweet, savory sesame paste, a version less sour and more rich. Don't get me wrong;

ized. During a recent trip, I saw one particular chain known for liang pi prominently pushing the slick noodles with broccoli. *What the hell*, I thought. *So weird.*

One favorite from my childhood is still around, though. Decades ago, three brothers opened up three competing soup dumpling shops, one next to another on a main road in the Muslim Quarter. My family and friends would debate about which one was better, and now, all these years later, only one is left standing: the third brother, with his Sichuan-spiced lamb dumplings, sauced with a light vinegar, delicate and meaty and tingly all at once.[3]

The space has expanded from one tiny store to a multilevel restaurant, but everything else is the same. The photos on the wall are the ones I looked up at as a kid, and the service is as old-school as it gets. Order at the counter, get a piece of paper, and the servers will run around checking off plates that have already been delivered. The hustle, the grind, everyone yelling loudly for more vinegar—it's like being transported in time.

---

2   A sweet, cold tea topped with a thick, cream cheese–based froth. It's surprisingly good, like a light fluffy creamy tea with a tiny bite (think of pairing cheesecake with black tea and you might get it).

3   Glad to say I won that round; the third brother was always my favorite.

I'll stumble upon moments like this every now and then. I might be wandering around the side streets of the Muslim Quarter and see dangerously thin metal skewers of lamb (albeit over a gas grill instead of charcoal). Or I might see a line forming outside a shop that only sells the daily bread of Xi'an, the bakers there masters of their craft. One day, when we were driving out through the villages to visit my ancestors' grave, we stopped through a small town in Qin Zhen (秦镇). Hungry, we walked into a random joint and ordered a bowl of liang pi. I immediately realized it was a version of what we made in our stores—handmade, cut with a giant two-handled rocking knife, seasoned with vinegar and salt. The purveyor finished off the dish by dipping a single strand of liang pi into chili oil and mixing that piece in with the rest of the noodles. It was just like the old times, the final dish served in a plastic bag–covered bowl so you have the option to take the bag to go without even getting the serving dish dirty.[4]

I've found that these moments are more prevalent outside of the city, near the countryside. So while this chapter does have some popular renditions of our standard fare (like sesame liang pi, page 247) and classics I overlooked as a kid (like a starchy, spicy breakfast soup, page 236), it also includes old-school homey meals with roots in farm cooking. These dishes were made to be enjoyed by commoners from ancient times until now. Some were created during wartime, some during times of famine. In most cases, they were masterminded out of desperation and innovation, with the drive to cook something comforting, something delicious even while lacking precious resources. Which, when you look at the rest of this book, sounds strangely familiar, right?

It was just like the old times, the final dish served in a plastic bag–covered bowl so you have the option to take the bag to go without even getting the serving dish dirty.

4   I've learned that this town was the birth home to my liang pi dish.

ONE OF THE MANY STREET STALLS IN THE MUSLIM QUARTER SELLING VARIOUS RICE CAKES.

THE HISTORIC BELL TOWER IN CENTRAL XI'AN, CHINA.

The No-Frills Guide to Xi'an as a Tourist

I SPEND THE MAJORITY OF MY TRIPS HOME EATING AND HANGING OUT WITH FAMILY, BUT EVERY NOW AND THEN I GET ASKED ABOUT THE MUST-SEE SPOTS AROUND TOWN (AND THE MUST-EAT DISHES). The problem is that Xi'an has a long history—it was the home of thirteen dynasties. There are countless historical sites to visit, and, as for the restaurants, well, places change as soon as you book a flight.

For those with limited time, though, these are eight spots that you should prioritize. You'll get a glimpse of the old city *and* the new city and eat many, many bowls of noodles.

XI'AN BELL TOWER AND DRUM TOWER | 西安钟鼓楼

In the old days, the Bell Tower in the heart of the old city marked the rise of dawn, when a large bell would be struck to welcome a new day. The Drum Tower, facing the Bell Tower, held a drum that was struck during sunset. While these daily traditions are no more, the two towers are still prominent landmarks in Xi'an, referenced by locals to specify location or directions in the city. Visitors can climb to the top of the towers for panoramic views; my favorite is from the top of the Bell Tower.

XI'AN CITY WALLS | 西安古城墙

First constructed during the Ming dynasty, the old Xi'an city walls are six-hundred-year-old, 8½-mile-long (13.74 km) long relics of my hometown's history. As one of the oldest, most complete walls in China, it's a prime spot for tourist photos, but the views are worth the crowds. The best time to visit, in my opinion, is at sunset.

THE MUSLIM QUARTER | 回民街

It's no surprise that this area is on my list. Not only is this central neighborhood historically significant, but it was also my favorite place to eat as a kid. The blocks are densely packed with vendors serving all sorts of snacks and crafts. A few notable items: sesame liang pi, with a heavy, nutty sesame paste; soft, orange persimmon cakes with a sweet syrup filling; yellow-green mung bean pastries with a powdery bite; and steamed *jing gao* rice cakes, or "mirror cakes," covered with sugar and other toppings of your choice. You should also find a pao-mo soup stand, where you'll have to break up the bread yourself before getting your bowl of broth, and make a stop at Jia San's Soup Dumplings (贾三灌汤包子) for the steamed lamb soup dumplings I grew up eating. The skewers of my childhood are no longer around, but you can still find similar ones, served on thin metal sticks, if you look hard enough. (Avoid the ones that use twigs or branches; those tend to be tourist traps.)

SHAANXI HISTORY MUSEUM | 陕西历史博物馆

This is one of the most important history museums in China, if not the world, with a collection that dates from prehistoric times to the nineteenth century. I went here often as a kid and would dream of digging up ancient gold coins in my grandmother's garden as a result of those visits. Not to brag, but locals often say that just one of the 370,000 artifacts in this institution would have enough clout to merit its own special exhibit at the Metropolitan Museum of Art.

DACI'EN TEMPLE AND THE GIANT WILD GOOSE PAGODA | 大慈恩寺/大雁塔

The area around the pagoda is now a bustling city center, surrounded by stores and malls and colorful lights, but at the heart of it all is the Daci'en Temple, a Buddhist temple built in the Tang Dynasty in 648 CE. The Great Goose Pagoda, a World Heritage Site, was built shortly afterward to house sutras and relics brought back from India, artifacts gathered by Xuanzang, a famous Chinese monk and traveler. In addition to the modernized tourist attractions (like the nightly fountain), a climb up the stairs of the pagoda will also reward you with overhead views of the city from the south.

TERRA-COTTA SOLDIERS OF THE FIRST EMPEROR OF CHINA | 秦始皇兵马俑

Sometimes referred to as the eighth wonder of the world, this collection of life-sized terra-cotta soldier statues was discovered in the burial ground of Qin Shi Huang, the first emperor of China. Each statue is unique, with its own hairstyle, facial expression, uniform, and gear. The soldiers were meant to serve the emperor in the afterlife, alongside terra-cotta chariots, horses, and weapons. Currently there are three pits excavated, but many parts of the mausoleum are still protected for fear that the air will disintegrate the works. Still, seeing six thousand unique statues assembled in one pit is definitely worth the two-hour drive from the city.

MOUNT HUA | 华山

Out of the five famous mountains of China, Mount Hua is the westernmost peak, with a height of 7,070 feet (2,154.9 meters). Known as a mystical and spiritual place, the mountain has precipitous drops, making it both beautiful and dangerous. I'm afraid of heights, so I've never dared to hike it, but don't let me stop you.

YONG XING FANG | 永兴坊

While there has been a push to modernize the city, there has also been an effort to preserve our history. This square just inside the eastern gate of the city walls is one of the latter efforts. The food center, meant to re-create the look and feel of a small historical village, houses shops and stalls dedicated to serving Shaanxi delicacies. It's here you might find traditional versions of Mt. Qi Pork Noodles (岐山臊子面) and Biang-Biang noodles, as well as more obscure dishes like cold buckwheat noodles dressed in vinegar and mustard oil (荞面凉饸饹), liang pi–like Qin Zhen–style rice "mipi" cold noodles (秦镇米皮), and Shanbei *jianbing* (陕北煎饼), made with spongey buckwheat crepes. You can also take part in the spectacle of drinking some light wine that's "so good that it'll make you smash your bowl." Literally, you're supposed to drink the wine and smash the bowl once you're done.

ABOVE: ME AT MY HAPPIEST, AFTER A FEW LAMB SOUP DUMPLINGS AT JIA SAN'S SOUP DUMPLINGS. **RIGHT:** THE CROWDED STREETS IN THE MUSLIM QUARTER IN XI'AN.

THE KITCHEN IN MY GRANDFATHER'S HOME IN XI'AN, CHINA.

What Exactly Does "Authentic" Mean Halfway Around the World?

I'LL OCCASIONALLY GET IRATE MESSAGES TELLING ME THAT THE MENU AT XI'AN FAMOUS FOODS IS NOT "AUTHENTIC." If I'm being completely honest, those commenters are both right and wrong.

In Xi'an, China, there's no such thing as spicy cumin lamb noodles, just like there's no version of our lamb burgers. There's spicy cumin lamb. There are noodles. There are burgers. But those combinations? They don't exist. I've checked my sources.

The dishes at Xi'an Famous Foods might not be what purists call "authentic." We put cilantro in the liang pi and stir-fried it, stuffed lamb meat into bread, and just straight-up invented Mt. Qi Vegetables. So when I see other restaurants serving lamb noodles and calling it authentic food from Xi'an, I think, *No, dude, that's not Xi'an food.* Spicy cumin lamb is authentic Xi'an food. Hand-pulled noodles are authentically Xi'an. Combined? That shit's straight-up OG XFF.

MY UNCLE MADE THESE PRETZELS WHEN I WENT TO GO VISIT MY GRANDFATHER, AND WE SNACKED ON THEM WHILE CHATTING AROUND THE DINNER TABLE WITH MY FAMILY.

What *does* make our food authentic is this: My family has lived in Xi'an for generations. We grew up eating Xi'an food. And this is the food that we crave.

How we got here, though, is important. We mastered the meats, the noodles, the balance of sour and salty, the elements of our hometown cuisine. And then, once we learned those rules, we broke them—respectfully, of course.

The same thing is happening in Xi'an, too. Mixing broccoli instead of bean sprouts into a classic bowl of liang pi is not traditional by any means, but it sells. And in some ways, the distance between China and New York City has isolated XFF, letting us preserve the food of the past in small ways. In Xi'an today, shops are turning to fully automated, machine-made, and machine-cut liang pi. I don't blame them; it's more economical. But we haven't been privy to those technological advances at XFF, so watching our liang pi process is a little like looking into a time vortex. We're still watching and checking the liang pi every step of the way, dressing it in sour vinegar instead of sesame sauce. It's a strange mixed-up world, where the food I used to have in Xi'an is now almost everywhere in New York, but back in Xi'an, it's transformed completely.

I'd call this a confession, but to be honest we haven't tried to hide it. This is what my family would choose to eat, over and over, above all else. Meats stewed until tender, falling off the bone, with a star anise kick and a dash of chili oil. Small pieces of lamb dusted with cumin, tossed with chewy, dense noodles. It's the premise that started it all: My dad missed the food of his home and started playing around in the kitchen. He liked what he made, started eating it all the time, and then started serving it, too. That, to me, is authentic.

Spinach Cakes
菜疙瘩

My older relatives from the countryside oftentimes whip up this snack for something quick and savory to tide them over until dinner. The ingredients in the cakes are surprisingly simple, with spinach taking the top notes of every bite and an earthy corn undertone throughout. The complicated part, it turns out, is in the vinegar-rich dipping sauce, which adds a tangy and spicy flourish. The sauce might feel like a surprising accompaniment to the mild steamed vegetable cakes, but it's what keeps you going back for more.

Serves 2
as an
appetizer

FOR THE CAKES:
7 ounces (200 g) spinach, coarsely chopped into ½-inch (12 mm) pieces

⅛ teaspoon baking soda

¼ teaspoon salt

¼ cup (30 g) all-purpose flour

¼ cup (30 g) cornmeal

FOR THE DIPPING SAUCE:
½-inch (12 mm) piece fresh ginger, peeled and finely chopped

2 garlic cloves, peeled and chopped

⅓ green onion, trimmed and diced

2 teaspoons Red Chili Powder (page 35)

1 teaspoon Roasted Sesame Seeds (page 34)

¼ cup (60 ml) vegetable oil

1 teaspoon Sichuan peppercorns

3 tablespoons (45 ml) black vinegar

⅛ teaspoon salt

¼ teaspoon sugar

1 tablespoon soy sauce

TOOLS:
Steamer

Cheesecloth

To make the cakes: In a large bowl, combine the spinach with the baking soda and salt. Squeeze the mixture with your hands repeatedly for 5 to 6 minutes, until the spinach releases all of its juice. Set aside the slightly dehydrated spinach pulp and reserve the spinach juice separately.

In another bowl, add the all-purpose flour and cornmeal. Mix in the spinach pulp. Gradually, a little bit at a time, add the reserved spinach juice, mixing with your hands until you form a loose, rough, clumpy "dough." You might not use all the liquid.

Add plenty of water to the bottom of a steamer pot. Line the bottom of one stack with a damp cheesecloth. Place the "dough" on the cheesecloth, wet your fingers, and use your fingers to flatten the "dough" into a rectangular cake, roughly 4 by 5 inches (10 cm by 12 cm) wide, 1 inch (2.5 cm) in height. The neater the cake, the easier it will be to cut later on. Cover the steamer pot and bring to a boil over high heat. Steam for 15 minutes.

Carefully remove the cake from the steamer and set aside to cool. Once cooled, cut into 1-inch (2.5 cm) cubes.

To make the sauce: In a small heat-safe bowl, add the ginger, garlic, green onion, chili powder, and sesame seeds. Mix to combine.

In a small skillet, heat the vegetable oil over low heat. Add the Sichuan peppercorns to the oil and cook until fragrant, about 1 minute.

Carefully remove the peppercorns from the oil with a slotted spoon and discard. Continue heating the peppercorn-infused oil until it just starts to shimmer but before it smokes, then quickly but carefully pour the oil into the bowl with the spices. Stir to combine.

Add the black vinegar, salt, sugar, soy sauce, and 1 tablespoon water. Stir to combine and serve alongside the cakes for dipping.

Hoolah Soup
糊辣汤

I definitely underrated this breakfast soup when I was a kid. In my defense, though, my only encounter with hoolah soup was at school. Every morning, we'd bring in little metal bowls from home and fill those bowls with a scoop of this starchy slop for breakfast. I rarely finished my meal, scrambling to eat as quickly as possible before tossing my bowl into my lunch bag, the metal still dripping with the remnants of the soup.

I'm a grown man now, though, and I've realized the error of my ways. The first time I went back to Xi'an, I had a vague memory of this breakfast soup, so I ordered myself a bowl at a stand one morning. It's not exactly an enticing-looking soup with a broth that's slightly translucent, starchy, and thick. But I took one bite and realized there's so much more to this than meets the eye. The recipe's heartiness comes from the potatoes, but the soup is also filled with meatballs, carrots, and cabbage. After several mouthfuls, you start feeling numb thanks to the Sichuan peppercorns, but a splash of chili oil easily wakes up your palate. Throw some of our bread (page 46) or "pretzels" (page 259) in if you'd like, shovel the rest into your mouth, and you might have what you need to start off your day. That first morning I tried it, I ended up eating three whole bowls. True story.

Serves
6 to 8

FOR THE BROTH:

7 ounces (200 g) beef soup bones (femur), cracked to allow the marrow to escape

9 ounces (260 g) beef chuck

1 teaspoon Sichuan peppercorns

4 (1-inch/2.5 cm) cinnamon sticks

5 star anise pods

¼ teaspoon dried thyme

3 black cardamom pods, cracked

FOR THE BEEF BALLS:

9 ounces (255 g) ground beef chuck

½-inch (1.25 cm) piece fresh ginger, peeled and finely chopped

1 tablespoon finely chopped white onion

½ teaspoon salt

1 teaspoon Chinese five-spice powder

4 teaspoons cornstarch, plus more for sprinkling

2 teaspoons Shaoxing cooking wine

1 egg white

FOR SERVING:

1 large yellow potato, peeled, cut into ⅜-inch (1 cm) cubes

1 small zucchini, cut into ⅜-inch (1 cm) cubes

½ medium carrot, peeled and cut into ⅜-inch (1 cm) cubes

½ small green cabbage, cut into 1-inch (2.5 cm) pieces

½ cup (100 g) string beans, cut into ½-inch (12 mm) segments

¾ cup (75 g) cubed cauliflower (½-inch/12 mm cubes)

1¾ ounces (50 g) wood ear mushrooms, hydrated in warm water, drained, and cut into 1-inch (2.5 cm) pieces

½ cup (40 g) cornstarch mixed with ½ cup (120 ml) water, to create a slurry

2 teaspoons Sichuan peppercorn powder

2 teaspoons white pepper powder

2 teaspoons salt

3 stalks green garlic, white sections only, diced

Black vinegar

XFF Chili Oil (page 40)

To make the broth: Rinse off the beef bones and chuck and add to a large pot. Submerge the bones and chuck in cold water. Let soak for 1 hour to get rid of impurities.

After soaking, remove the meat to a bowl, dump out the water, then add the meat back to the cleaned pot. Fill the pot with 3½ quarts (3.3 L) cold water to cover the meat, and add the remaining broth ingredients.

Cover the pot and bring to a boil over high heat. Once boiling, turn the heat down to a simmer. Cook for 2 hours, occasionally skimming off the impurities that rise to the top of the pot with a ladle.

After 2 hours, carefully strain the soup into a heat-safe container, keeping only the liquid. This broth can be kept refrigerated in an airtight container for up to 1 week, frozen for 1 month.

To make the beef balls: Place the ground beef in a large bowl together with the ginger, onion, salt, Chinese five-spice powder, cornstarch, cooking wine, egg white, and 2 tablespoons water. Use your hands to evenly combine.

Note: Grab and throw a chunk of the mixture against the side of the bowl every so often. This helps with cohesion, making sure it all sticks together.

Sprinkle a large plate with extra cornstarch. Take a small piece of the meat, about ⅓ ounce (8.5 g), to form a small meatball, about ¾ inch (2 cm) in diameter, and place on the prepared plate. You should be able to make 50 to 60 meatballs.

To serve: In a clean pot, add the reserved broth and bring to a boil, covered, over high heat.

Carefully add the beef balls one at a time, gently stirring to prevent sticking.

When the broth starts boiling again, add the potato, zucchini, carrots, cabbage, string beans, cauliflower, and mushrooms. Bring the soup back to a boil once more.

Slowly stir in the starch slurry so that it thickens the soup. Add the Sichuan peppercorn powder, white pepper powder, and salt and stir to combine.

Divide the soup into bowls and top with the green garlic, black vinegar, and chili oil to taste.

XFF

Beef Xiao Chao Pao-Mo Soup
牛肉泡馍小炒

In my earliest years in Xi'an, back when I wasn't big on food and all that, my grandfather would make me lamb pao-mo soup (page 161) every day for lunch. I hated it. I would sit there not eating until the soup congealed and the bread got mushy, and pray that I could sneak away unnoticed for an extra fifteen minutes of playtime.

Once I moved to the States, though, the soup became a signifier of home—it was my version of chicken noodle soup. Today in Xi'an, they've made a few updates, and the modern version is less lamb-forward, more spice-centric. Swapping beef for lamb gives the soup a less gamey aroma, allowing the chili powder and Sichuan peppercorn to shine, while tomatoes add a hint of acid and sweetness. I like to think if I were a kid in Xi'an today, I'd love having this for lunch with my grandpa.

Serves
4

FOR THE PAO-MO BREAD:

3 cups (375 g) all-purpose flour

¼ teaspoon active dry yeast

1 cup (240 ml) cold water

FOR THE SOUP:

1 pound (455 g) beef loin or strip

6 cups (1.4 L) unsalted beef broth or Bone Broth (page 42), divided

2 green onions, trimmed and chopped

3-inch (7.5 cm) piece fresh ginger, peeled and sliced

1 garlic clove, peeled and chopped

2 teaspoons Sichuan peppercorns

1 tablespoon fennel seeds

¼ cup (60 ml) vegetable oil

2 stalks green garlic, diagonally sliced

2 tablespoons Red Chili Powder (page 35)

8-ounce package (225 g) dougan (dried tofu) cut into ½-inch by 2-inch (12 mm by 5 cm) strips

⅓ cup (about 70 g) dried lily flowers (found in the dried ingredients section of Chinese supermarkets), hydrated in warm water for 30 minutes and drained

16 wood ear mushrooms, hydrated in warm water for 30 minutes and coarsely chopped

½ large tomato, roughly chopped

4 baby bok choy, roughly sliced

2 tablespoons black vinegar

4 ounces (110 g) thin dry mung bean noodles, hydrated in warm water for 10 minutes

2 large eggs, beaten

Salt

TOOLS:

Cheesecloth or coffee filter

Twine

XFF

To make the bread: Follow the directions in Lamb Pao-Mo Soup on page 161.

To make the soup: Break the bread into ¼-inch (6 mm) pieces by hand. Set aside.

Add the beef to a large pot and submerge in cold water. Let sit for 1 hour to remove impurities.

Remove the beef from the water and cut into 1-inch (2.5 cm) cubes. Discard the soaking water.

Heat a wok or flat-bottomed pan over medium-high. Carefully place the beef into the wok or flat pan and cook without oil over medium heat, constantly stirring to keep it from sticking and to reduce the liquid. Cook until the outsides are seared.

Meanwhile, in a separate pot, bring 2 cups (480 ml) of the broth to a boil. Keep it simmering over low heat on the stovetop.

Add the green onions, ginger, and garlic to the pan with the beef and cook until the green onions and ginger are tender and fragrant, about 1 minute.

Ladle the hot beef broth into the pan to just cover the beef.

Place the Sichuan peppercorns and fennel seeds in a cheesecloth or a coffee filter and tie it up to create a spice bag. Add to the pan of beef and bring to a boil over high heat.

Turn the heat down and simmer for about 40 minutes, reducing the mixture until the stock evaporates. Remove from the heat and set aside.

In a large pan or a wok, heat the vegetable oil over medium-low heat. Add the green garlic and cook until tender and fragrant, about 2 minutes.

Add the chili powder, stirring to combine, and cook for 30 seconds more.

Add the dougan, lily flowers, and mushrooms. Stir to combine, and follow up with the tomato, bok choy, and vinegar.

Stir in the reserved beef and the remaining 4 cups (960 ml) beef broth. Turn the heat up to medium-high and bring the broth to a boil.

Add the mung bean noodles and as many of the reserved bread pieces as you desire.

Pour in the beaten eggs and cook until all the ingredients are cooked through. Leave as is and enjoy as a soup, or reduce the liquid by a third or more for a stew-like consistency. Season with salt and serve.

Little "Fish" in Celery Broth
浆水鱼鱼

This dish is a little difficult to make, but so refreshing in the summer. Served cool or lukewarm, its bright, celery bite is almost gazpacho-like. The "fish" in this soup aren't really fish, but actually tiny, slippery morsels of dough, much like Western-style dumplings or spaetzle (but cooked in reverse). These "QQ" mouthfuls are then dropped into a fermented celery broth, sharp, with a touch of sour vinegar. Think of it like savory lemonade. It might sound weird, but hey, I thought Bloody Marys were weird when I first saw them, too.

Serves
2

FOR THE FERMENTED CELERY:

1 tablespoon all-purpose flour

3¼ cups (780 ml) cold water

2 stalks Chinese celery, cut into 2-inch (5 cm) segments

2 teaspoons white vinegar

FOR THE "FISH":

1 cup (125 g) yellow cornmeal

2 tablespoons cornstarch

1 teaspoon salt

FOR SERVING:

4 teaspoons vegetable oil, divided

2 dried red chile peppers, cut into ⅛-inch (3 mm) segments

⅓ green onion, trimmed and chopped

1 garlic clove, peeled and sliced

½ teaspoon salt, divided

½ bunch Chinese chives, cut into ¼-inch (6 mm) segments

XFF Chili Oil (page 40)

TOOL:

Paper or plastic cup with ¼-inch (6 mm) holes on the bottom, or a dried gourd shell with holes drilled into it

Thermometer

To make the fermented celery: In a large bowl, stir together the flour and cold water.

In a large pot set over high heat, add 6 cups (1.4 L) water, cover, and bring to a boil. Once boiling, turn the heat down to medium. Add the flour mixture from the previous step and keep stirring with a spatula or ladle to avoid lumping and burning.

Once the liquid comes back to a boil, turn off the heat. Put the contents of the pot into a heat-safe container and let cool for 1 to 2 hours, until the temperature drops to 90 to 100°F (40 to 45°C).

Prepare a bowl of ice water. Bring a small pot of water to boil over high heat. Once boiling, add the celery and cook for 30 seconds. Immediately remove the celery to the bowl of ice water to stop the cooking process.

Once cooled, transfer the celery with a slotted spoon to the container of water and flour, along with the white vinegar. Cover the top of the container with plastic wrap and poke a few holes in the plastic wrap to allow gas to escape. Place the container in a shady but well-ventilated spot and allow it to sit for 1 day at room temperature (about 70°F/21°C).

After 1 day, use a clean, sanitized utensil to stir the celery around in the liquid. Cover the container and allow to sit and ferment for 2 to 3 more days, stirring the celery once each day.

In 2 to 3 days, the celery should turn yellow and the broth should be sour. Watch carefully; if there's any foam, the celery has spoiled and should not be consumed. Once done fermenting, use immediately.

To make the "fish": Once the celery is ready to use, prepare the "fish" by combining the cornmeal, cornstarch, and salt in a large bowl. Add 1½ cups (355 ml) water to the cornmeal and cornstarch mixture so it forms a thick batter, slightly thinner than polenta.

In a pot, add 2 cups (473 ml) water and bring to a boil over high heat. Once boiling, slowly add the cornmeal mixture, stirring continuously with a spatula. Once the liquid starts boiling again, turn the heat down to low and cook for 4 to 5 more minutes, stirring constantly to prevent burning. At this point, the mixture should be fragrant with the corn. Remove the pot from the heat.

Fill a bowl with ice and cold water. Hold the cup with holes in the bottom over the bowl while you use a ladle to scoop the "fish" mixture into the cup. Once the mixture moves through the holes in the cup and hits the water, it should solidify and look like little fish. You can store the fish in the water for up to 30 minutes. For longer storage (up to 1 day in the refrigerator), drain and transfer the "fish" to a dry container.

To serve: Remove the fermented celery, reserving the liquid. Drain well, and cut into ¼-inch (6 mm) pieces.

In a large saucepan, heat 2 teaspoons of the vegetable oil over medium heat. Add the dried chiles, green onion, and garlic and cook until fragrant.

Add ¼ teaspoon of the salt. Add the fermented celery and 4 cups (960 ml) of the fermented celery liquid and bring to a boil. Turn off the heat and set aside.

In a small skillet, heat the remaining 2 teaspoons vegetable oil over medium heat. Add the chives and cook for 1 minute, until wilted and fragrant. Stir in the remaining ¼ teaspoon salt. Turn off the heat and set aside. Cool, covered, in the fridge if you wish to enjoy the broth at a lower temperature.

Divide the fish into two bowls. Evenly pour the celery broth into the bowls and top with the cooked chives and chili oil to taste.

Spicy and Sour Mung Bean Jelly
绿豆凉粉

Mung bean jelly is a typical snack all over China, especially during the summer. I like to make a big batch of the jelly, store it in my fridge, and cut out pieces for a refreshing bite on hot days, dressing the cool gelatinous slivers in our signature spices and chili oil. It's what I would consider junk food, except tastier than a bag of Doritos (there, I said it). It's also messier, since the jelly is super slick and easily dropped into stain-making sauces, so be careful with your chopsticks.

Serves
7 or 8 as an
appetizer

1 cup (about 130 g) mung bean starch

2 tablespoons soy sauce

1 tablespoon black vinegar

¾ teaspoon salt

1 tablespoon sugar

1 longhorn pepper, diagonally sliced into slivers

3 garlic cloves, peeled and sliced

1 tablespoon XFF Chili Oil without seeds (page 40)

1 tablespoon XFF Chili Oil seeds (page 40)

In a large pot, add 5 cups (1.2 L) water, cover, and bring to a boil. Turn the heat down to a simmer.

In a small bowl, add the mung bean starch and 1 cup (240 ml) water and stir to combine.

Slowly pour the mung bean mixture into the simmering water, stirring gently with a ladle while pouring. Continue to stir until the mixture in the pot starts to thicken and small bubbles start forming. It should start turning somewhat translucent. Cook for another 6 to 8 minutes while stirring, then carefully transfer the mixture to a rectangular baking dish, just large enough to hold the mixture snugly but small enough so that the mixture is at least 2 inches (5 cm) thick. Allow to cool at room temperature for 7 to 8 hours, until solidified. At this point, you can store the jelly in the refrigerator, covered, for up to 2 days.

Mix the soy sauce, vinegar, 1 tablespoon water, the salt, sugar, longhorn pepper, garlic, chili oil, and chili oil seeds together to create a sauce.

Place the solid mung bean jelly block onto a cutting board. Cut into slivers, roughly ½ inch by ½ inch by 2½ inches (1.25 cm x 1.25 cm x 6.35 cm) long. Transfer to a bowl, top with the sauce, and serve immediately.

XFF

Five Nuts and Seeds "Chowder"
五仁油茶

When I was growing up, I didn't really think of this as a soup. Instead, it was a savory breakfast porridge, a Chinese oatmeal if you will. The thick chowder was always sold to me as something that's "good for you"—and upon further inspection, I can see why my mom would say that. The base of the chowder includes ingredients like ground walnuts and sesame seeds, rich in textures and flavors. Naturally, this was my mother's favorite dish when I was a kid, particularly because you could basically "meal prep" this (before "meal prep" became a thing). Make the powerful, nutty mix ahead, store it in the fridge, and when you need a quick and filling bite, stir in boiling water until a creamy soup is formed. I like to serve this with the West Fu "Pretzels" (page 259) or some pieces of Daily Bread (page 46).

Serves
3

2 tablespoons walnuts, crushed

2 tablespoons blanched almonds, cut in half

2 tablespoons pine nuts or melon seeds

2 tablespoons black sesame seeds

2 tablespoons white sesame seeds

3 cups (375 g) all-purpose flour

1 tablespoon salt

¼ teaspoon Sichuan peppercorn powder

¼ teaspoon Chinese five-spice powder

TOOL:
Mortar and pestle

Heat a medium skillet over low heat, then add the walnuts, almonds, and pine nuts. Roast for 2 minutes.

Then add the black and white sesame seeds and roast for an additional 2 minutes, stirring occasionally. Set aside to cool.

Crush the seeds and nuts with a mortar and pestle and set aside.

Set a clean medium skillet over low heat and add the flour. Stirring constantly to prevent burning, cook until the flour turns lightly golden (like a roux) and fragrant, 40 to 50 minutes. This low-and-slow toasting gently coaxes out the maximum amount of flavor from the flour. If you need to speed this up, you can cook for 30 minutes over medium heat, but be wary of burning. Remove from the heat, and keep stirring while adding the salt, Sichuan peppercorn powder, and Chinese five-spice powder.

Add the reserved nuts and seeds mixture. Stir to combine. This can be stored, cooled and refrigerated, in a closed container for up to 2 weeks.

To serve, divide the mixture among three bowls. Bring a pot of water to a boil. Add ⅓ cup (75 ml) room temperature or slightly cool water to each bowl, stirring to evenly combine, and then add 1½ cups (350 ml) boiling water to each bowl, stirring until there are no lumps. Serve.

Sesame Liang Pi "Cold Skin Noodles"
麻酱凉皮

When it comes to liang pi, I still prefer the old-school vinegar-salt mix, followed by a decent spoonful of our chili oil (page 40). But I've started to appreciate the sesame version as well—not only because it's tasty, but also because it's easier to make (see the next page for a photograph). With this dish, there's no washing of the dough to get the gluten out, no seitan making. Instead, the liang pi here is softer, not quite as chewy, with a rounder bite to pair with this slick, nutty sesame dressing.

Serves 2

---

2 cups (250 g) all-purpose flour

1 teaspoon salt

Vegetable oil for brushing

¼ cup (60 ml) sesame paste

½ cup (120 ml) XFF Liang Pi Sauce (page 44)

2 small Persian or spiny cucumbers, cut diagonally into slivers

2 teaspoons Garlic Puree (page 37)

XFF Chili Oil with seeds (page 40)

TOOLS:

Double-stack steamer pot, at least 12-inch (30.5 cm) diameter capacity

3 deep-dish pans, 9 inches (23 cm) in diameter

Pair of tongs, at least 8 inches (20 cm) long

Brush (for oil)

In a large bowl, add the flour and salt and mix together.

While stirring, gradually add 3 cups (720 ml) water to the flour until it becomes an even mixture with no lumps. Cover with plastic wrap and let sit for 30 minutes in the refrigerator.

In a double-stack steamer set over high heat, add 6 cups (1.4 L) water, cover, and bring to a boil.

Evenly coat one of the deep-dish pans with vegetable oil. Scoop a third of the starchy flour mixture into the pan, making sure it is evenly spread over the bottom.

Place the pan on the lower stack of the steamer pot and cover immediately. Steam for 3 minutes. When bubbles form on a sheet of liang pi, which should now be translucent, it is done.

Prepare an ice bath. With tongs, carefully remove the pan from the steamer and set on top of the ice bath to cool for 1 minute.

Using chopsticks, circle the sides of the liang pi, much like how you would circle the sides of a sunny-side up egg to get it off the pan, and then peel the sheet off with your hands.

Put the cooked liang pi on a flat pan brushed with vegetable oil to prevent sticking and repeat the steaming process with the remainder of the batter. You can store the cooked sheets for up to 4 hours, stacked on top of each other, as long as you brush plenty of oil between each sheet to prevent sticking.

In a small bowl, add the sesame paste along with 10 tablespoons (150 ml) water, stirring in one direction continuously until evenly mixed.

Fold each sheet of liang pi into thirds, then stack the sheets on top of one another. Cut from one side to the other, making ⅜-inch (1 cm) wide ribbons.

Add the liang pi to a bowl, along with the diluted sesame paste, the liang pi sauce, cucumbers, garlic puree, and chili oil to taste. Mix and serve.

A MEAL AT MY FAMILY'S HOUSE IN XI'AN (CLOCKWISE, FROM TOP): HONG SHAO "RED BRAISED" SPARERIBS (PAGE 89), AN ITERATION OF A DISH SIMILAR TO OUR SPINACH CAKES (PAGE 235), HOOLAH SOUP (PAGE 236), HONG SHAO BRAISED STRIPED BASS (PAGE 250), SESAME LIANG PI (PAGE 247).

Hong Shao Braised Striped Bass
红烧鲈鱼

Xi'an is pretty landlocked, so when my family would have fish, it was always a treat, reserved for larger family meals on a weekend. And you bet when we did fish, we did it proper—cooked whole with the head on, bones intact (watch out for those little ones), and the important (tasty) innards left inside. You know, China style. If you can find a fishmonger to do you a solid, you'll have them remove the gallbladder (bitter, gross) but keep the brain (rich in fish oil and flavor), roe (if it's there), and fish swim bladder (a crunchy treat once it's popped). Take extra care to descale the fish, too. If you do this right, the fish skin will be the most flavorful part.

Serves
2

page 60

FOR THE FISH AND MARINADE:

1 striped bass, about 1½ pounds (680 g), cleaned, scaled, and gutted (but ask your fishmonger about those extra tasty bits like the bladder and roe)

2 green onions, trimmed, cut into 2-inch (5 cm) segments, then cut into slivers

2-inch piece (5 cm) fresh ginger, peeled and cut into slivers

1 teaspoon salt

2 tablespoons Shaoxing cooking wine

FOR THE SAUCE:

1½ teaspoons light or regular soy sauce

½ teaspoon dark soy sauce

1½ teaspoons fermented bean curd (see page 141 for usage in hot pot)

1½ teaspoons sugar

½ cup (120 ml) chicken stock

FOR FRYING:

2½ tablespoons cornstarch

4 cups (950 ml) vegetable oil

1 teaspoon Sichuan peppercorns

2 star anise pods

½-inch (12 mm) piece fresh ginger, peeled and sliced

FOR BRAISING:

½ green onion, trimmed and cut into 2-inch (5 cm) segments

½-inch (12 mm) piece fresh ginger, peeled and cut into slivers

2 garlic cloves, peeled and sliced

2 teaspoons black vinegar

2 teaspoons Shaoxing cooking wine

1 teaspoon toasted sesame oil

TOOL:

Digital instant-read thermometer

To make the fish and marinade: Cut two bone-deep slits on each side of the fish.

In a small bowl, combine the remaining ingredients and rub the marinade into each of the slits and inside the stomach.

Place the fish in a container, cover, and refrigerate for 30 minutes.

To make the sauce: Mix the sauce ingredients in a small bowl and set aside.

To fry: Pat the fish dry. Remove the solid aromatics from the fish and coat the fish on all sides with cornstarch.

In a large, deep flat pan set over high heat, heat the vegetable oil to about 260°F (127°C). Turn the heat down to medium and add the Sichuan peppercorns, star anise, and ginger and cook for 3 to 4 minutes, until fragrant.

Carefully remove the solid spices from the oil and raise the heat to high. When the oil reaches 400°F (205°C), gently add the fish and fry on each side for 1 to 2 minutes, until golden brown all over. Remove the fish to a plate.

To braise: Remove all but 1 tablespoon of oil from the pan and heat over medium heat.

Add the green onion, ginger, and garlic and cook for 1 minute, or until fragrant, then add the fish.

Pour the black vinegar and wine over the fish, then the prepared sauce. Turn the heat down to medium-low and cook the fish for 2 minutes.

Flip the fish and cook the other side for another 2 minutes, until the fish is well integrated into the sauce. Remove the fish to a serving plate.

Turn the heat in the pan up to medium-high and reduce the sauce as much as desired. Remove any solid spices. Pour the sauce over the fish and drizzle with sesame oil. Be careful of bones when eating!

Iron Pot Lamb Stew
横山铁锅羊肉

If you're cooking for a group and you want a major photo op, this is your dish. The draw here is the heavy iron pot—both cool-looking and useful at the same time. Its material and weight allow the stew to hold its heat for much longer while keeping the meat tender, making this the best meal for a group on a cold winter night. Serve this stew as a centerpiece dish alongside greens and rice, and watch as your friends hover to take overhead shots. Then spend the rest of the night digging in and chatting over an ice cold beer.

Serves
4

page 60

Note: Traditionally this is served in an iron pot, but if you don't own one (I get it, they're heavy), you can use another heavy-bottomed pot instead.

2 pounds (910 g) lamb shank (bone-in)

2 green onions, trimmed and cut into 2-inch (5 cm) segments

1-inch (2.5 cm) piece fresh ginger, peeled and sliced

1 garlic clove, peeled and chopped

3 dried red chile peppers

2 teaspoons Red Chili Powder (page 35)

1 teaspoon white peppercorns

2 tablespoons Sichuan peppercorns

1 teaspoon dried thyme

½ teaspoon cumin seeds

1 teaspoon fennel seeds

1½ teaspoons salt

1 sprig cilantro, chopped

1 green onion, trimmed and diced

TOOLS:

Iron pot 12 to 16 inches (30.5 to 40.5 cm) in diameter

Cheesecloth or coffee filter

Twine

Cut the lamb into 2-inch (5 cm) square pieces. Discard the bone. Submerge in cold water and soak for at least 20 minutes, preferably 1 hour. Rinse the meat and rub off any excess blood. Discard the water.

In an iron pot or another heavy-bottomed pot, add the meat, submerge in water, and bring to a boil over high heat. Boil for 2 minutes, then remove the meat and discard the water. This helps remove impurities.

Clean the pot and add the lamb along with 6 cups (1.4 L) water.

Add the green onion segments, ginger, garlic, dried chiles, and chili powder.

Place the white peppercorns, Sichuan peppercorns, thyme, cumin seeds, and fennel seeds in a cheesecloth or coffee filter and tie with twine to make a spice bag. Add to the pot. Bring back to a boil.

Once boiling, turn the heat down to a simmer and cook, covered, for 1 hour. Add the salt and stir to combine.

Garnish the stew with cilantro and diced green onion before serving. I recommend bringing the entire pot to the table, as it'll keep the stew warmer for longer.

Steamed Celery Bites
芹菜麦饭

Just take a look at these ingredients and you'll see what I mean when I say "peasant food," or nong jia food. This dish uses a common technique found in more rural areas, where fewer provisions meant utilizing grains in more versatile ways. Chopped celery gets another life when breaded with flour and steamed, and the result is almost like a non-fried, soft "tempura" celery, where the bright peppery flavor gets toned down with mellow cornmeal. Much like other side dishes, like our Spinach Cakes (page 235), the extra zing comes from the sauce—classically garlicky and sour, with a tingle of Sichuan peppercorn. This probably isn't showy enough to be a centerpiece dish, but it's an easy side dish to complement the table and snack on over a few beers.

Serves 4 as an appetizer

FOR THE CELERY:

4 leafy Chinese celery ribs, about 7 ounces (200 g)

1 cup (125 g) all-purpose flour

½ cup (70 g) yellow cornmeal

¼ teaspoon Chinese five-spice powder

FOR THE SAUCE:

¼ cup (60 ml) soy sauce

2 tablespoons black vinegar

1 teaspoon Sichuan peppercorn oil, available at most Chinese grocery stores

2 teaspoons toasted sesame oil

1 tablespoon Garlic Puree (page 37)

½ teaspoon salt

½ teaspoon sugar

FOR SERVING:

1 teaspoon Red Chili Powder (page 35)

1 garlic clove, peeled, smashed with the side of a knife, then diced

2 green onions, trimmed and thinly sliced

6 tablespoons (90 ml) vegetable oil

TOOLS:

Steamer

Cheesecloth

To make the celery: Wash the celery well. Cut into ½-inch (12 mm) segments and set aside in a bowl filled with clean water.

In a medium bowl, mix together the all-purpose flour, cornmeal, and Chinese five-spice powder until evenly incorporated.

Drop the wet celery into the flour mixture and mix with your hands. The flour should stick to the celery pieces.

Fill the steamer pot with water. Line the bottom of one stack with cheesecloth. Put the celery pieces onto the cheesecloth. Any flour that doesn't stick to the celery can be evenly pressed on top.

Cover the steamer and bring to a boil over high heat, then cook for 10 minutes, until the flour is cooked through and the celery is tender. Carefully remove the celery from the steamer and put on a plate to cool.

To make the sauce: In a small bowl, mix together the sauce ingredients.

To serve: Portion the cooled celery into four serving bowls and evenly divide the chili powder, smashed garlic, and green onions among them.

In a small pan set over high heat, heat the vegetable oil until it just begins to simmer but before it begins to smoke.

Carefully pour equal amounts of the hot oil on top of the contents of each bowl. Top each bowl with the sauce and serve.

Steamed Rice-Coated Lamb
粉蒸羊肉

You know me—I like my lamb spicy, grilled, smoky with charcoal. But if you're into something more subtle, this might be your dish. The lamb, mixed with an aromatic oil tinged with ginger, green onions, shallots, and garlic, gets only a light tingle of spice with Sichuan peppercorns. All those flavors, plus the natural juices of the lamb, are then absorbed by crushed rice for a soft, fluffy base. Steamed until tender, the end result resembles the interior of a meat pie—but with Chinese aromatics. This is great served with rice or steamed buns, which can be found in the refrigerated section of Chinese grocery stores.

Serves
4

page 60

FOR THE AROMATIC OIL:

3 tablespoons (45 ml) vegetable oil

1 teaspoon Sichuan peppercorns

1-inch (2.5 cm) piece fresh ginger, peeled and finely diced

¼ shallot, finely chopped

1 green onion, trimmed and finely chopped

2 teaspoons Garlic Puree (page 35)

FOR THE SPICE POWDER:

½ teaspoon dried thyme

1 teaspoon Sichuan peppercorns

1 teaspoon fennel seeds

2 star anise pods

1½-inch (4 cm) cinnamon stick

FOR THE LAMB:

½ cup (92 g) long-grain non-glutinous rice

½ cup (92 g) glutinous rice

1 pound 5 ounces (600 g) boneless lamb leg, with some fat

1½ teaspoons sweet flour sauce

1 teaspoon Pixian bean sauce

1 teaspoon oyster sauce

½ teaspoon soy sauce

1 teaspoon toasted sesame oil

2 tablespoons Shaoxing cooking wine

1 teaspoon XFF Chili Oil (page 40)

½ teaspoon sugar

1 teaspoon Chinese five-spice powder

½ teaspoon white pepper powder

2 teaspoons salt

2 teaspoons cornstarch

TOOLS:

Mortar and pestle or spice grinder

Steamer

Cheesecloth

To make the aromatic oil: In a small skillet, heat the vegetable oil with the Sichuan peppercorns over medium-low heat until the Sichuan peppercorns are fragrant, about 30 seconds, then carefully remove the peppercorns from the oil with a slotted spoon.

Add the ginger, shallot, green onion, and garlic puree to the aromatic oil and cook until fragrant, about 1 minute. Carefully pour the aromatic oil into a heat-safe container and set aside.

To make the spice powder: In a small, clean skillet set over low heat, add the thyme and spices and roast until fragrant (3 to 5 minutes), stirring constantly to avoid burning. Remove the thyme and spices from the pan to cool.

Once cooled, grind all the ingredients into a powder using a mortar and pestle or spice grinder.

To make the lamb: In a medium skillet set over low heat, add the non-glutinous and glutinous rice. Stirring constantly to prevent burning, cook for about 10 minutes, or until the rice turns slightly yellow. Turn off the heat and allow to cool.

Once cooled, grind the rice with a mortar and pestle or a spice grinder so it forms a fine sand. Set aside.

Rinse the lamb under cold running water, then pat dry with paper towels. Set the lamb on a work surface and pound both sides evenly with the blunt side of a knife to tenderize it.

Cut the lamb into slices roughly 1½ inches long, 1 inch wide, and ⅛ inch thick (4 cm long, 2.5 cm wide, and 3 mm thick).

In a large bowl, add the lamb, aromatic oil, and spice powder and mix to combine.

Add the sweet flour sauce, Pixian bean sauce, oyster sauce, soy sauce, sesame oil, cooking wine, chili oil, sugar, Chinese five-spice powder, white pepper powder, salt, cornstarch, and 2 tablespoons water. Stir to combine.

Cover the bowl with plastic wrap and place in the refrigerator to marinate for 40 minutes.

After 40 minutes, sprinkle the rice crumbs over the marinated meat and use your hands to make sure each piece is evenly coated.

Prepare the steamer by filling it with water. Line the bottom stack with cheesecloth and place the meat in an even layer over the top.

Cover the steamer and bring to a boil over high heat. Once boiling, turn the heat down to low and steam for 40 minutes, or until the meat is fully cooked and tender. Serve.

West Fu "Pretzels"
西府麻叶

It took a long time for me to come up with this English name, because there's nothing quite like these deep-fried dough bits here, but calling them pretzels just about captures the appeal of this salty snack with an intriguing shape. They are crunchy, almost like thin breadsticks or crackers, and are made from sheets of dough that are then sliced, intricately folded, and deep-fried in peanut oil.

My great-grandma was a pro at making these, but she'd reserve them for large family gatherings during holidays like the Lunar New Year. Everyone knew it was a treat; not only is it a hassle to make (folding each individual one is no joke, and you must fry the dough the same day you make it), but the ingredients themselves were at one point considered excessive in China. You need a decent amount of oil to make these right, and in the past, oil was hard to come by thanks to rations. But while crunchy pretzels—especially flowery, ornate ones—are not essential to a meal, sometimes it's worth the effort to have this extra-fancy garnish on the table.

These typically accompany a savory dish such as Hoolah Soup (page 236) or Five Nuts and Seeds "Chowder" (page 246), but during a photo shoot our food stylist Tyna topped them with honey and sesame seeds in a stroke of genius. The team couldn't stop eating them.

Serves 2, or a small party

2 cups (250 g) all-purpose flour

1½ tablespoons whole white sesame seeds

½ teaspoon Chinese five-spice powder

½ teaspoon sugar

¼ teaspoon salt

1 egg, beaten

2 tablespoons vegetable oil

¼ cup (60 ml) cold water

Peanut oil for frying

TOOL:
Digital instant-read thermometer

Add the flour, sesame seeds, Chinese five-spice powder, sugar, salt, egg, and vegetable oil to a large bowl and stir to combine.

Slowly add the cold water while mixing with your hands or in a stand mixer to form a dough. Cover with plastic wrap and rest for 10 minutes.

Knead the dough for 2 minutes, then let it rest again for another 10 minutes.

Form the dough into a ball, then flatten with a rolling pin into a thin round sheet about ⅛ inch thick, roughly 15 inches (38 cm) in diameter. Dust each side with loose flour if it's sticky, but the dough shouldn't be very sticky, as it contains oil and is rather hard.

Using a knife and a straight edge (a rolling pin works), trim the dough into a 14-inch (35 cm) by 14-inch (35 cm) square sheet.

Cut the sheet into two equal pieces measuring around 14 inches (35 cm) by 7 inches (17.5 cm).

Note: Trimmings and excess dough can be combined and kneaded into a separate dough and then rolled out on its own and made into pretzels.

Take one of the two pieces and fold it in half length-wise, leaving you with a piece that's 14 inches (35 cm) by 3½ inches (9 cm) large. This piece is now ready to be cut into pretzels. There are many ways to shape the pretzels, and you can be creative with it. See below and the following spread for a few simple, more common ways, from easiest to hardest.

After folding your pretzels, line a plate with a paper towel. In a medium-sized pot or pan, add enough peanut oil to submerge your pretzels. Heat the oil to

320°F (160°C), then fry one pretzel at a time, using chopsticks or tongs to move them around in order to prevent over-browning. Once you get the hang of it, you can try frying a few at a time. You just don't want to overwhelm the oil.

Once evenly golden all the way around, carefully remove the pretzel with tongs or a slotted spoon and set on your prepared plate. Do not stack them on top of each other right out of the pot; they need to breathe. Repeat with the rest of the dough.

Allow to cool, then serve at room temperature. You can store the pretzels in a cool, dry place for up to 3 days, avoiding moisture so they keep their crunch.

6-CUT SIMPLE METHOD:

Using a knife, with the folded edge of the sheet closest to you, cut the folded sheet from the bottom, ³⁄₁₆-inch (5 mm) away from the side edge but leaving up to ¼ inch (6 mm) at the top (see step 1 for reference). So, in other words, don't cut through fully.

Make 5 total such cuts, and on the sixth cut, cut all the way through to remove the end piece (step 2).

Unfold the piece (step 3). Carefully pick up two middle strands (step 4) and tuck one end of the piece under and through the two strands (step 5), then pull the ends to straighten (step 6) and gently throw the piece onto the counter so it holds its shape. The strands should appear tangled up in the middle but in a controlled manner, almost braided.

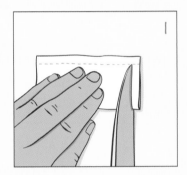
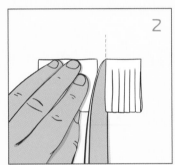
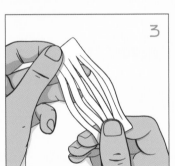
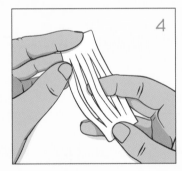
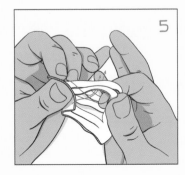
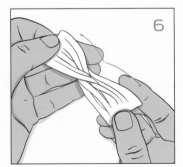

13-CUT "PINE CONE"
SONG-TA METHOD:

Repeat the 6-cut simple method's first step (see step 1 for reference).

Make 12 such cuts, and on the thirteenth cut, cut all the way through to remove the end piece (step 2).

Bring the two thick ends together one on top of another (about a ¼ inch/6 mm overlap), and press together into each other to create a large ring with the strands (step 3).

With a finger or two from each hand, hold the ring and rotate it so that the thick part of the ring is on the bottom (step 4). Then take the dominant hand's finger out. You should be holding up the rings with your non-dominant hand.

Using your free hand, pull one ring at a time down toward the counter, making a slight point by pinching the top of the ring before setting it down (step 5). Put the first ring down in the center, next one to the left, next one to the right, laying them on top of each other, and repeat until all the rings are set down on the counter (step 6).

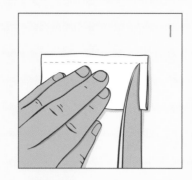

**13-CUT "SPREAD LOOSE"
SAN-ZI METHOD:**

Repeat the 6-cut simple method's first step (see step 1 for reference).

Make 12 such cuts, and on the thirteenth cut, cut all the way through to remove the end piece (step 2).

Unfold the piece, flip it over, and pull to stretch the strands slightly (step 3).

Take one thick corner and fold it diagonally over to meet the other diagonally opposite corner and press into each other (step 4).

With the dough still on the counter, use your thumb and index finger to "turn" one corner toward the overlapping corners, and then press that corner onto the top of the overlapping corners (step 5). Repeat with the other corner (step 6).

Grab the thick end, shake slightly to loosen the strands, then gently throw down again onto the counter.

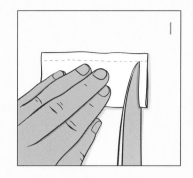

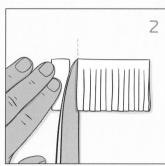

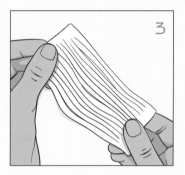

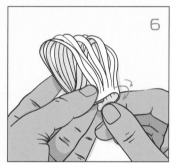

7

THE (BITTER)SWEET STUFF

Our Past and Our Present

ABOVE: XI'AN LOCALS PLAYING CHINESE CHESS ON THE SIDEWALK. **RIGHT:** THE MUSLIM QUARTER LIT UP IN ALL ITS TOURISTY GLORY AT NIGHT.

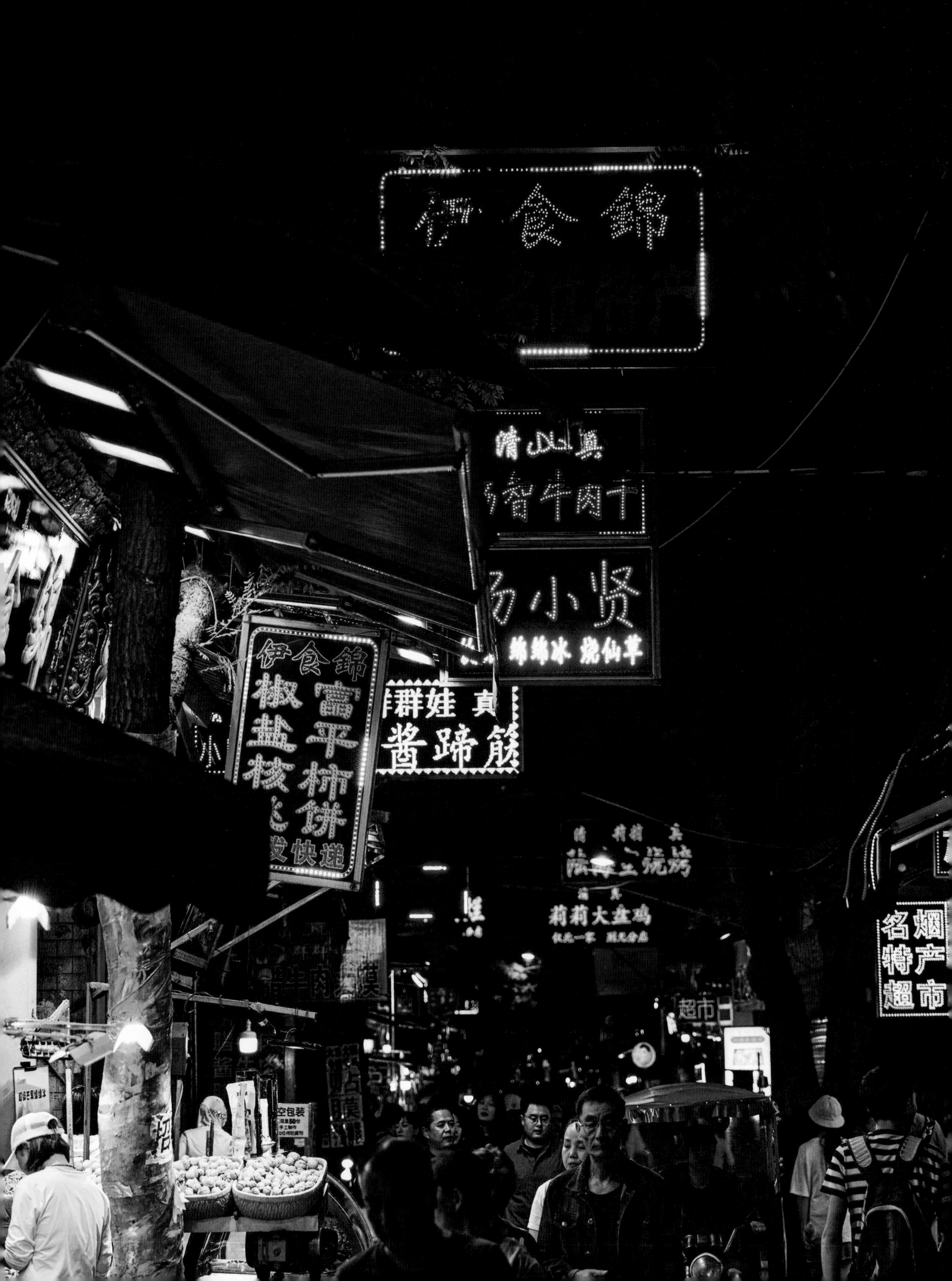
伊食錦
小贤
绵绵冰 烧仙草
伊食錦
富平柿饼
椒盐核
快递
酱蹄筋
莉莉大盘鸡
名烟
特产
超市
超市

A VIEW OF THE NEW AND THE OLD FROM THE TOP OF THE GIANT WILD GOOSE PAGODA.

THE LAST TIME I WENT TO XI'AN, I STOOD ON THE SOUTH SIDE OF THE CITY WALLS, FORTY FEET ABOVE STREET LEVEL. I looked north, into the old city center, and saw a sea of gray rooftops, barely changed from the architecture of my youth. Then I turned around, outward, toward the rest of the world, and was confronted with a wall of skyscrapers just across the moat, the glass windows reflecting the setting sun back at me.

It was a bittersweet view. It's cool to see Xi'an become modernized, a cosmopolitan city with classy speakeasies lining the city walls. It's exciting to see other people visiting and touring Xi'an, recognizing its place in history, making a pilgrimage to the Terracotta Army, the "eighth wonder of the world." And yeah, it's pretty great that I no longer have to explain where my hometown is to every single person I meet. Xi'an has become an international destination, and in that process it has developed along with the rest of the nation. The benefits of this transformation can be small but significant; my grandfather's apartment now gets four days of hot water instead of just one (like it used to when I was a kid).

At the same time, though, I can't help but feel like some things are lost or buried. Chain restaurants and tourist traps have pushed out many of the mom and pop shops in the Muslim Quarter, and the city monuments have lost some of their old-world glamour to dazzling lights. Obviously I'm biased, but I feel more and more like an outsider as the years go by.

It's a similar story with Xi'an Famous Foods. Our stores look nothing like what they used to. To quote Drake, we started from the bottom (literally, in the Flushing basement), and now, well, we're here, with a mini empire of stores across all of New York City.[1] My dad and I transformed what used to be a two-man operation into an empire, and it's (not always, but some days) a well-oiled machine.

There are times I miss the days when we didn't have a slick website, when we were just small fish in the big city. I think back on that random blizzarding day when I cashiered and my dad cooked, and we kept the store afloat with only the heat of the burners to keep us warm. I think about the late nights at East Village, stacking the stools and chasing drunk guys away from my storefront. And then I think, man, that sure beats my current gig, where I'm stuck catching up on bullshit emails after midnight.

It's probably why I love store openings so much. We're usually slammed from day one, just getting on our feet, so I go in the restaurant to help out and get the line moving. We blast the '90s hip-hop, churning out bowl after bowl of noodles. Every swoop, every duck, every arm gesture is purposeful and efficient. On a good day, when we get in a groove, it's flawless.

I think my dad also misses being in every restaurant. He's always been a doer, a maker, but as the company has grown, his role has changed. He's not cooking every day or talking to customers regularly, and he's not able to oversee each and every single employee to

---

1 The hustle never stops, so here's to many, many more stores.

make sure every noodle is pulled to perfection. As I've expanded the company, he's realized that not everything is going to go his way—and it's a source of tension for us, even today.

It's fitting, then, that this is our dessert section. Most of the Chinese desserts I grew up with centered around sticky rice, a sweet glutinous rice often associated with togetherness

Personally, I like to think our differences in opinion are what makes us stronger. He's there with the passion and vision for the food. I'm there to make it all happen in a way that won't drive our employees crazy. It's a delicate system of checks and balances, and the conflicts we have bring out our best ideas. We're already in this; we're already committed to the restaurant. And at the end of the day, us work-

The reason I always fought with him, he concluded, was because I didn't eat enough sticky rice as a kid.

and family in Chinese culture. While making the dishes in this book, my dad took the connection one step further. According to him, people who ate more sticky rice are closer to their family, less likely to fight, calmer and more loving. The reason I always fought with him, he concluded, was because I didn't eat enough sticky rice as a kid.

I'm sure this is bullshit, but I get it. We do fight a lot. He lets me know when he thinks I'm fucking up; I let him know if I don't agree with his half-developed plans. Sometimes I get fed up with his (supposedly constructive) criticism. I'll take some blame for this: On the days I'm low on sleep, I just don't have the patience for his constant opinions. But he's also as impulsive and hotheaded as he's always been. This time, though, he can't quit on a whim like he did when he worked at Chinese buffets. He's stuck, 'cause we're family.

ing through it all despite our differences might be the key to our success. He's seen what I can do with expansion, with growth, and I've seen what his confidence and stubbornness can do.

But sure, I could still try to eat a little more sticky rice. And honestly, it'll be easy with these recipes. Not only are most of these relatively basic (definitely not as scientific as, say, baking a cake), they're also insanely snackable, a sweet play on textures: chewy, crunchy, crispy, and velvety. And the thing about Chinese desserts, in my experience, is that they don't require a ton of sugar, relying instead on the natural flavors of decadent ingredients: smooth red bean, tart goji berries, nutty sesame seeds, and, of course, sweet, "QQ" sticky rice. So as far as desserts go, these might actually be somewhat better for you, if not for your familial bonds.

RIGHT: SOME PEOPLE MIGHT SAY MY DAD AND I LOOK SIMILAR, BUT I DON'T SEE IT AT ALL. WE DO AWKWARDLY LAUGH TOGETHER SOMETIMES, THOUGH.

Q&A: With the Man Who Started It All

MY DAD AND I DON'T OFTEN SEE EYE TO EYE, BUT THIS WHOLE ENDEAVOR STARTED WITH HIS PASSION PROJECT. XFF has become a massive company, where any small change can trigger a chain reaction in all of our stores. It's not exactly the best environment for a man who likes to tinker around in the kitchen, throw things at the wall, and see what sticks. This is oftentimes the source of our fights—he wants to try something new, add a menu item, tweak a recipe to make it "better." I like to have systems and standards, and change often fucks that stuff up. He thinks I'm a robot; I think he's a hothead.

Truthfully, both my dad and I have egos—and tempers. But somehow we've made it through. So I decided to sit down and do a little reminiscing with him.

When you first started making the food, did you think the restaurant would ever get this big? Why or why not?

I didn't think it was going to be as big back then. I wasn't aware of the market. I just wanted to try it because I like the food and I like cooking it to share with people.

Is there anything you miss from the old days when you were selling this food from a cart outside in Flushing? And what are the things you don't miss?

I miss my old guests who were always giving me ideas, giving me feedback, and chatting with me. They would come to me from near and far and say the smell of the food brought them back. They would also chat with me about the experience they had with this food back in China, reminiscing about the old days. What I do not miss is having to deal with the weather and standing outside in a hole in the wall next to a bus station.

Describe the Xi'an of your childhood. What was it like?

Some glimpses of my childhood include walking to school, bringing a bread for breakfast to trade with others for their different breads, getting five cents or ten cents for a popsicle on some days. Going to old abandoned buildings to look for bird nests for eggs. Catching cicadas in the summer. Biking to the outside of the city to the farms to trade light bulbs for grains with farmers.

What do you miss about Xi'an?

I miss being surrounded by history. The city itself is ancient, and that is not found in the US. Besides that, I miss the night market culture, as there was always food around that was very tasty and cheap.

The Lintong persimmons were my favorite: translucent, soft, small, very sweet. You twist off the stem, and it opens a hole on top, and you can suck out the meat from there. When I was a kid, I would blow up the

empty skins to make fake ones to trick friends. We would squat and eat fresh ones grown by farmers and get charged by how many stems we left behind after eating. I could usually eat ten to fifteen at once; they were that small.

What do you want to do when you retire?
Become more cultured. Read some books, plant some plants, and practice my calligraphy.

When did you consider XFF a success?
Ever since the late Anthony Bourdain approved of our food upon his visit, it was a sign of success for us. When he accepted this food, it represented to me the eventual acceptance of the food by Americans.

Are you proud of what we've created?
Very proud of it. We are given a chance to spread the culture of our hometown to the US, all the while creating a successful business in the US that's bringing jobs and money to the economy.

Even though we have our differences, are you proud of me?
Of course, I'm most proud of you. You were instrumental in introducing our hometown food and culture to this new world. What we have is really unique. If I had gone to culinary school, if I had trained to become a top chef, I wouldn't have been able to achieve what we have today.

Hard-Candied Fruits on a Stick
冰糖葫芦

Walk through any street market in China and you'll likely see skewers of candied hawberries, sticking out like flowers from a stand. These hawberries aren't like the ones we have in the States—Chinese hawberries are larger, perfectly round, and dry and crunchy, almost like mealy baby apples (but in a good way).

I loved candied hawberries as a kid. Right before my college graduation, I took a road trip down to Louisiana to visit a few hawberry farms to see if we could start selling these. While we did find a few purveyors with a hawberry haul on occasion, the fruits would be so small we couldn't skewer them. They would be juicy, tart, and tiny, meant to be eaten in jams rather than whole. So we decided to skip out on trying canned hawberries and moved on to strawberries and tangerines instead. Ironically, this Western version is now also popular in China.

Makes
5 skewers

25 strawberries, stems removed, or 15 segments peeled tangerines

1 cup (200 g) rock sugar

TOOLS:
5 bamboo skewer sticks

Digital instant-read thermometer

Clean the fruit and dry with paper towels. Thread 5 strawberries or 3 tangerine segments on each of the skewers. Do not spread the fruits out too far and keep them at the top of the skewer so they're easier to roll in syrup.

In a medium skillet set over high heat, add the rock sugar and 1 cup (240 ml) water. Once boiling, turn the heat down to medium. Cook until the sugar melts and turns into a syrup, first forming big and then small bubbles.

Once the sugar is melted, stop stirring (or it will crystallize) and let cook until the temperature of the syrup reaches 350°F (176°C), about 10 minutes. The syrup should be caramelized and golden brown.

Test to see if the syrup is caramelized enough by dipping a spoon into it and then dropping it in ice water. The syrup should solidify. If the sugar sticks to your teeth when you bite it, it is not ready. If it's crunchy when you bite into it, you're good to go.

Once the syrup is golden brown and caramelized, turn the heat down to low to keep the syrup hot.

Prepare a board or surface and spread water on it. You will set the skewers on here to cool and shape. Quickly roll the skewered fruit in the syrup until evenly coated, using a spoon to pour syrup over any parts that aren't covered.

Set the coated skewers onto the prepared board to cool, 5 to 6 minutes, before serving.

Sweet Soup with White Wood Ear Mushrooms
枸杞银耳羹

Serves
2 to 3

When I was a kid, my mom would plop a bowl of this down and tell me, "Drink this, it's good for you." Now, to be fair, Chinese people say that about a lot of things (see Five Nuts and Seeds "Chowder," page 246), but with this soup, I believe it. I've had it when I was feeling feverish, when I've been overheated, when I've had headaches—and it always made me feel better. The secret is the white wood ear mushroom, or snow fungus, with its anti-inflammatory benefits. (It's also allegedly good for your skin.)

You might be weirded out by dessert mushrooms. Don't be. White wood ear mushrooms are similar in texture to the black versions with crunchy-chewy folds, but the variety's lighter taste makes it more versatile. You could cook it up in savory dishes, but it's almost a waste then. In sweet soups, it adds a slightly earthy, floral aroma and a silky texture; I like to describe it as crunchy jelly. Serve the soup cool for a refreshing, slightly sweet ending to a meal in the summer, or warm for a nourishing bowl on rainy days.

½ ounce (14 g) dried white wood ear mushrooms

¾ ounce (21 g) dried red jujube fruits, seeded and cut into ⅛-inch (6 mm) cubes

1¾ ounces (50 g) rock sugar

20 goji berries

Put the white wood ear mushrooms in a medium pot along with 5 cups (1.2 L) water. Soak for at least 12 hours or overnight.

Drain the mushrooms, remove the roots if there are any, and cut the mushrooms into ¼-inch (6 mm) squares.

Add the mushrooms to a large pot along with 16 cups (3.8 L) water. Cover the pot and bring to a boil over high heat. Turn the heat down to a simmer and cook, covered, for 4 hours, or until the mushrooms are very soft and have begun to form a thick broth.

Add the dried jujubes and cook, covered, for another 1 hour.

Turn off the heat. Add the rock sugar and stir for 2 minutes or until melted.

Add the goji berries and stir to combine. Cover the pot and cook over medium heat for another 30 minutes, until the berries are plump and soft.

Serve either hot or cold. The soup can be refrigerated, covered, for up to 3 days.

Mountain Yam with Osmanthus Syrup
桂花山药

The thing that tends to throw people off when they try Chinese desserts for the first time is the texture. There's the creaminess of red bean paste, the density of sweet sticky rice, the slickness of white wood ear mushrooms, and then there's this: crunchy and slimy mountain yams, sliced into rounds and dipped in a thin, sweet syrup.

    To appreciate this dish, though, you have to fully embrace its texture. The yams here are watery and juicy, like a perfectly ripe Asian pear, complemented by the floral osmanthus syrup, with its bitter, sweet component.

Serves
2

½ mountain yam, peeled and sliced into ¼-inch (6 mm) thick rounds

1 tablespoon sugar

2 tablespoons osmanthus syrup

TOOL:
Steamer

Note: You could use strawberry jam if osmanthus isn't on hand, but it will be much sweeter. Honey also works.

Stack the slices of mountain yam onto a plate that will fit in a steamer pot. Form a pyramid with the yam pieces, starting with a flat base, and then continuing upward with smaller and smaller pieces. Sprinkle the sugar on top.

Fill the steamer pot with water. Place the plate of yams on the first stack in the steamer pot and cover. Bring the water to a boil over high heat. Once it starts boiling, turn the heat down and steam for 10 minutes.

Remove the plate carefully from the steamer. Move the yams to a new plate or clean the current one of any condensation. Rearrange your pyramid for presentation.

Pour the syrup on top and enjoy.

Candy "Silk" Sweet Potatoes
拔丝红薯

In China, hot dishes are typically served excruciatingly hot, to the point where if you're not careful, you could get burnt. It's both a sign that the food is fairly fresh and, let's be real, safe to eat. My dad, who grew up with siblings to fight over food with, has a higher tolerance for heat than I do (I'm an only child). So when he orders this dish (one of his favorites), I'm only able to eat two pieces while he downs the rest of the fiery hot potatoes.

Timing is everything. Wait too long, the potato-sugar combination loses its crunchy-creamy consistency. Get too impatient, the potato will burn your tongue. The sweet spot is right when the syrup gets stringy enough to make fun little sugar strands with, adding just a hint of bite to the caramelized potatoes.

Serves
2

1 sweet potato (about 5½ ounces/ 150 g), peeled

1 tablespoon cornstarch

2 cups (480 ml) vegetable oil

½ cup (100 g) sugar, plus more for dusting

TOOL:
Fryer probe thermometer (high temperature range)

Cut the sweet potato into roughly 16 evenly sized cubes. In a medium bowl, add the potato pieces and cornstarch and mix, making sure every cube is coated.

Line a plate with a paper towel. In a small pot, heat the vegetable oil to 420°F (215°C). Carefully add the sweet potato and fry until golden on all sides, 2 to 3 minutes. (The sweet potato should be submerged in the oil when frying.)

Once fried, transfer the sweet potato with a slotted spoon to the paper towel–lined plate. They should not be held too long, as they need to stay hot, so proceed immediately to the next steps.

Prepare a serving plate by sprinkling with sugar to prevent sticking.

In a small pan set over medium heat, add the ½ cup (100 g) sugar and 2 tablespoons water, stirring continuously with a wooden spoon to melt the sugar. Stir until bubbles start appearing.

Once the sugar is melted, stop stirring (or it will crystallize) and let cook until the temperature of the syrup reaches 350°F (176°C), about 10 minutes. The syrup should be caramelized and golden brown.

Test if the syrup is caramelized enough by dipping a spoon into it and then dropping it in ice water. It should harden as it cools. Take a bite. If the sugar sticks to your teeth, it is not ready. It should be very crunchy.

Remove the pan from the heat and quickly add the drained sweet potato to the pan. Toss the sweet potato until coated with the syrup. Pour onto your prepared plate and serve immediately.

Note: Serve alongside small bowls of cold water to dip pieces of the candied potatoes into. This helps cool the surface for easier eating.

Sweet Fermented Rice Soup
醪糟圆子

One of my favorite summer treats in Xi'an is a cold, sweet fermented rice drink, oftentimes sold at street stands. It's essentially just sugar and funky rice, a grain version of kombucha, something to sip on while walking back home. When I was a kid, this drink always felt taboo because of its trace amount of alcohol. I never got drunk off it, but I always knew I *could* if I had enough.

This is the grown-up, more complex version of that summer drink, less sweet and more tart, served either hot or cold. Amp it up with some filled *tangyuan* (page 283) for a true Chinese banquet experience.

Serves
2

2 tablespoons cornstarch

½ cup (60 g) glutinous rice flour, preferably water-milled

1 cup (240 ml) fermented rice (found at Chinese or Korean grocery stores)

3 tablespoons sugar

1 tablespoon goji berries

In a small bowl, make a slurry by mixing the cornstarch with 2 tablespoons water and set aside.

In a small bowl, combine the rice flour with about 3 tablespoons (45 ml) water, or as much as you need to make a smooth, elastic dough. Cover the dough with plastic wrap and set aside.

In large pot set over high heat, add 3 cups (720 ml) water and the fermented rice and bring to a boil. Meanwhile, roll the rice flour dough into a long snake about ½ inch (12 mm) in diameter.

Cut the dough into ½-inch (12 mm) segments. Roll the segments into balls and drop them into the pot of boiling fermented rice and water.

Once the rice balls start to float, cook for an additional 1 to 2 minutes to ensure they cook through. Then add the sugar and slowly pour in the slurry, stirring to incorporate.

Add the goji berries and serve.

Tangyuan (with Sesame or Hawberry Filling)
汤圆

You probably don't need me to say this, but the Lunar New Year is a big deal in China. Most people get a full two weeks off, and families travel from all around the world to see each other. As a kid, this holiday was filled with family members I only saw once a year, endless feasts, and these little guys: sticky, chewy rice dumplings filled with sweet paste, boiled and served in a syrupy soup.

Tangyuan soup is a staple during Lunar New Year because its roundness brings to mind both the full moon and the idea of togetherness, with its sticky, chewy texture. I have distinct memories of listening to firecrackers, still full from dinner, and biting into pillows of ground-up sweet rice to find a sweet filling in the middle. Some would have a smooth, nutty sesame paste, the filling so hot I'd have to breathe quickly out through my mouth to swallow it all down. Others would have a tangy sour hawberry filling, slightly jammy with a sharp sweetness. Every bite was a little surprise.

Both of those options are presented below, and you can play a similar game of roulette yourself (just divide the filling recipes in half to match the amount of tangyuan dough, or double the tangyuan dough recipe). At home, we'd serve this straight with the water we boiled it in (and maybe a touch of sugar), but if you want to be fancy, toss some filled tangyuan into fermented rice soup (page 281).

Makes 25 rice balls, or 5 servings

FOR THE HAWBERRY FILLING (to make 25 tangyuan):
10 ounces (280 g) dried hawberries, soaked in water for 30 minutes before removing the pits
1 cup (200 g) sugar

FOR THE SESAME FILLING (to make 25 tangyuan):
4 teaspoons black sesame seeds
2 teaspoons white sesame seeds
2 tablespoons sugar
4 teaspoons unsalted butter, melted
1 tablespoon toasted sesame oil

FOR THE TANGYUAN DOUGH AND ASSEMBLY:
2 cups (320 g) glutinous rice flour
⅓ cup (75 ml) boiling water
½ cup (120 ml) cold water

TOOL (if you're making a sesame filling):
Clean spice grinder, coffee grinder, or mortar and pestle

To make the hawberry filling: In a small saucepan set over medium heat, add the hydrated hawberries and 1 cup (240 ml) water. Bring to a boil, and continue to boil, uncovered, for 10 minutes. After 10 minutes, add the sugar and cook for 30 more minutes, stirring often. Remove from the heat and allow the sauce to cool and solidify to a paste.

Line two large plates with plastic wrap. Set one aside for later. Fill a small bowl with water. Dip a teaspoon into the water, then use it to scoop up a bit of the hawberry paste. Using your clean hands, roll the paste into a ½-inch (12 mm) ball (about ¼ ounce/8 to 10 grams) and place it on one of your prepared plates. Repeat with the rest of the hawberry paste (you should have enough for about 25 balls), being sure to space the mounds out so they don't stick to each other. Store in the freezer, covered, for 30 minutes to solidify.

To make the sesame filling: Place both types of sesame seeds into a small flat pan. Set over medium heat and roast the seeds for about 3 minutes, stirring them often to prevent burning. Turn the heat down to low and continue to roast for about 3 minutes more. Turn off the heat and let the seeds sit in the pan for 2 minutes more before transferring to a bowl to cool.

Put the cooled seeds into a clean spice grinder, coffee grinder, or mortar and pestle. Add the sugar and grind into a powder.

Put the powder into a bowl along with the melted butter and mix evenly to combine. Cover the bowl and place in the freezer for 1 hour to allow the filling to solidify.

Cover two large plates with plastic wrap. Set one aside for later. Using a paper towel, coat the inside of a round teaspoon measuring spoon with sesame oil. Use the oil-coated spoon to scoop the sesame filling, pressing down on the mixture with your finger to create a compact half-sphere.

Place the mound on one of your prepared plates. Repeat this process with the rest of the filling to create about 25 mounds, spaced far enough from each other so they don't stick together. Set in the freezer for 1 hour to solidify.

To make the tangyuan and assemble: In a medium bowl, add the rice flour and slowly pour in the boiling water, using chopsticks to stir in one direction to combine, for 1 to 2 minutes. Add the ½ cup (120 ml) cold water and continue to mix for 1 to 2 minutes. Use your hands to knead the mixture into a smooth dough. Cover the dough with plastic wrap and set aside for 10 minutes.

Divide the dough into 25 equally sized pieces, or as many pieces as you have filling for, and roll each piece into a ball, at least ½ inch (12 mm) in diameter.

Remove the filling from the freezer. Take one piece of dough. Using your thumb, press a small indentation in the middle of the ball and place one of the frozen paste mounds inside.

Wrap the sides of the dough around the paste, then roll it in your hands to form it back into a smooth ball. Place the tangyuans on your second plastic wrap–lined plate, covering the batch with plastic wrap to keep your tangyuans from drying out and cracking.

Note: Any extra balls you don't intend to cook right away can be frozen for 1 to 2 hours, then removed from the plate, placed into an airtight bag, and frozen for up to 2 weeks.

Fill a pot with water and set over high heat. Cover and bring to a boil. Once boiling, add the tangyuans and immediately stir them around with a ladle or chopstick to prevent them from sticking to each other or the sides of the pot.

Once the water comes back up to a boil, turn the heat down to low and add ¼ cup (60 ml) cold water to slow the boiling process.

When the water starts to boil again, add another ¼ cup (60 ml) cold water.

When the tangyuans start floating to the top of the pot, turn the heat down to low and simmer until a total cooking time of 10 minutes is reached. Serve the tangyuans in small bowls along with some of the water they were cooked in.

Chilled Rice Cake with Honey
蜂蜜凉粽子

Most people's first introduction to *zong zi* is a bamboo-wrapped sticky rice packet filled with savory goodies at dim sum—pork belly, peanuts, soy sauce, the works. But when I was growing up, those bamboo packets were always a sign of something sweet, in part thanks to this dish. Sweet zong zi was my grandmother's favorite snack, and she would make this recipe often in the summer so we could have the cool, slick rice cakes as a treat in the hot afternoons. The trick here is to really pack in the rice, binding up the triangular pyramids tightly with twine. During the cooking process, the rice grains will expand, melding together as the pressure increases. The best-wrapped packets end up with a dense, chewy cake, smooth and slick with a uniform bite, and when they're freshly made, straight out of the fridge, the soft cake is perfectly cold and sweet, especially with a little drizzle of honey.

Makes 12 small cakes

2 cups (400 g) short-grain glutinous rice

1 package bamboo leaves, with at least 12 leaves

Honey for serving

TOOL:
1 roll cooking twine

Put the rice into a large bowl and top with enough water to reach two times the level of the rice. Let soak for 12 hours; this will soften the rice and create a better texture.

Put the bamboo leaves in a separate bowl and cover with water. Top with a heavy plate or pot so the leaves remain fully submerged and let soak for 12 hours as well.

Strain the hydrated rice and discard the water.

Remove and pat dry the bamboo leaves, trimming off any pointy ends or stems that poke out.

Hold one or two leaves, depending on the size of your bamboo leaves, with the veins facing down (see illustration step 1). Create a cone, folding the larger end of the leaf behind itself, a third of the way up from the bottom of the leaf (step 2).

Spoon ¼ cup (50 g) of the rice into the cone, pressing down hard to pack it in tightly (step 3). Fold the top of the leaf down to "cap" the cone (step 4), then fold the rest of the leaf around the sides to completely close off the cone (step 5).

Use twine to wind around the middle of the cone to tie up the leaf, going around twice, then crisscross the strings and wind two more times in the other direction and make a slip knot for easy opening when eating (step 6). Repeat this process to make twelve wrapped cakes.

In a large pot, add the wrapped bamboo packages and submerge with enough water to reach three times the level of the cakes. Cover and bring to a boil over high heat. Once boiling, turn the heat down to low and simmer for 2 hours.

Remove the cakes to a plate to cool to room temperature, then place in the refrigerator to chill for 1 hour before eating. Wrapped in bamboo, these cakes can sit in the fridge, covered with plastic wrap, for up to 3 days. However, you will have to reheat them in the microwave for roughly 1 minute, or by boiling or steaming, prior to eating to regain the original texture. They can also be frozen for up to 2 weeks. Defrost them at room temperature, then steam or boil them to reheat and enjoy.

When eating, remove the rice from the bamboo leaves. Cut the rice cake into smaller pieces with scissors or a knife and drizzle with honey to taste.

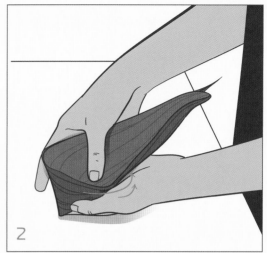

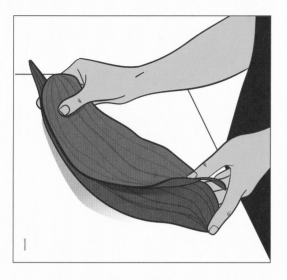

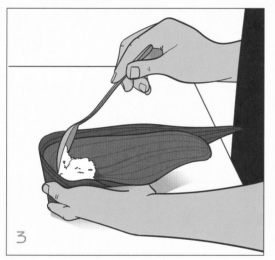

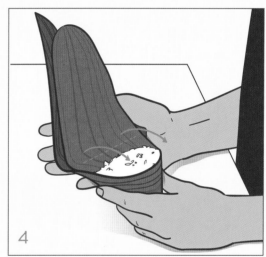

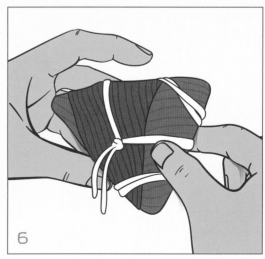

"Zeng Gao" Rice Cake
甑糕

In my experience, really old-school Chinese desserts offer very little when it comes to visual presentation. It's mostly because way back when, just *having* dessert was a luxury. When someone has already gone through the hassle of obtaining sweet sticky rice (not native to the region), there's no reason to ask them to make it pretty. They just have to make it taste good.

Zeng gao perfectly encapsulates this prioritization of taste over looks. Less of a cake and more of a generic mass of sticky rice, sweet beans, and jujubes, zeng gao is made to feed a group of people. You'll see Xi'an locals lining up for this in the morning, as it makes for a sweet breakfast treat, with vendors scooping the sticky rice out from giant steamer pots. Our version is a little more presentation-oriented, using a bowl to help shape the cake, but the idea is still the same.

Serves
4
(unless you're my dad; he eats a lot)

½ cup (80 g) dried pinto beans, or ½ cup (80 g) canned unseasoned pinto beans (although the flavor and texture won't be as good)

2 cups (400 g) short-grain glutinous rice

26 red jujube fruits

10 seedless jujube fruits, cooked in syrup, cut into halves (can be found in the dry goods section in Chinese grocery stores; not the actual candy)

Sugar or honey for serving

TOOL:
Steamer

Cheesecloth

Cover the dried pinto beans in water and soak for 12 hours, then drain and set aside. Soak the rice and red jujubes, separately, in water for 6 hours. Drain and set aside.

Fill a small pot halfway with water. Add the red jujubes and bring to a boil over high heat. Boil for 10 minutes. Remove the jujubes from the water and cool. Once cooled, slice in half to remove the pit and set aside.

In a medium pot, add the rice and submerge in water, with the water hitting 1 inch (2.5 cm) above the rice. Bring to a boil, covered, over high heat. Once boiling, turn the heat down to low and boil for 10 minutes more. Drain the rice and set aside.

In a small pot, add the pinto beans and submerge in water, with the water 1 inch (2.5 cm) above the level of the beans. Bring to a boil, covered, over high heat. Once boiling, turn the heat down to low and boil for 15 minutes more. Drain the beans and set aside.

Fill a steamer pot with water. Line the first stack with cheesecloth. Inside a round heatproof bowl that can both fit all the ingredients as well as fit inside the stack of the steamer pot, place some jujubes into the bowl, before adding one-third of the rice, spreading the grains out into a ¼-inch (6 mm) thick layer, packing the rice lightly.

In my experience, really old-school Chinese desserts offer very little when it comes to visual presentation. It's mostly because way back when, just having dessert was a luxury.

Top the rice with half of the red jujubes and candied jujubes; pack lightly.

Add another one-third of the rice on top and spread into a ¼-inch (6 mm) thick layer; pack lightly.

Top with an even layer of the pinto beans; pack lightly.

Put the rest of the rice on top of the beans and spread into a ¼-inch (6 mm) thick layer; pack lightly. Then top with the rest of the red jujubes and candied jujubes, applying some pressure to pack it all in.

Place the bowl upside down with the contents packed inside it onto the cheesecloth (it's OK if it separates from the bowl).

Note: The bowl should remain through the process of steaming.

Cover the steamer pot and bring to a boil over high heat. Once boiling, turn the heat down to low and steam, covered, for 1 hour. Once the rice is fully cooked through with a slight bite, turn off the heat and let sit, covered, for 20 more minutes.

To serve, cut the cake into pieces and add sugar or honey to taste on top. You can refrigerate this for up to 1 day, covered; otherwise, cover and freeze for up to 2 weeks. Defrost and steam to heat up and enjoy.

Eight Treasures Congee
八宝甜稀饭

The term "eight treasures" is often bestowed on dishes both savory and sweet that combine eight high-quality ingredients in one recipe. Typically, they're meant to show just how bougie of a host you are when you serve all eight incredible ingredients together. *Ba bao fan* is the most common version you'll see, a steamed sticky rice dish with red bean, dried fruits, and nuts. Our version takes the same idea but turns it into a thick congee, full of lotus seeds, jujubes, peanuts, and more.[2] Each of these ingredients is supposed to be good for you in a different way, but sometimes I think we just make this shit up so we feel better about dessert.

Serves
2

FOR THE CONGEE:

8 red jujubes

½ cup (100 g) short-grain glutinous rice

2 tablespoons peanuts, crushed

2 tablespoons walnuts

19 lotus seeds

2 tablespoons dried lily bulbs

4 seedless jujube fruits cooked in syrup, cut into halves (can be found in the dry goods section in Chinese grocery stores; not the actual candy)

1 tablespoon golden raisins

2 slices dried mango, cut into ¼-inch (6 mm) cubes

3 tablespoons brown sugar

½ tablespoon osmanthus syrup

FOR SERVING:

½ tablespoon peanuts, crushed

½ tablespoon Roasted Sesame Seeds (page 34)

To make the congee: Cut the red jujubes in half and remove the seeds.

Soak the rice in water for 4 hours, then drain and set aside. Meanwhile, soak the peanuts, walnuts, and red jujubes in water for 3 hours, then drain. Soak the lotus seeds and lily bulbs for 2 hours, then drain and set aside.

Remove any skin from the peanuts and break the walnuts up into peanut-sized pieces. Set aside.

In a large pot, add the rice and 9 cups (2 L plus 240 ml) water. Cover and bring to boil over high heat, then turn the heat down to low and simmer, covered, for 45 minutes.

Add the crushed peanuts, walnuts, red jujubes, lotus seeds, lily bulbs, candied jujubes, raisins, and mango. Turn the heat up to high and boil for 5 minutes.

Add the brown sugar and osmanthus syrup and stir to combine.

To serve: Portion into bowls, sprinkle with peanuts and roasted sesame seeds, and serve immediately if you prefer to enjoy this warm. It also can be stored in an airtight container in the refrigerator for up to 1 day and enjoyed cold. If you don't plan on finishing this in a day, cover and freeze for up to 2 weeks. Defrost and boil to reheat.

Note: You can swap out osmanthus syrup for strawberry syrup or honey if you don't have the former on hand.

2 Come on—did you think I would deliver a Chinese cookbook *without* an eight treasures dish? I would get scolded by all my aunties if this weren't in here.

Layered Rice Cake
江米凉糕

Of all the desserts in this book, I like to think that this is the most delicate one, requiring the most finesse to get the right balance of dense, even layers of sticky rice and creamy red beans. First, you have to presoak the rice and beans separately, before cooking the rice and carefully layering the ingredients. Then the entire cake goes into the fridge, allowing the shape to remain intact while the flavors meld together and the rice forms a thin, gooey, sticky crust. The result? A rice cake with a smooth ribbon of thick red bean running through, almost like the Chinese version of a sweet tea sandwich. It's pretty damn classy, and—bonus—goes great with (oolong) tea.

Serves 2

½ cup (100 g) red beans or adzuki beans

1 cup (200 g) short-grain glutinous rice

1 teaspoon toasted sesame oil

1 tablespoon sweetened condensed milk

1½ tablespoons sugar

2 tablespoons Roasted Sesame Seeds (page 34)

2 teaspoons osmanthus syrup or honey

TOOLS:
Steamer

Cheesecloth

Rectangular pan about 1 inch (2.5 cm) deep

Note: You could buy precooked red bean and skip the soaking step, but it won't be as good.

Separately soak the red beans and rice in water for 12 hours.

In a large pot set over high heat, add 3 cups (720 ml) water and the soaked red beans. Bring to a boil, then turn the heat down to low. Cover and cook for 30 minutes.

After 30 minutes, strain the beans from the water and use a food processor or blender to puree the beans into a paste.

In a small pan set over medium heat, heat the sesame oil for 1 minute. Add the red bean paste and stir, then add the condensed milk and sugar and cook for 3 to 5 minutes, until the mixture is evenly combined. Set aside.

Drain the soaked rice from the water. Fill a steamer pot with water and line the first stack with cheesecloth. Place the rice on top of the cheesecloth, cover the steamer pot, and bring to a boil over high heat. Once boiling, turn the heat down to low and steam, covered, for 40 minutes.

In the rectangular pan, add half of the rice, spreading evenly with your fingers until the grains form a flat, solid layer roughly ½-inch (12 mm) thick. Add the red bean paste on top of the rice and spread into an even layer.

Place the rest of the rice on top and spread evenly with your fingers until it forms a flat, solid layer roughly ½-inch (12 mm) thick. Sprinkle the top with the roasted sesame seeds and allow the cake to cool, covered, in the fridge, about 2 hours.

Once cooled, cut the cake into pieces and drizzle with the osmanthus syrup or honey for a refreshing treat. When it's warm out or when it's not being immediately consumed, this cake should be stored, covered, in the refrigerator, for up to 1 day. Otherwise, cover and freeze for 2 weeks. To serve, defrost at room temperature and then steam to reheat.

SOME OF MY FAVORITE DESSERTS (LEFT TO RIGHT): SWEET SOUP WITH WHITE WOOD EAR MUSHROOMS (PAGE 281), "ZENG GAO" RICE CAKE (PAGE 288), LAYERED RICE CAKE (PAGE 291).

The Future:

So, What's Next?

The simple answer is, I want to be able to serve our family's recipes for as long as I can. I want to make sure the business is strong enough to become a century-old business. But who knows what will happen? As someone who has experienced quite a few unexpected turns in life, I know plans are set to be changed. For now, I will push on and strive to meticulously improve and cautiously expand the business for as long as I can, because Xi'an Famous Foods, to me, is the pride of my family, the culmination of all our years of work. It's a place where Chinese people in America can experience a taste of home, be transported for a moment, and feel proud of the culture, the food, and the country of their roots. To be able to live up to that every single day in every single store is already enough of a challenge to me, so let's just say that's the only thing I plan to do.

Acknowledgments

TO MY FATHER, FOR SHARING HIS VAST KNOWLEDGE AND EXPERIENCE WITH ME TO HELP ME GROW ALL OF THESE YEARS, SHAPING ME INTO WHO I AM.

To my XFF team, for helping make XFF into a legend.

To my high school friends, for keeping things real and fun when we hang, despite how different all of our lives are compared to when we were kids. Thanks for always reminding me of the good old simple days. Mario Kart on N64, CS LAN parties, and Pineapple Fanta for life.

To my high school teachers, for providing me with knowledge and giving me confidence during a time when I had little of it, especially Ms. Cabrera, Mr. Potter, Dr. Weissman, and Mrs. Yi.

To my college friends, for inspiring me to be smarter, more culturally aware, and more worldly in my views, and for providing me with advice and comfort all of these years, long after graduation.

To my book team: Sarah Smith for holding my hand through my first book. Jessica Chou for doing pretty much everything. Jenny Huang for capturing beautiful images to properly convey our story. Tyna Hoang and Imogen Kwok for the organized execution of the food styling. Beatrice Chastka, Stephanie De Luca, and Sophie Leng for the prop styling that made our dishes look like works of art. Julie Kane for the cool illustrations. Sarah Zorn for working out the recipe kinks.

To the Abrams team: Thanks to Laura Dozier, for guiding us on our first book. Diane Shaw, for putting our vision onto paper. The marketing and publicity team, Kimberly Lew, Natasha Martin, Jessica Weiner, and Mamie Van Langen, for getting our story out there.

To the late Anthony Bourdain, for enjoying our food in its earlier days and giving us the opportunity to share it with more people in America and beyond.

And, finally, to **Xi'an Famous Foods fans** all over the world. You give my life meaning.

About the Authors

JASON WANG

is the CEO and owner of Xi'an Famous Foods, who expanded his family-founded business into a New York City institution beloved by locals and tourists alike. Starting first as a cashier in Chinatown, he moved his way into the kitchen before taking on all operations for XFF restaurants, with multiple locations. In 2013, Wang was named an Eater Young Gun as well as a *Zagat* 30 Under 30. In 2014, Wang was listed as a *Forbes* 30 Under 30 and a *Crain's* 40 Under 40. And in 2020, he received a James Beard Award nomination for Outstanding Restaurateur. After all these years, he still eats the Liang Pi "Cold Skin Noodles" (page 51) and the Spicy Cumin Lamb Noodles (page 173) on the regular. He lives in Queens, New York.

JESSICA K. CHOU

has written and produced for the likes of Refinery29, Insider, Potluck Video, Opening Ceremony, Lonny, *Edible Manhattan*, and *Edible Brooklyn*. She got her start interning in the photo department of *Bon Appétit*, eventually making her way to Refinery29, where she founded the popular "Money Diaries" series. She lives in Manhattan but will always miss the restaurants of the San Gabriel Valley.

Index